WELCOME

HALIFAX

I remember the first time I saw a Halifax. It was at the Yorkshire Air Museum (YAM) in about 1998. That aircraft – Grim Reaper et al – is known the world over as 'Friday the 13th'. I can remember looking over that slab-sided beast, saying something about it being "huge" to my dad, before running off in search of the next one. Back then, as a seven-year-old kid, it was all about seeing whatever aeroplanes I could – very rarely did an information board get a look in. I knew this was a bomber built by Handley Page and flew during World War Two – that was enough. As I grew up, it was a different story… I took every opportunity to learn absolutely everything I could about every aeroplane I cast my eyes on. It was only then I realised there was much more to the Halifax – and with YAM just 'up the road', I was lucky to see 'Friday' on a fairly regular basis.

I discovered the Halifax represented the epitome of resilience, adaptability, and collective effort in 'her' service as a vessel of human determination. Despite this, it was clear the Halifax was a near forgotten pillar in Bomber Command's order of battle that delivered time after time, lost in the shadow of the Avro Lancaster. As a result, it also became a symbol of near injustice with not a single example saved for posterity or in remembrance of the 'Halifax Boys' – many of whom gave their all for freedom.

While the 'Lanc' became a legend – its massive bomb loads, and celebrated raids capturing the public imagination – the Halifax quietly bore almost half of Bomber Command's burden. Steadfast and understated, this versatile workhorse of war carried crews into the unknown, night after night. To these young men, often barely out of their teens, the Halifax was both their duty and their lifeline as it guided them through history's darkest skies. Today, their brotherhood stands as a testament to unity and the enduring power of trust forged in the crucible of war.

Vital to victory, the Halifax may have lacked the spotlight, but it carried an equal weight of sacrifice, courage, and enduring legacy. It is now an unyielding symbol of loyalty and quiet valour. Beyond combat, the Halifax embodied innovation, with a versatile design that evolved in line with both wartime and postwar needs.

When I accepted this project, I considered sharing production lists, serials, groups, exacting specifications, paint codes, part numbers, and the sort – but all of this can be found online. While so much has already been said about the Halifax, I wanted to share stories that epitomise the type – the challenge and response, the people who designed, built and flew it, and the want to remember.

All of this helps connect new generations to a truly magnificent machine, particularly in an age of rapid technological advancement when reflections of ingenuity and bravery offer valuable lessons in perseverance and invention under the horrific pressures of war, and the human cost of conflict – aspects that are more than apparent today.

In showcasing this history, my intention is to deepen the understanding of the sacrifices made and emphasise the importance of remembering them. I hope the words and images in this publication offer an insight into a type that, in the annals of flight, is our quiet link to those who fought.

Jamie Ewan
Editor

'Friday the 13th' watches over 'her' Yorkshire Air Museum home as the sun sets over the former Halifax base. The legacy of the Halifax is not built on glamour, but on grit and service, as well as the unspoken bond between crew and aircraft.
ALAMY-DAVID KILPATRICK

CONTENTS

CONTENTS IMAGE: A wonderful image captured by famed lensmen Charles E Brown of Halifax III LV857 airborne out of Handley Page's Radlett Aerodrome in Hampshire on January 28, 1944, shortly after being rolled out by the firm. Delivered to 51 Squadron a week later, it was lost with its crew during Bomber Command's disastrous raid against the German city of Nuremberg on March 30-31 that same year. See 'NIGHTMARE OVER NUREMBERG', p18, for more.
ROYAL AIR FORCE MUSEUM

COVER IMAGE: Fg Off Cyril Barton fights for control of his Halifax III, LK797/LK-E, *Excalibur* after a devastating head on attack by a Luftwaffe Junkers Ju 88 night-fighter during Bomber Command's raid on Nuremburg. See 'ON A WING AND A PRAYER', p60, for Barton's story.
ANTONIS KARIDIS

ISBN: 978 1 83632 191 0
Editor: Jamie Ewan
Proof reading: Tom Allett, Steve Beebee
Senior editor, specials: Roger Mortimer
Email: roger.mortimer@keypublishing.com
Cover Design: Steve Donovan
Design: SJmagic DESIGN SERVICES, India
Advertising Sales Manager: Sam Clark
Email: sam.clark@keypublishing.com
Tel: 01780 755131
Advertising Production:
Becky Antoniades
Email: Rebecca.antoniades@keypublishing.com

SUBSCRIPTION/MAIL ORDER
Key Publishing Ltd, PO Box 300,
Stamford, Lincs, PE9 1NA
Tel: 01780 480404
Subscriptions email:
subs@keypublishing.com
Mail Order email:
orders@keypublishing.com
Website: www.keypublishing.com/shop

PUBLISHING
Group CEO: Adrian Cox
Publisher: Steve O'Hara

Published by
Key Publishing Ltd, PO Box 100,
Stamford, Lincs, PE9 1XQ
Tel: 01780 755131
Website: www.keypublishing.com

PRINTING
Precision Colour Printing Ltd, Haldane,
Halesfield 1, Telford, Shropshire.
TF7 4QQ

DISTRIBUTION
Seymour Distribution Ltd,
2 Poultry Avenue, London,
EC1A 9PU
Enquiries Line: 02074 294000.

We are unable to guarantee the bonafides of any of our advertisers. Readers are strongly recommended to take their own precautions before parting with any information or item of value, including, but not limited to money, manuscripts, photographs, or personal information in response to any advertisements within this publication.

THE ROAD TO HALIFAX

Often taking second place to Avro's more 'glamorous' Lancaster, the Halifax offered much greater versatility and bore the brunt of the RAF's bombing campaign in the early, difficult days of the war. Jamie Ewan traces the need for the type and its journey into RAF service

RIGHT: Handley Page's innovative chief designer and the creator of the Halifax, George Volkert.

BELOW: The sheer size of the so-called 'Berlin Bomber' – the V/1500 – is evident in this photograph thought to be taken at HP's Cricklewood Aerodrome, circa mid-1918. Had it not been for the Armistice of November 11, 1918, the type would have been the first British machine to hit Germany while operating from home soil.

It was always Handley Page's proud boast that, ever since the formation of the Royal Air Force on April 1, 1918, the service had *never* been without an aircraft of 'HP' design – something that remained true until the retirement of its Jetstream T.1 twin-turboprop multi-engine trainers in 2003.

During World War One, the company – which was founded by Frederick Handley Page (later Sir Frederick) in 1909 – had supplied twin- and four-engined bombers such as the O/100 of 1915 and the O/400 of 1918. It also delivered the mammoth V/1500 – another four-engined design that could carry an unprecedented 3,000lb of bombs to the German capital Berlin from bases in East Anglia, the first British aircraft capable of doing so, as hostilities drew to an end. In fact,

on November 11, 1918, a V/1500 (often dubbed the 'Berlin Bomber') of No. 166 Squadron at RAF Bircham Newton in Norfolk tasked with attacking Berlin on the type's first operational mission, was stopped while taxiing by an excited member of groundcrew who ran out to tell them the armistice had just been declared.

Going on, HP continued to supply the RAF with bombers during the 'interwar' years – including the H.P.24 Hyderabad that entered service in 1925 and remained in use until 1933, and the H.P.33 Hinaidi introduced in 1929 – the latter going on to remain in the RAF's inventory until the early 1930s as a military transport.

Furthermore, HP was heavily involved during the United Kingdom's rearmament phase between 1934 and 1939 (deemed necessary after defence spending had been slashed from £766m between 1919 and 1920 – an eye watering £43.7bn today – to just £102m between 1931 and 1932) producing the ungainly looking, high-winged H.P.54 Harrow

> **Issued on May 8, 1935, it called for a 2,000lb load to be carried over a range of 1,500 miles, at a cruising speed of at least 195mph at 15,000ft**

braced monoplane, and the more sophisticated H.P.52 Hampden – both of which flew in 1936.

Following on from these, the HP design office at Cricklewood in north London, was studying the requirements for a new twin-engined heavy bomber that would meet Air Ministry (AM) Specification B.1/35 – itself in line with Operational Requirement (OR) 19.

Issued on May 8, 1935, it called for a 2,000lb load to be carried over a range of 1,500 miles, at a cruising speed of at least 195mph at 15,000ft. The span was limited to 100ft, making it compatible with the RAF's ground equipment and infrastructure – including hangars, motor transports, and even packing cases. It was to be powered by two new-generation British 1,000hp engines, utilising variable-pitch propellers.

The specification had also been issued to Airspeed, Armstrong

Whitworth, and Vickers. Eventually, all the firms, except Airspeed, were awarded contracts for prototypes, Armstrong Whitworth touting its Armstrong Whitworth A.W.39, and Vickers its Warwick – a larger counterpart to its Wellington.

The HP design, designated the H.P.55, featured a pair of air-cooled Bristol Hercules HE-ISM engines and in some ways resembled Douglas' DC-2 airliner – its low-mounted wing, spanning some 95ft, boasting a sweptback leading edge and the main undercarriage retracting into the rear of the nacelles – albeit with a cantilever monoplane tail with twin fins and rudders. George Volkert, the H.P.55's chief designer (though his title was then production engineer) had just returned from a trip to the US to review the latest

ABOVE: Reginald 'Reggie' Stafford was the firm's chief aerodynamicist through the type's journey from H.P.55, to H.P.56, to H.P.57. He is seen here holding a model of a Handley Page H.P.42 (another of George Volkert's designs) in 1952 while Handley Page's chief designer.

production techniques in use, so the layout may have reflected his good impressions of that aircraft.

The fuselage itself, like the tail unit, very much harked back to the Harrow.

The AM's Director of Technical Development (DTD) – responsible for the focus on research and application of emerging materials, technologies, and processes for the RAF – wanted the resultant aircraft to be as small as possible, so it was necessary to split the bomb load between the fuselage and the proposed two-spar wing.

With the contract formally signed on October 24, 1935, for delivery of an airworthy prototype on or before August 23, 1937, the first ▶

LEFT: Frederick Handley Page (November 15, 1885 - April 21, 1962) founded Handley Page on June 17, 1909, as Britain's first publicly traded aircraft manufacturing company. The RAF was never without a type of 'HP' design on strength from its inception through to 2003...

> **With the increasingly dark shadow of war looming on the horizon, the resultant machines were urgently needed to radically enhance the RAF's bomber force**

'mock-up' was to be completed in February 1936 – and it was. However, in May 1936 it was decided to swap the Bristol powerplants for a pair of 1,200hp liquid-cooled V-12 Rolls-Royce Merlin XX engines – a mock up in this form being shown for the first time to the then DTD, Air Commodore John Henry Verney, on July 11 that same year. On returning from a second look 11 days later, the sheer number of criticisms he had for the H.P. 55 resulted in the planned Mock-up Conference being indefinitely postponed. Work was stopped while the possibility of accommodating a much bigger bomb load was investigated.

After a year's work, it became clear that this design was not going to be successful. In his book *Handley Page Aircraft Since 1907,* published in 1976, C H Barnes notes: "This led to a meeting between Handley Page and Verney on 14th September, when a new draft specification was discussed,

the proposed engines being up-rated Hercules, although it was hoped that Rolls-Royce Vultures of still higher power would be available in three years' time."

In HP's design offices, attentions were quickly turned to two new specifications: B.12/36 in line with OR.40 for a four-engined heavy bomber capable of a 250mph cruise, a 1,500-mile range, and a 4000lb bomb load, issued during July 1936, and P.13/36 in line with OR.41 for a high-performance twin-engined medium bomber for "world-wide use" soon after; B.12/36 would eventually result in the RAF fielding the huge Shorts Stirling in August 1940.

With the increasingly dark shadow of war looming on the horizon, the resultant machines were urgently needed to radically enhance the RAF's bomber force then made up with the likes of Vickers' huge Virginia and HP's own H.P.50 Heyford – both open cockpit twin-engine biplanes. While the Heyford could carry a respectable 2,500lb bomb load, and the Virginia 3,000lb, both boasted top speeds under

ABOVE: The second Halifax prototype, L7245, airborne from Boscombe Down while undergoing full-service and armament trials with the Aeroplane & Armament Experimental Establishment, circa September/October 1941. Of note, is the type's original triangular tail fins, which were seriously – and tragically – flawed. ALL IMAGES KEY COLLECTION UNLESS STATED OTHERWISE

LEFT: Delayed, unreliable, overweight, underpowered, and over budget. The Rolls-Royce Vulture was originally slated to power the winner of the Specification P.13/36. When this complex 24-cylinder X-format brute finally made it into service, it was considered by many to be "downright dangerous". GETTY IMAGES-ROLLS-ROYCE

"the war to end all wars". Almost immediately, the British military services and munitions industry were quickly and drastically cut down, while funding was substantially reduced. This was driven by the assumption – for the basis of policy planning at least – that Britain would not be involved in another significant armed conflict during the then next decade. Orders for the Royal Air Force were typically based on the assessment of "operational requirements" by the AM. These in turn were mediated by its perception of progress in aviation, engine technology and armaments, the relevant international events and agreements, and the political realities at home.

In his 2002 title, *The RAF and Aircraft Design: Air Staff Operational Requirements 1923-1939*, author Colin Sinnott acknowledged the difficulties in doing just that: "The Air Ministry had to take decisions on the aircraft performance characteristics needed to fight an air war at an unknown time, against an unknown enemy, and against a rapidly changing technical background." It could be said, the AM was putting all its eggs in one basket in an attempt to catch up.

The 1930s were a decade of historic change driven by the insurmountable evidence that one European nation's central policy was long-term deception and an aggressive period of rearming, in blatant and open disregard of Treaty of Versailles. As a result, the rise of air power in Germany under the Nazi Party caused considerable alarm. With concerns growing and the public's open expression of fear as Chancellor Adolf Hitler's foreign policy became increasingly belligerent, it soon became obvious that Britain would have to respond. It wasn't a matter of *if* there would be a war, but *when*. But that shadow

150mph, and were barely capable of breaking the 1,000-mile range mark.

In line with this – as well as the British Government's growing fear of Germany's increasing air power, often due to overestimates in its size, reach and hitting power – the RAF formed Bomber Command on July 14, 1936. At the time, it was argued that a strong bomber force provided a deterrent to aggression, as bombing would result in complete and inescapable destruction on both sides – after all, it was then believed "the bomber will always get through". As such, a nation's ability to secure itself hinged on its ability to control the air. In his influential 1921 doctrine *The Command of the Air*, Italian Gen Giulio Douhet, argued that strategic bombing – particularly targeting civilian populations and infrastructure – could break a nation's will to fight, while it could put the enemy on the brink of defeat in a short time.

Consequently, the early conception of Bomber Command was an entity that threatened the enemy with utter destruction. The reality was of course very different, but that's for another time.

The need

At the end of World War One, there was firm resolve that it had been

of war was beset by government disorganisation, misunderstanding, and a lack of future proofing, as well as public perception hung over many aircraft manufacturers trying to keep up with the near constant and rapid technological advances across aviation as they pushed speeds, ranges and performance figures towards realms never before considered. Countless aircraft designs and concepts appeared on the drawing boards and in the skies as ▶

LEFT: The basic lineage of the Halifax is more than apparent in these early layout diagrams of the H.P.55 (top), H.P.56 (middle) – although neither design made it off the drawing board, instead making way for the H.P.57 (bottom).

BELOW: Seen here at RAF Linton-on-Ouse, L9499 was one of the first Halifaxes delivered to 35 Squadron – the aircraft arriving at the North Yorkshire base on March 3, 1941. Assigned the codes 'TL-Q', the aircraft failed to return from a daylight raid on the German port city of Kiel on June 30 that year having been shot down by Luftwaffe fighters – all but one of the crew were killed. They were, pilot, Flt Lt Thomas Douglas Inglis Robison, 23, 2nd pilot Sgt Laurence Hancock, 21, flight engineer Sgt Percy Ingham, 25, wireless operator / air gunner Flt Sgt Alexander James Davie, 23, air gunner Sgt Richard Norman Hares, 27, and air gunner Sgt Robert Dunn, 20. Flying as an observer, Sgt Ernest Joseph Harding managed to escape the stricken machine when he bailed out through the bomb bay doors.

manufacturers attempted to do so – only to fall behind the ever-changing performance curves. Possession of the needed technology, the associated costs, and how to endure it, industry requirements needed to sustain progress, strategic concept and polices, as well as reprisals, all being questioned. This wasn't helped by countless, and often conflicting, demands upon its relatively limited resources – but again, that is for another time.

The response

One wonders what went through Frederick Handley Page's mind when he read the advanced operational requirements for Specification P.13/36 for the first time. Similar documents had been sent to Avro, Boulton Paul, Bristol, Shorts and Vickers. That said, he soon realised that an aircraft designed to such requirements would do virtually everything required by B.1/35 – something he pointed out in a letter to the AM. Even so, the numbers were challenging. This state-of-the-art, all-metal, twin-engined monoplane required the ability to carry some "8,000lb of munitions internally at no less than 275mph and 15,000ft over a maximum range of 2,000 miles". In terms of range, speed and bomb load, a single example of this new aircraft would

> **66** *Countless aircraft designs and concepts appeared on the drawing boards and in the skies as manufacturers attempted to do so – only to fall behind the ever-changing performance curves* **99**

be equivalent to three Fairey Battle light bombers then less than a year from entering RAF service. But the AM wanted more.

Initially issued in May that same year by Gp Capt Robert Dickinson Oxland, Director of the AM's ORs, Specification P.13/36 called for the winning design to be crewed by five, including a second pilot, filling the roles of wireless operator, front gunner and bomb aimer; be able to carry an "alternative load" of two 18in torpedoes for anti-shipping work; switch between the general reconnaissance/maritime patrol role with minimal equipment changes; and be capable of carrying out dive-bombing attacks at an angle of 60. It should 1) improve the accuracy of weapon aiming and 2) reduce time over the target area. There should be provision for power-operated gun turrets in the nose and tail and it should have the ability to transport up to 16 fully equipped troops, thus

"reinforcing Overseas Commands". If that wasn't enough, the aircraft, which had to operate from existing RAF airfields with a full warload (in other words get airborne in around 700yds) should have the ability to undergo an engine change on the dispersal within two hours, be compatible with RAF ground equipment and infrastructure, fly at its top speed on just two thirds power, and maintain 10,000ft on one engine. It also had to sustain the stresses of a catapult assisted take off – a so-called 'frictionless take off' – at its all up weight. Moreover, the resultant bomber was to be powered by a pair of "British engines which shall have passed the service-type test".

Of course, the powerplant wanted by the AM was Rolls-Royce's monstrous, yet unproven, near 2,000hp, 24-cylinder Vulture then in development. While not specifying its use, the ministry would 'drive' the manufacturers to take it up. It could be said, this then soon to be long-delayed and over budget powerplant sowed the seeds of the type's future issues. Armament was to be two nose guns with 2,000 rounds, a rear four-gun turret with 6,000 rounds, with a further 4,000 rounds carried in the fuselage.

Away from the operational requirements, the aircraft was required to be "simple" to aid easy manufacture at scale, as well as easy to maintain, while the design, construction, and testing of all aspects of the aircraft to be as quick as possible for service entry. It really was a remarkable 'shopping list' and one that represented a huge challenge for Handley Page.

Almost immediately, Volkert looked at an enlarged version of the H.P.55 – designating it the H.P.56. When the ministry saw HP's initial results, it agreed that the firm could stop work on the H.P.55 and continue with the H.P.56.

And with the final specification approved by the AM's Director of Technical Development in September 1936, it was issued by the Contracts

BELOW: A wide view of the Drawing Office at Handley Page's Cricklewood facility, showing rows of people working their drawing boards to translate the initial design of the Halifax into formulated plans and blueprints for each of the individual parts – of which there was some 256,000! GETTY IMAGES-PIEMAGS-ARCHIVE-MILITARY

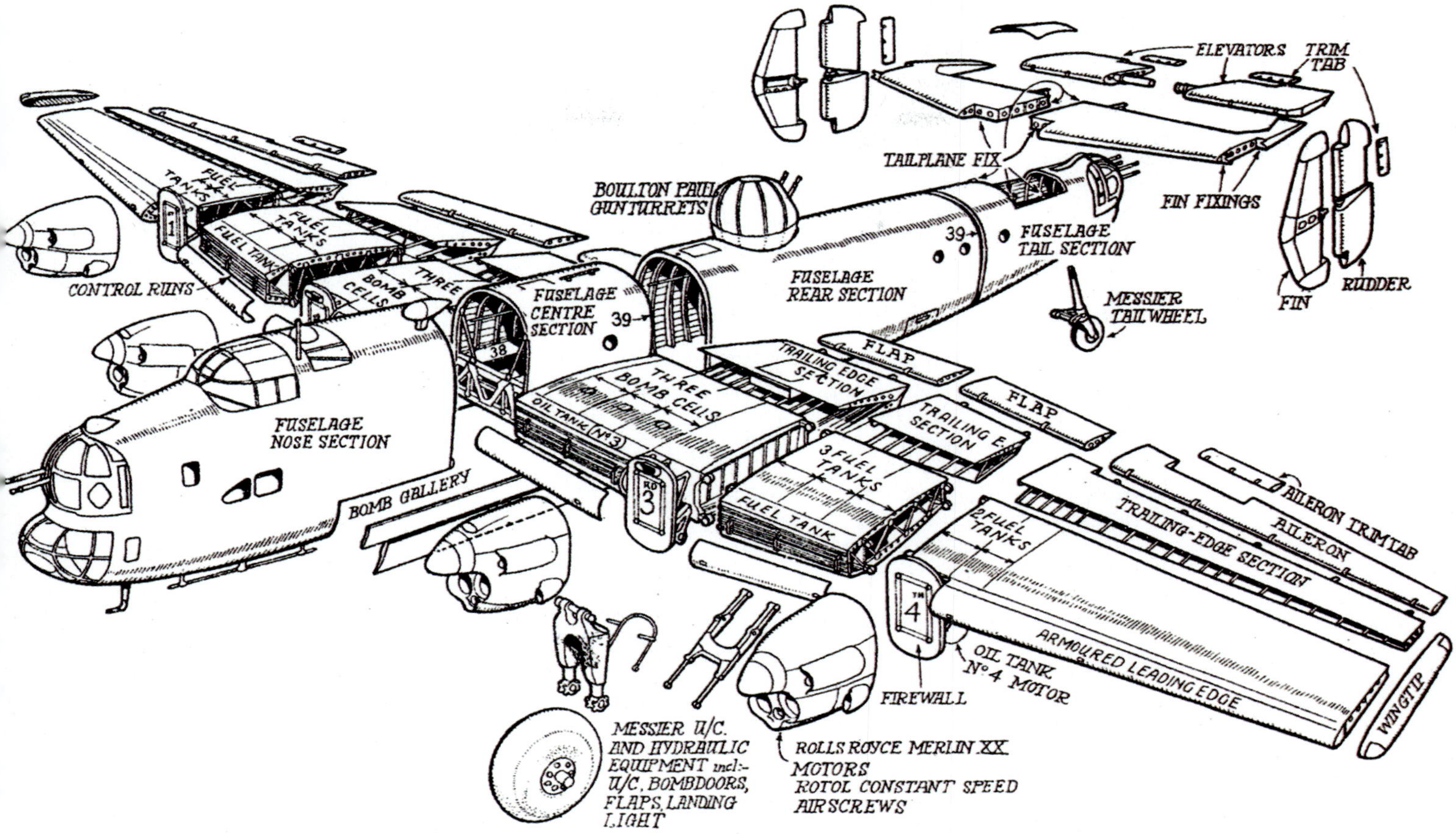

Branch that November with formal invitations to tender being sent to the original six manufacturers, as well as Fairey and Hawker.

At Radlett, a near constant stream of design, evaluation, and redesign soon resulted in a slender, moderately tapered mid-wing monoplane with with incredibly clean lines, boasting a broad, deep, oval-section slab-sided fuselage housing a large internal bomb bay. At the front a short squat glazed nose, an integrated cockpit with a "greenhouse" canopy providing visibility but not breaking the overall line, while the rear fuselage narrowed gradually to support the low-set tailplane and twin-tail layout with end-plate fins and rudders. Underslung engine nacelles housed the main undercarriage.

When deemed ready, HP submitted its tender to the AM in early February 1937 – just six months after OR.41 had been issued. Within days, Boulton Paul, Bristol, Fairey, Shorts, and Avro had all tendered their own proposals. While Boulton designated its bid, the P.91,

Bristol, Fairey and Shorts all opted for the generic P.13/36 designation, while Avro chose the Type 679. Although Vickers had a design, it chose not to submit it – the firm also opting to dub its design the P.13/36. Of course, Avro's proposal would become the Manchester – the predecessor to the Lancaster.

With Specification P.13/36 essentially calling for a multirole platform, most, if not all, of the tendering firms noted that the expected bombing requirements had dictated their basic designs.

Contemporary reports note the H.P.56's principal dimensions included a projected wingspan of 88ft, a length of 70ft, a height of just 20ft, maximum take-off weight in the region of 45,000lb and an empty weight of 25,000lb – 7,120lb of which was taken up by the Rolls-Royce Vultures alone, these being rated at an estimated (and needed) 1,710hp each while turning a three-bladed constant-speed feathering propeller. Performance wise, its maximum speed was estimated at 265mph at

its service ceiling of 23,000ft. It had a range of 2,000 miles with maximum fuel, as well as an internal bomb load up to 14,000lb.

Powerplant woes

Later in February 1937, following the Tender Design Conference, the AM selected Avro and Handley Page first and second place, respectively, "off the board". Like the HP machine, the '679' was to be powered by Rolls-Royce Vultures.

On April 30 that same year, both manufacturers were informed – on the recommendation of the DTD – of the AM's request for a pair of airworthy prototypes within 12 months. Ordering duplicate prototypes had only recently become an accepted opinion. While such process had until then been considered too costly, not only did it help reduce the development period, but the urgency also generated by the prospect of war had drastically altered the situation. Having fostered a belief in an independent ▶

ABOVE: This wonderful drawing first published in the April 24, 1942 issue of *The Aeroplane* reveals the innovative 'split construction' aspect of the type's design. Not only did this this technique safeguard Halifax production from enemy action, but it also resulted in a very strong airframe built like a "brick s*house!"**

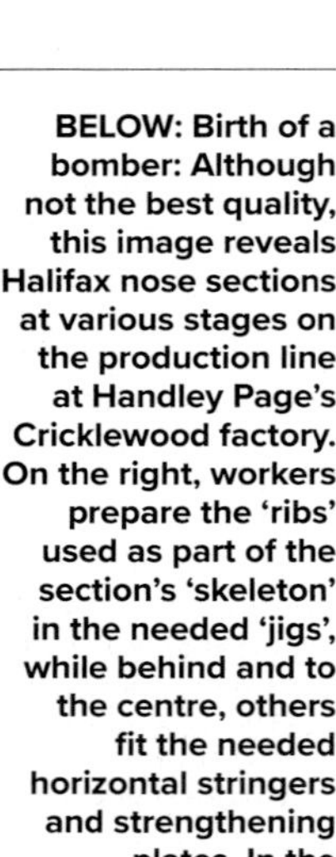

RIGHT: Handley Page workers file H.P.57 blueprints at Cricklewood during production of type, circa 1942. GETTY IMAGES-PIEMAGS-ARCHIVE-MILITARY

BELOW: Birth of a bomber: Although not the best quality, this image reveals Halifax nose sections at various stages on the production line at Handley Page's Cricklewood factory. On the right, workers prepare the 'ribs' used as part of the section's 'skeleton' in the needed 'jigs', while behind and to the centre, others fit the needed horizontal stringers and strengthening plates. In the background, workers attach the body work to another frame. GETTY IMAGES-PIEMAGS-ARCHIVE-MILITARY

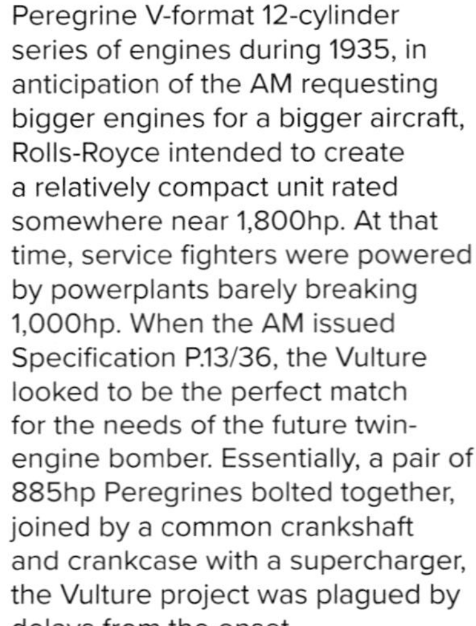

strategic approach to air power using bombers, the theoretical expectations of strategic bombing were the foundations of the 'Western Air Plans' that established in 1937, listing suitable targets for attack such as airfields, roads, railways, canals, battleships, industrial targets, and forests. But these needs were already being thwarted by the huge gap between expectation and capability. As such, in March 1937, it was decided that all medium bombers not delivered by April 1, 1939, should be replaced by the resultant P.13/36 type or types – something the Chancellor of the Exchequer, Arthur Neville Chamberlain, approved the following month.

The Radlett-based firm completed an immense expansion to cope with the needed work. Following the H.P.56 Mock-up Conference on July 8, the prototypes were allocated the serials L7244 and L7245.

Despite near constant design changes requested by both the AM and the RAF as they continued to revise the aircraft's requirements from those originally specified, the H.P.56 took shape under Volkert's leadership. To add to the challenge, almost all the non-bomber requirements were eventually dropped – both the wanted torpedo requirement and the anachronistic message pick-up hook were also removed. Elsewhere, the dive-bombing angle was reduced to 25° before being deleted altogether, and the maximum number of 500lb bombs carried was reduced from 16

to 15 – bizarrely, the troop-carrying requirement role lingered on well into 1940.

From the onset, the firm was under intense pressure from the AM to foreshorten the development time. As it was, HP had been at work for only a month or two when it is said rumours emerged that there could be a shortage of Vultures. That said, it's likely the firm had heard of the somewhat considerable 'teething' troubles with the powerplant.

Building on the technology of its successful Kestrel and

Peregrine V-format 12-cylinder series of engines during 1935, in anticipation of the AM requesting bigger engines for a bigger aircraft, Rolls-Royce intended to create a relatively compact unit rated somewhere near 1,800hp. At that time, service fighters were powered by powerplants barely breaking 1,000hp. When the AM issued Specification P.13/36, the Vulture looked to be the perfect match for the needs of the future twin-engine bomber. Essentially, a pair of 885hp Peregrines bolted together, joined by a common crankshaft and crankcase with a supercharger, the Vulture project was plagued by delays from the onset.

When this 24-cylinder, X-format brute eventually ran on the test bench for the first time on September 1, 1937, it represented the cutting edge of technology. A year later, it was clear to see it was just too complex for the technology of the time. It proved prone to catastrophic failures, continual difficulties with the crankcase distorting, and the reliability of the main bearing, along with less-than-ideal performance – issues that followed it into service. With the Vulture finally taking to the skies attached to a heavily modified Hawker Henley in 1939, it was found the performance figures barely broke 1,600hp.

On July 1, 1937, it was decided to order 100 examples of both the Avro 679 and H.P.56 designs "off the drawing board" to speed up

delivery timetables. But by then Avro was stuck with the Vulture. Handley Page had dodged that bullet.

That same month, the rumours surrounding the Vulture came true – Rolls-Royce advising HP that the number available would most likely be smaller and massively delayed. By then the AM was anxious not to have to rely on it too much, which is why it 'encouraged' HP to consider various four-engined layouts.

Unlike Avro, which was later forced to substantially modify an aircraft already in service (under the pressure of war, cost, reliability, performance problems, and mounting losses), HP was able to effect considerable revision at the cost of only the paper. That said, Volkert was somewhat unwilling to alter his design due to the fact the wings would have to be completely redesigned to each take two engines. At that time, such a layout was considered highly experimental, and had to be submitted for stringent strength tests with the Royal Aircraft Establishment at Farnborough in Hampshire. On top of this, the weight of the wing, and indeed the whole aircraft, would rise significantly which would necessitate the strengthening of the structure and supporting members. Despite this, he got to work and before long, the wingspan was increased from 88ft to 99ft. In parallel, the weight increased by some 13,000lb, from 39,000lb to 52,000lb. The question was, however, which engine?

Discussions leading to the change in the type's powerplant

> **Most, if not all, of the tendering firms noted that the expected bombing requirements had dictated their basic designs**

were all-embracing, with HP's chief aerodynamicist, Reginald 'Reggie' Stafford, considering Bristol's 14-cylinder two-row supercharged radial Taurus, and nine-cylinder, single-row Pegasus, Rolls-Royce's in-line V-12 Kestrel, along with Napier's 24-cylinder H-pattern air-cooled Dagger. However, none of these (the Hercules, earmarked for the Stirling, was not then considered) would be capable of overcoming the increase in drag and weight resulting from the four-engined layout.

But when an uprated Merlin X was considered, Stafford found that the take-off performance at maximum overload, albeit with a longer take-off run, meant the 'catapult launch' requirement could be done away with. (Merlin X was the only engine likely to be available in sufficient numbers, although the demand later outstripped production – leading ultimately to Hercules later being used.)

While Volkert preferred air-cooled engines, none of sufficient power were available at the time. To make matters worse, it didn't suit the projected weights of what would become the Halifax.

As it was, on July 24, then Chief of the Air Staff, Marshal of the Royal Air Force Sir Edward Ellington, decided that the aircraft should be refitted with four engines. Less than a week before, AM Wilfrid Freeman, the Air Member for Research and ▶

LEFT: Monocle and all, Handley Page's chief test pilot, Maj James Cordes, was at the controls of prototype L7244 for the type's maiden flight from RAF Bicester on October 25, 1939.

Development whose job it was to choose the aircraft with which to rearm the RAF, requested a version showing four Taurus – such was the question as to what engine to use.

At Cricklewood, work on the H.P.56 was abandoned on August 18 – the design effort being switched to the new four engine bomber. Essentially a new aircraft, it was designated the H.P.57. Volkert admitted that the change was a terrible blow, but very quickly realised the advantages that were going to accrue. On September 3, HP was officially notified of the decision that the four water-cooled, 12-cylinder 1,075hp Merlin Xs were to be used. This decision would ultimately delay the prototype by some six months while extensive design changes were made.

The drag to Halifax

With a revised Mock-up Conference held in December, production drawings were started soon after. By the end of the year, the initial material cuts had been made. Such was the promise of the H.P.57, on January 7, 1938, the AM chose to place its first production order for the type "off the drawing board", ordering 100 examples; the serials that had already been assigned to the H.P.56 were switched to the H.P.57. This number was later increased, the Air Staff envisaging 500 of the new bomber would be in service by April 1942. Ironically, that same plan also called for 1,500 Manchesters in use by the same date.

But with hostilities looming, the numbers were changed, doubled, then increased again. As a result, manufacturing plans were soon

extended to include English Electric, which was already producing Hampdens at its "shadow factory" at Samlesbury, near Preston in Lancashire. The Halifax had been designed for dispersed production – dubbed 'split construction' – with large components, made elsewhere, being brought together for final assembly. To aid this, Volkert devised a method of 'photo-lofting' based on a system used in the US to produce accurate copies of master drawings on sensitised metal, to ensure accurate machine work. Another three aircraft manufacturing plants were given over to Halifax production – Rootes Securities at Speke, Fairey Aircraft at Stockport, and the London Aircraft Production Group, the latter a consortium established by the Ministry of Aircraft Production (MAP) led by the London Passenger Transport Board. In all, some 41 plants were tasked with Halifax production and HP established the 'Halifax Group' to oversee the manufacturing programme.

A month later, the first panels had been pressed and the bulkheads rivetted, while preparations were made for serial production at Cricklewood. It was there, in March 1938, that the hand-building of both prototypes began. By July, with most of the design work deemed complete, construction of the fuselage was well under way. The aircraft was then about 20% bigger than the H.P.56.

The heavier engine mass ahead of the wing, which followed the light-alloy structure and used in the Harrow and Hampden, utilised a NACA (National Advisory Committee for Aeronautics) 23021 airfoil at the root, and a NACA 23007 system at the tip, and boasted an area of 1,250ft^2, had pushed the design's centre of gravity (CG) forward. This resulted in the sweep on the wing's leading edge being drastically reduced (0° inner mainplane, 9°outer) – but also allowed the rear spar (made from a T-section boom, solid web, and vertical extruded angle stiffeners riveted to the front surface) to be straight. This resulted in sufficient room between the two spars (the front being built up using U-shaped upper and lower booms

with vertical stiffeners between them and diagonal tie members, built up in box section, like a girder bridge) for bomb cells (three in each wing) inboard and then integral (worries about sealing and the effects of combat damage later resulted in this being changed), and six fuel tanks with 1,552 imp gal capacity, between the inner and outer engines – although the wing section had to be thickened by 21% to accommodate them.

The smaller 13ft diameter of the three-bladed Rotol hydraulic constant-speed fully feathering propeller attached to the Merlin, compared to the 16ft de Havilland example used by the Vulture, stemmed a significant loss of efficiency resulting in a reduced cruise speed and lower range. The drag figure was affected by the fact it was no longer possible to enclose the larger mainwheels (two 24 x 19in Dunlop AH 2238s) necessitated by the higher gross weight fully within the engine nacelles.

Wind tunnel testing revealed that mid-positioned nacelles gave the least drag at the expected maximum

ABOVE: Seen here airborne out of Boscombe Down in October 1941, L7245 (its Boulton-Paul power-operated turrets in the nose and tail, giving the aircraft a much more "business-like appearance") was handed over to No. 28 Conversion Flight (CF, the first such unit set up to convert crews to the new type – many of whom came from the Armstrong Whitworth Whitley force) at RAF Leconfield in the East Riding of Yorkshire on November 17, although it did not take it on charge until December 7. Moving west with the unit to nearby RAF Marston Moor in North Yorkshire soon after, No. 28 CF was absorbed by No. 1652 Conversion Unit on January 2 the following year, but not before L7245 had been damaged in a flying accident on December 27 – very little is known about the incident, but the aircraft was repaired at Marston Moor and returned to service. Receiving 'Category B' damage (beyond repair on site, but repairable at a Maintenance Unit or by a contractor) in another flying accident at Marston Moor on February 24, 1942, the aircraft was not repaired and later struck off charge – this being back dated to the date of the accident. Stored at Marston Moor, 'she' was converted into a ground instructional airframe, receiving the maintenance serial '3474M' on Christmas Eve that same year. After this nothing more is known about the aircraft.

speed so these were adopted. In turn, this brought the exhaust into view from the rear, which was acceptable at the time because it was envisaged most bombing would be done in daylight. In the event, night bombing was the rule, and it became essential to quickly find a means of shielding the exhaust flame. One semi-successful solution was to put a large shield over the outlets, but this upset the flow for something like 3ft of the span either side of each nacelle, thus affecting around a third of the net wing area… no wonder the drag was up!

Of note, when low-drag nacelles were developed for the Merlin installations on both the Bristol Beaufighter and Lancaster, examples were fitted to the Royal Aircraft Establishment's (RAE) Merlin 65-powered Halifax II test bed HR756 in mid-1943. Testing revealed a top speed of 324mph at light load – considerably faster than the same aircraft with standard nacelles and Merlin 22s, which topped out at 288mph. While most of this increase was due to the extra power, it was found the nacelles themselves were worth about 12mph. Despite this, it was not considered worth interrupting production for and the changes were never made – such was the need to keep the type rolling off the lines.

Another contribution to drag was the wing-section thickness – a maximum of 21% of the chord at the centre section, tapering to 9% at the tip, it was chosen on the basis of tests of thick wing sections at the National Physical Laboratory, which

showed quite low drag. By the time it was realised that the figures were faulty and that the drag was in fact much higher, it was too late to change the design.

Further drag was caused by the generous 'headroom' that allowed the crew easy access over the main spars – something that was always a problem in the Lancaster with its tight confines. The maximum diameter, or depth, of the HP machine's fuselage was 9ft 6in, compared to the Avro bomber's 8ft 2in. It was said this contributed to the larger number of Halifax aircrew who successfully abandoned the aircraft. A January 1944 *Bomber Command Operational Research Study* revealed that during 1943, the survival rate among Lancaster aircrew shot down over Germany was only 11%, whereas in Halifax it was 29%. Understandably, these figures were of the strictest secrecy and not disclosed to the crews flying either type to begin with.

Structurally, the Halifax was quite conventional, but it was designed to be built in some 15 main components – each of which could be subdivided to achieve a highly dispersed manufacturing base. While this technique safeguarded production from enemy action, it also resulted in a slightly heavier airframe owing to the number of transport joints. An unexpected benefit was that, provided there was no fire, the aircraft tended to break into its main component parts in a crash landing, often ▶

LEFT: Halifaxes undergoing assembly at Handley Page's Cricklewood factory – which was responsible for building some 1,592 examples during the type's production run. Of note in this view is the sheer thickness of the inner wing.

RIGHT: Spray painters at work in the paint shop at Handley Page's Cricklewood factory. When tested by the Royal Aircraft Establishment, the rough nature of the paint was found to be a major contributor to the type's early drag issues – to the extent it negated the flush riveting used across the airframe during its early days in service.

BELOW: Like all aircraft manufacturers, Handley Page continually worked to improve its designs – the Halifax being no exception. Here, engineers prepare to test a model in the wind tunnel at the Handley Page factory at Cricklewood, circa 1942, to study the effect that the opening of the bomb doors had on the aircraft. GETTY IMAGES-PIEMAGS-ARCHIVE-MILITARY

enabling crews to escape relatively unscathed. As many Halifax aircrew put it, it was built like a "brick s***house!"

To cap it all, when tested by the RAE, the rough nature of the paint applied as part of the standard Bomber Command camouflage of Dark Green/Dark Earth over Night Black added considerably more drag – to the extent it negated the flush riveting used across the airframe. The outside of the aircraft also boasted many non-aerodynamic protrusions, such as the non-retractable landing lamps and barrage balloon cable-cutters on the leading edges. Many of these were improved on later production aircraft, but it all took time, and changes delayed production.

To war

To get the type into its initial service trials at the Aeroplane & Armament Experimental Establishment (A&AEE) at Boscombe Down in Wiltshire as soon as feasible, it had been decided that L7244 was to be finished as a 'flying shell', while the fully-equipped second machine, L7245, would follow as soon as possible for full-service and armament trials. However, it was deemed that the firm's airfield at Radlett in Hertfordshire didn't have the wanted safety margin – especially for a first flight and testing. Completed on September 2, 1939 – the eve of the war it was manifested for – at a cost of some £90,000 (the equivalent of more than £7.5m today) '244 was taken in semi-assembled sections by road to RAF Bicester in Oxfordshire – the nearest suitable and convenient airfield of insufficient importance to warrant enemy attention. There, working in strict secrecy in a specially set aside hangar, HP personnel assembled and prepared the aircraft for its maiden sortie. In parallel, company chief test pilot, Maj James L Cordes, made several flights in a borrowed Miles Magister to familiarise himself with the local area.

And so it was, Cordes took the H.P.57 for its first flight on October 25, with the firm's chief test observer, 'Ginger' Wright, alongside him – the undercarriage being locked down as a safety precaution. Climbing out, he was somewhat surprised to see what looked like either a canal or a river close to the airfield boundary – how had he missed that while out in the Magister?

He remained puzzled until the test flight was nearly over, and then, as he came into land, he could see it was a line of cars parked along the roadside, the autumn sun catching their windscreens. So much for security in face of local gossip! On landing, Cordes found the Lockheed hydraulic brakes were slow acting – vindicating the use of Bicester. It took three days to swap

> **66** *This decision would ultimately delay the prototype by some six months while extensive design changes were made* **99**

these out for a pneumatic system from Dunlop prior to the next flight.

With initial manufacturer testing continuing using L7244 (which despite being just a 'shell', tipped the scales at a whopping 55,000lb) from Bicester, Cordes was forced to make a hasty landing after one of the fabric-covered elevators fractured in flight.

While L7244 was handed over to the A&AEE at Boscombe Down during November 1939 (the same month the MAP called for 500 Halifaxes to be built at a rate of 22 per month), 'she' flew little while HP engineers addressed a near constant stream of issues. Time on the ground was not wasted, however, with various bomb combinations up to 11,000lb being fitted and assessed. The few occasional air tests undertaken did allow stalling speeds in various configurations to be noted for the operating manuals, while the type's structural flight limits were found to be "fairly tight".

Despite the increasing urgency to get the new bomber into production, it would be August 17, 1940, before L7245 finally took to the skies – Cordes again in the cockpit, albeit climbing away from Radlett a frustrating 11 months after L7244. By then, series production was well underway.

Fitted with most of the equipment and armament (a Boulton-Paul Type C turret with two 0.303in guns in the nose, and a Type E in the rear from the same manufacturer with four 0.303s – the latter without

the guns fitted) then planned for production examples, '245 was quickly transferred across to the A&AEE the following month. It was followed that October by the first production example Mk.I – L9485, the aircraft taking to the skies on 11th of that month, just 72 weeks after the first production drawings had been issued; this airframe was never used operationally.

The type, still shrouded in secrecy, had been given the name Halifax following the long-running practice of naming heavy bombers after major towns and cities, in this case the town in West Yorkshire. The aircraft was unveiled to the public when Lady Halifax christened L9608 – a late production Mk.I – at Radlett on September 12, 1941. At that stage, the type was less than a month from entering service with the RAF. And when it did get there, it was soon nicknamed the 'Halibag' – an ironic nod towards its relatively low performance and some of the large, unwieldy aspects of its design.

Increasing weights did not help, but mechanically it was not ready – there were issues with its so-called 'archaic' fuel and hydraulic systems, the latter resulting in countless issues with main undercarriage and retractable tailwheel, as well as 'rudder overbalance' – the latter a fatal design flaw that would follow the type into service (See HALIFAX VERSUS LANCASTER: A PERSONAL PERSEPCTIVE, p90). On top of this, performance figures proved disappointing. At 58,000lb, the climb to 15,000ft took an extra eight minutes, while the specified 20,000ft was unobtainable. Further tests showed that with full fuel and 8,000lb of bombs, the max range dropped to 1,700 miles from the expected 1,860. To make matters worse, the aircraft's weight did nothing for its underpowered Merlin engines, and the aircraft tended to enter a gear straining swing

on take-off – all of which factored when L9485's gear collapsed while departing for an early test flight. Ironically, repairs involved local strengthening to permit an increased take-off weight of 60,000lb. However, this extended the take-off distance by 50% and at unstick, a 'soggy' feel in the controls as the machine quite literally "staggered" into the air! These changes were the first that saw the type evolve through a confusingly large family of marks – themselves reflecting rapid wartime development, production at multiple subcontractors and equipment changes, as well as conversion into secondary roles.

At its peak, around 51,000 people were involved in production of the type – including staff at some 600 individual sub-contractors. As a result, it was said one Halifax, even with 30,000 components, 256,000

airframe parts, 70,000 rivets, three to four miles of cabling, a mile of piping, three miles of stretch-formed or rolled stringers and seven tons of light alloy skins covering an area more than half an acre, was completed every hour.

Accordingly, the first Halifax for operational use was delivered to 35 Squadron at RAF Leeming in North Yorkshire on November 13, 1939 – it having been formed at Boscombe Down that same month for the express purpose of introducing the Halifax into Bomber Command service under the leadership of Wg Cdr Raymond William Pennington Collings.

To aid with this, L9484 – by then fitted with dual controls – was borrowed from the MAP, and the second production aircraft (L9486) were handed over to the unit for training. Early that December, '35' – under the umbrella of No. 4 Group, Bomber Command – moved 'down the road' to Linton-on-Ouse where deliveries continued into the new year. Come March 1940, HP had some 20 examples had arrived.

And so it was, on the night of March 11-12 – just five months after the appearance of the first production machine – the type was 'blooded' in its first operation. With seven aircraft dispatched, it was supposed to be an easy "nursery run" to attack the docks in the major northern French port city of Le Havre. While one aborted ▶

21793 Wt. 38805/3503 400,000 12/39—MeC A Co—51-5b58

R.A.F. Form 540 *See instructions for use of this form in K.R. and A.C.I., para. 2349, and War Manual, Pt. II., chapter XX., and notes in R.A.F. Pocket Book.*			**OPERATIONS RECORD BOOK** of (Unit or Formation) **NO. 35 SQUADRON.**	**Page No. 1.** No. of pages used for day

Place	Date	Time	Summary of Events	References to Appendices
	1940			
BOSCOMBE DOWN	5.11		SQUADRON reformed as a Unit in the BOMBER COMMAND, attached to A. &. A.E.E. for formation.	
			W/Cdr R.W.P. COLLINGS, AFC., assumed command and officers posted to strength as follows :– S/L P.A. GILCHRIST, DFC., PILOT	
			F/L T.P.A. BRADLEY, DFC., PILOT	
			F/O M.T.G. HENRY, DFC., PILOT	
			F/O R.V. WARREN, DFC., PILOT	
			P/O A.E. COOPER, GUNNER OFFICER	
			P/O L. MORGAN ENGINEER OFFICER	
	13.11		HALIFAX aircraft L. 9486 taken over and ferried by F/O M.T.G. HENRY, DFC. and crew	
LEEMING	20.11		Squadron moved to R.A.F. STATION, LEEMING and placed under HEADQUARTERS, No. 4 GROUP	
	23.11		Halifax aircraft (prototype) L. 7244 taken over temporarily from M.A.P. for dual purposes and ferried here by W/CDR R.W.P. COLLINGS, AFC, and crew.	
LINTON-ON-OUSE	5.12		Squadron moved to R.A.F. STATION, LINTON-ON-OUSE, remaining under HQ, No. 4 GROUP	
			P/O H. ANDREW reported on posting from No. 10 Squadron, LEEMING (Gunner Officer)	
			P/O A.E. COOPER, Gunner Officer, remained at Leeming, detached to that Station.	
	12.12		The following officers reported on posting, for the duties and from the Units as stated :– F/L G.A. LANE, DFC Pilot 51 Squadron, DISHFORTH	
			P/O E.G. FRANKLIN Pilot 78 Squadron, DISHFORTH	
			P/O G.A.L. ELLIOT, DFC Pilot 77 Squadron, TOPCLIFFE	
			P/O L.J. MACDONALD Pilot 77 Squadron, TOPCLIFFE	
			P/O W.A. TETLEY Observer 78 Squadron, DISHFORTH	
			748544, Sgt WOOLNOUGH, A., Pilot, reported on posting from 78 Squadron, DISHFORTH	
	13.12		566881, Sgt BOVINGTON, L., Pilot, reported on posting from 51 Squadron, DISHFORTH	

ABOVE: Air and groundcrews assigned to 35 Squadron pose with one of the unit's Halifaxes at RAF Linton-on-Ouse in September 1941. Going on to field some 2,493 operational sorties – 717 with No. 4 Group, and 1,776 with No. 8 Group – with the Handley page type before converting to the Avro Lancaster in March 1944, records show it lost 100 examples – equating to 5.6% of those dispatched. NATIONAL ARCHIVES

RIGHT: Surrounded by wartime secrecy during its early career, the Halifax emerged into public view when the type was officially named by Lady Halifax at Radlett on September 12, 1941. The aircraft selected for the ceremony was L9608, a late production Mk.I. Ultimately assigned to No. 1652 Heavy Conversion Unit, the aircraft fell foul to the Handley Page's "vicious swing" while flying "circuits and bumps" with a sprog crew at RAF Marston Moor on November 29, 1942. While those on board were unhurt, L9608 was deemed a write off and struck off charge.

with hydraulic issues, a regular early problem with the type, four successfully hit the docks. One crew, unable to see the primary or the alternative target of Boulogne-sur-Mer – about 100 miles northeast – dropped their bombs on Dieppe, halfway between the two. As for the seventh machine, it also failed to locate Le Havre after repeated attempts and, running short of fuel, turned for home and jettisoned its bombs in the English Channel.

The relative success of the mission turned to tragedy when L9489/ TL-F, one of the aircraft to hit Le Havre, was mistaken for an enemy machine and shot down by a British night-fighter over Surrey. While the pilot, Sqn Ldr Peter Gilchrist and navigator, Sgt Ron Aedy, managed to escape the stricken bomber, flight engineer Sgt Reginald Lucas, 29; bomb aimer/air gunner PO Edward Arnold, 25; wireless operator/air gunner Sgt Stanley Broadhurst, 20; and air gunner FO Albert Cooper, 34, were all killed. Gilchrist summed up the incident later as "A rather sad beginning…" It was the first of

1,833 examples ultimately lost during World War Two.

The following night, a pair of Halifaxes attacked Hamburg and in so doing became the first RAF four-engined bombers to attack the German homeland, thus achieving what the Handley Page V/1500 never managed more than two decades before.

The Halifax went on to play a crucial, if overlooked, role in the Allies' long fight against the Axis powers. Alongside the Lancaster, primarily it formed the backbone of Bomber Command's offensive – albeit under the shadow of the distrust and near hatred of the type by Arthur 'Bomber' Harris, the Air Officer Commanding-in-Chief

> **66 *It was a line of cars parked along the roadside, the autumn sun catching their windscreens… so much for security in face of local gossip!* 99**

Bomber Command. He thrust a cold shoulder towards the Handley Page machine and its parent company from its earliest days of existence, going as far as calling it "a deplorable aircraft". As for HP, he once said: "Nothing whatever is being done to make this deplorable product worthy for war. The two strongest motives of Englishmen in the aircraft industry are patriotic devotion and commercial gain. They will never think of new designs when more orders for the old ones are to be had. To obtain or maintain an order book, aircraft companies will promise anything…" – but that too is for another time.

Despite this, during their service with Bomber Command, Halifaxes flew an incredible 82,773 operations and dropped a massive 227,805 tons of bombs, striking at the heart of the enemy's industrial and military might. Its eventual adaptability also allowed use in paratroop drops, electronic warfare, and maritime patrols. Rugged and reliable, the Halifax contributed significantly to weakening German production and morale, supporting the Allied invasion of Europe, and maintaining control of the Atlantic. Its service demonstrated the importance of heavy bombers in strategic warfare and cemented its legacy as one of Britain's most important aircraft. ∎

1943
Handley Page HALIFAX
Heavy Bomber of the ROYAL AIR FORCE to-day

1918
Handley Page O-400
then the Heavy Bomber of the R.A.F.

Since the birth of the
Royal Air Force, the name
HANDLEY PAGE has been
inseparably linked with development of heavy bombers and large
transport aircraft. Handley Page
HALIFAX four-engined bombers
are now on many fronts playing an
important part in the great offensive
of the R.A.F., with which the manufacturers are proud to be associated.

HANDLEY PAGE
HANDLEY PAGE LIMITED, LONDON

NUREMBURG

With six of its Halifax IIIs falling, 51 Squadron of the Royal Air Force proportionately suffered the highest losses of any unit during Bomber Command's worst night of World War Two – as Andrew Thomas explains

"Last night aircraft of Bomber Command attacked the German city of Nuremburg – 95 of our aircraft are missing…" It was these words during the British Broadcasting Company's one o'clock news on March 31, 1944, that revealed the extent of the losses on what was the worst night of the bomber offensive.

Less than 24 hours before, briefing officers at airfields across eastern England had opened with the words: "Gentlemen, your target for tonight is… Nuremburg."

Within hours, almost 800 bombers and crews would climb away from those same airfields and into the unknown. At the austere wartime airfield of RAF Snaith, near Goole, 51 Squadron listened intently as one of its flight commanders, Sqn Ldr Peter Hill, said those ominous words in the absence of the CO, Sqn Ldr G A Glen DFC. Outside, groundcrews worked to 'bomb up' its Handley Page Halifax IIIs heading to war.

The road to Nuremberg

A long-established heavy bomber unit with No. 4 Group, '51' was thrown into action on the very first night of the war – three of its Amstrong Whitworth Whitleys dropping propaganda leaflets over the German city of Hamburg.

Converting to the Rolls-Royce Merlin-powered Halifax II in 1942, it contributed to all of Bomber Command's major attacks through 1943, including the successful Battles of the Ruhr and Hamburg.

In November that year, the Battle of Berlin commenced – 51 Squadron was, however, still flying the Halifax II. Despite its respected contributions to operations, its performance by then was deemed unsatisfactory for the most part. This was primarily due to its underpowered Merlin engines preventing it from flying at the higher altitudes needed to avoid enemy fighters – the latter having become increasingly more effective throughout that same year. As such, towards the end of 1943, '51' began receiving the much-improved Bristol Hercules-engined Halifax III.

LEFT: Sqn Ldr Paul Jousse – left, the Rhodesian senior navigator on '51' – helps Fg Off Harry Bowling with his flight plan for what was his first and only operation. He was killed just hours later.

BELOW: The red line that led many to their fate – the announcement of the night's target was always a moment of high tension in any bomber briefing.

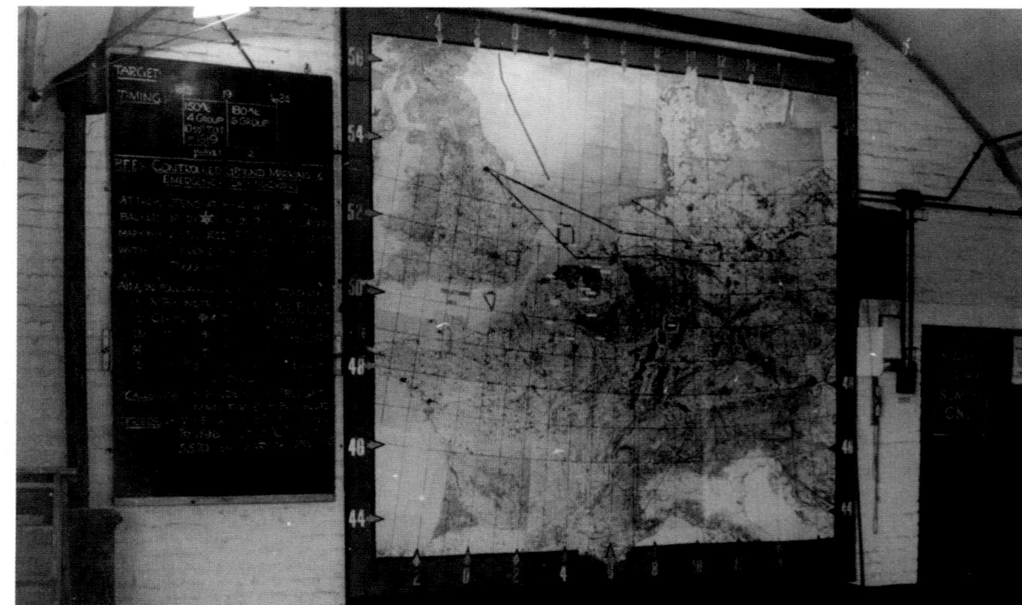

NIGHTMARE

ABOVE: "Gentlemen, your target for tonight is" – Sqn Ldr Peter Hill briefs his crews at Snaith onhe afternoon of March 30. Within hours, he and 34 others in the room would be dead... ALL IMAGES 51 SQUADRON RECORDS

RIGHT: Air and ground crew with 51 Squadron take a moment between tasks to pose with an unknown member of the British Army (third from right with walking stick) in front of Halifax at Snaith.

> 66 *Seaman was a native of Goole and tragically, he had been with '51' for such a short time before his death that he'd not made it home on leave* 99

Quickly pressed into service alongside its surviving Halifax IIs, the IIIs were used for the first time against the enemy capital on the night of January 20, and returned twice more before the end of the month, while another two againts it were flown in mid-February.

Bomber Command's then worst night fell later that month when 78 bombers were lost while attacking the Messerschmitt works in Leipzig on the 19th. Of the 78, 34 were Halifaxes – a loss rate (not including those that had turned back early with problems) of almost 15%. These losses resulted in the Merlin-powered Halifax being withdrawn from operations with immediate effect.

Throughout March, 51 Squadron participated in several successful attacks – but at the cost of several crews. Among those killed was pilot Flt Sgt Roland Seaman, air gunner/bombardier Flt Sgt Edward Andrew Glover, and air gunner

Sgt Leslie Harold Baldwin, their Halifax (LK750/MH-Y2) apparently hit by a Luftwaffe night-fighter using the deadly upward firing 'Schräge Musik' cannon during a raid against Frankfurt on the night of March 18-19.

Seaman was a native of Goole and tragically, he had been with '51' for such a short time before his death that he'd not made it home on leave. Theirs was one of 24 heavy bombers lost that night. Another 35 were lost attacking the same target just four nights later. Then on the 24th came the final major attack on the enemy capital – it was almost as bad as the strike against Leipzig less than a week before with 74 heavy bombers shot down, two of them, MZ507/MH-P2 and LW539/MH-N2 from '51' with the loss of six crew, the rest becoming prisoners of war (POW).

So far, Bomber Command's bitterest winter had cost some 600 bombers, with more than 3,000 aircrew killed, and 700 ▶

more captured. Although Bomber Command would not return to the German capital in such strength again, the final chorus of what was dubbed the 'Battle of Berlin' reached its dreadful crescendo a few nights later.

The target for tonight

At around 1830hrs on March 30, Sqn Ldr Hill stood up and addressed the Station Commander, Gp Capt Noel Fresson, the assembled aircrew, and No. 51 Squadron's mascot 'Butch'. The latter was described as "an evil smelling ragbag of a dog, nearer to a sheepdog than anything else, but he could do no wrong. He never missed a briefing, and his presence was as essential as that of the Met Officer".

Unhappily for many of those in the room, there were others present as, and with a particularly ironic twist, HQ Bomber Command's public relations department had selected that night to invite a party of press reporters and photographers to view the preparations for a raid at a "typical bomber station". Subsequently, they were on hand to record a tragedy. The images they captured that fateful night became some of the most poignant of the entire bomber offensive.

With the visitors attending the briefing, little did they know that hours later, 35 of the 119 aircrew they shared that room with, including Hill, would be dead. Another seven would soon to be POWs.

ABOVE: Smiles all round: a crew from '51' – seeming in good spirits – draw their equipment from the parachute store at Snaith before heading to their aircraft.
ALAMY STOCK PHOTO

BELOW: Sqn Ldr Roxborough of 51 Squadron (sitting, second from right) poses with his crew atop the warload of incendiary bombs bound for his Halifax at Snaith sometime during 1944.

Following the intelligence brief, the Met Forecaster gave the base weather as "fine, becoming cloudy with wintry showers, fine again in late evening. Visibility – good, deteriorating in the late evening. Wind mainly north-north-west – light. Hoar frost in the early morning."

What followed were individual briefs on the target weather, communications procedures, and, most importantly, details of the target marking. During this, Nuremburg's importance as an industrial centre and a communications hub for the Russian Front was emphasised.

With the route ominously marked out in red on the large wall-mounted

map, it took the bombers to an assembly point over the North Sea, then to a point south of the Belgian

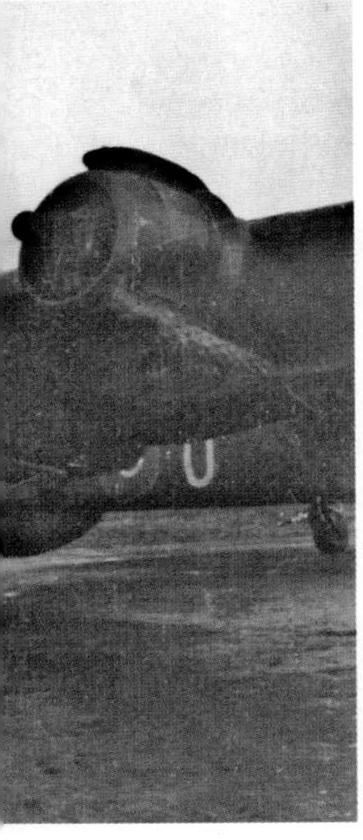

ABOVE: Seen here running up, LW588/MH-O was forced to return to Snaith after the pilot's hatch blew off while departing for Nuremburg on March 31, 1944. It was later lost with its crew on August 11 that same year. Reports at the time suggest it was hit by a bomb dropped by another Halifax above it during a strike against the railway yards at Somain in Northern France.

ABOVE RIGHT: This crew pose for one last picture before getting to work. Note some of them are carrying parachutes – often, crews didn't have the chance to use them.

RIGHT: The perils of night bombing, as well as the robust construction of the Halifax, are evident in this view of LW642/MH-L following a mid-air collision during a raid on Frankfurt on December 20, 1943. Soon repaired, it was flown by Flt Lt Pawell's crew on the Nuremburg raid. After landing safely at Snaith, they reported a quiet trip!

capital, Brussels, where they picked up the infamous 'Long Leg' – a more than 200-mile straight line in which many crews would fight their greatest battle of the European war – before turning south towards the target.

After this, crews left to conduct their individual planning. This was always a particularly busy time for the squadron's navigators. One of those was 32-year-old Plt Off Harold 'Harry' Bowling – this was to be his first operation.

While this went on, the press saw the aircraft being prepared. Each Halifax was loaded with 40 30lb bombs and 540 4lb incendiaries.

Although a bulkier load, it was lighter than those typically carried by the type to improve performance.

Sgt J McCoss, the navigator in Plt Off Mike O'Loughlin's crew, who would be flying his tenth operation, noted that it would be a maximum effort "which surprised most of us because it was still in a 'moon' period". He added: "The briefing produced a shock for everyone in more ways than one. The target was Nuremburg, a city deep in southern Germany and most of the outward journey would be in the moonlight. We were informed that the moon's effect would be offset by a layer of

high cloud, and a late take-off time would mean that the moon would have set by the time we reached the target area."

Although they voiced concerns about the selected route, '51's crews had more to worry about – they would be in the fifth and final wave to bomb. But they had a job to do.

With the briefings complete, the crews took advantage of some free time to prepare. While some rested, others penned those "just in case I don't get back" letters to their loved ones, before coming together for their pre-mission meal. A typical affair of bacon and eggs, many referred to it grimly as the 'Last ▶

Supper'. Before long it was time to kit up.

With the press following the crews to the dispersals, they soon gathered at the Watch Office to see the Halifaxes climb into the unknown. What the more superstitious of the aircrew, many of whom had a regular and unvarying 'lucky' routine, thought is not recorded, but it probably raised some unease. It was as if they were tempting fate and the Grim Reaper...

The 'long leg'

At Snaith, like at other airfields, the shining half-moon led many to expect the mission to be cancelled. But the ominous, desired, glow of a Red Very flare indicating the raid had been 'scrubbed' didn't come. Instead, a Green Aldis light from the Watch Office pierced the air. It was 2153hrs. Almost immediately, Flt Sgt F A Hall pushed the throttles open and eased LW538/MH-N into the air, followed four minutes later by Flt Sgt Sarjantson's crew in LW541/MH-Y. Fifteen more followed them, including Flt Sgt Geoff Brougham with his new navigator, Harry Bowling, in LW544/MH-Q at 2214hrs. With a scratch crew 'down the back',

> **66** *The clear, cold, skies at the height band of the bomber stream also caused many of them to form condensation trails – a deadly marker for the waiting night-fighters* **99**

Hill was the last to depart three minutes later in LV777/MH-F.

Once airborne, the navigators switched on their H2S ground scanning radars carried in a bulbous 'canoe' below the fuselage, then unaware the enemy's own radar could detect its transmissions. Even before the bombers had crossed the English Coast, the Germans knew they were coming – and as they say, "forewarned is forearmed".

Routing south overhead Cottesmore in Rutland, '51' headed east as the bomber stream began forming up over the English Coast. By then, two of '51's aircraft, flown by Flt Sgt O'Neill and WO Hayes, had been forced to abort with technical problems and return to Snaith; LW588/MH-O returned at 0050hrs after the pilot's hatch blew off taking off and LW522/MH-J 17

ABOVE: A pair of 51 Squadron Halifax IIIs in flight from Snaith during 1944.

LEFT: Sqn Ldr Peter Hill eases LV777/MH-F back into Snaith following a pre-op air test in 1944. He and his crew were killed during the Nuremberg raid. Note the radome housing the H2S radar aerial visible on the underside of the fuselage.

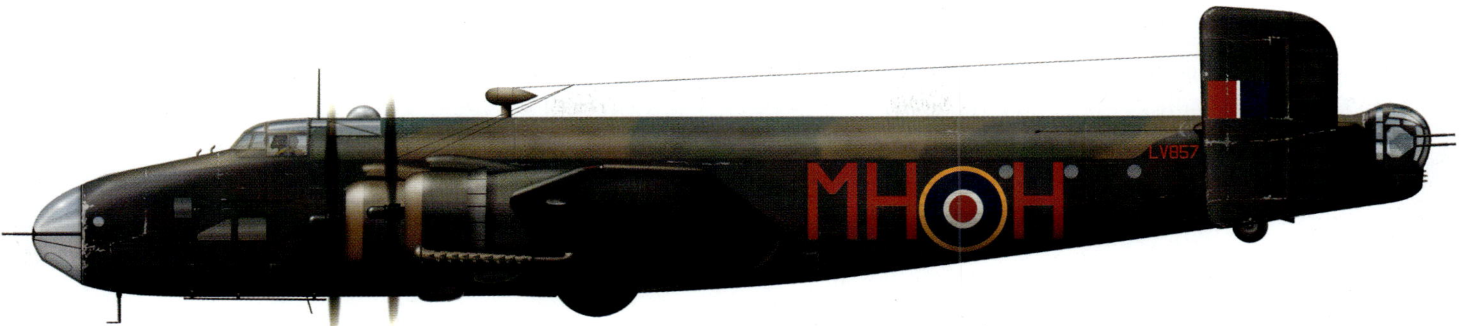

minutes later after its port-inner engine developed issues.

With the remaining 15 heading out over the habitually unforgiving waters of the North Sea in a steady climb, they soon reached the turning point south of Brussels, and the start of the leg that had given rise to such unease. By the greatest of ill fortune, as the raid approached, the Luftwaffe was already marshalling scores of night-fighters at two radio beacons – *Ida* near the German city of Aachen close to the borders of both Belgium and the Netherlands, and *Otto* near Frankfurt, 120 miles or so to the southwest. Both were immediately adjacent the bombers' selected inbound route.

Under the Luftwaffe's then still relatively new 'Zahme Sau' (Tame Boar) tactics, whereby the fighter controllers broadcast the position of the bomber stream, night-fighters from all over the Reich were heading to these points. Once in the stream, the fighters would make radar contact with the bombers and attack them

ABOVE: The first of 51 Squadron's aircraft to fall was LV857/MH-H – there were no survivors.
ANDY HAY-FLYINGART

RIGHT: As Australian Flt Sgt Geoff Brougham wrestled to keep LW544 airborne, he calmly called out the heights on the intercom in the hope that some of his crew might get out. Thanks to his gallant actions, two managed to escape the stricken bomber.

BELOW: Ground staff wave off the crew of Halifax III LW544/MH-Q as they depart for a daylight raid from Snaith, circa early-to-mid 1944. It and its crew never returned from Nuremberg.

for as long as their fuel and/or ammunition held out.

That night, natural factors also conspired against the bombers. Not only were the winds markedly different from that forecast, but the

anticipated cloud cover had never materialised. More worryingly, the clear, cold, skies at the height band of the bomber stream also caused many of them to form condensation trails – a deadly marker for the waiting night-fighters.

While most of the bombers were unsighted to one another in the dark, occasionally a crewman would report the appearance of a ghostly outline of another nearby. As O'Loughlin's Halifax approached the turning point for the 'Long Leg', it was clear that there was considerable activity ahead. Soon the gunners were reporting a steady stream of blazing wreckage lying along the route.

However, although witness to carnage all around them, ironically this crew, like many others part of the great battle, were not actively involved. In fact, O'Loughlin's gunners didn't fire their guns that night. Sgt Bill Morrish, the flight engineer, later recalled: "We actually flew parallel with a German fighter for some time. Luckily, I saw him, but he didn't see us, for some strange reason. I was never very hot on identification so I could not say what type; I just know that there was a swastika on the side... so he was unlikely to be friendly!" Such was the wheel of fate, but others were not so lucky.

The first of 51 Squadron's aircraft to fall was LV857/MH-H. Flown by 21-year-old Sgt Jim Binder, it was shot down close to the German village of Rossbach at 0023hrs by a Messerschmitt Bf 110G of II. Staffel (squadron) Nachtjagdgeschwader (NJG, night fighter wing) 3 (II./NJG 3) flown by Staffelkapitän Oblt Martin Becker. It was his 21st 'kill' – there were no survivors. On board with Binder that tragic night was flight engineer Sgt James Brear, 22; Flt Sgt Walter Austin Guy, 23; bomb aimer Flt Sgt Raymond Hathaway Wilson, 22; wireless operator/air gunner Sgt Edmund Joseph Paul ▶

Monk, 19; mid-upper gunner Sgt Frank Kasher, age unknown; and rear gunner Sgt Basil Hughes 22.

Ten minutes later, over Fladungen, 120 miles to the east, LW537/MH-C was attacked, most likely by 9./NJG 3's Ltn Hans Raum. While two of the crew escaped the stricken Halifax to become POWs, 21-year-old pilot Flt Sgt Malcolm Stembridge, along with the rest of his crew, was killed. It was just their sixth operation.

Six minutes later at 0040hrs, LV822/MH-Z flown by Australian Flt Sgt Edward Wilkins, fell victim to Oblt Becker's guns and came down near Wetzlar, about two-thirds of the way down the leg – again there were no survivors.

At around 1250hrs, Australian Flt Sgt Brougham's crew (which comprised four more Australians, mid-upper gunner Flt Sgt Lloyd Peel, rear gunner Flt Sgt Arthur Williams, wireless operator Flt Sgt Kenneth Radley and bomb aimer Flt Sgt J Gowland, and two Englishmen, flight engineer Sgt H Williams and navigator Bowling) in LW544/MH-Q came under attack while at 19,000ft just to the north of Alsfeld. Hit by a barrage of canon fire, likely from Oblt Becker's Bf 110G, the Halifax began spiralling in an uncontrolled dive. As its Australian pilot wrestled with the controls, he calmly called out the heights over the intercom in the hope that some of his crew might get out. While Williams and Gowland escaped, the rest didn't.

RIGHT: The shattered remains of LW544/MH-Q.

FAR RIGHT: Station Commander Gp Capt Fresson stands forlornly on the balcony of Snaith's Watch Tower, while personnel in the control room wait in vain for the return of 51 Squadron.

With the aircraft ablaze, it was seen to explode at 4,000ft. The gallant 21-year-old pilot was later found in the wreckage still strapped in his seat.

Already a successful Luftwaffe night-fighter expert, Becker was credited with downing seven heavy bombers that night alone – making him an 'ace in a day' for the second time. The following day he was presented with the Ritterkreuz des Eisernen Kreuzes (Knight's Cross of the Iron Cross) by German Führer Adolf Hitler. After the war, Becker said of that night: "They seemed to be lining up to be shot down. I just had to stop after the seventh one... I was sick of the killing."

> **We actually flew parallel with a German fighter for some time. Luckily, I saw him, but he didn't see us, for some strange reason**

Cloud cover

Despite the losses, the bomber stream, including the 11 surviving '51' machines, pressed on. Surviving the 'Long Leg', they turned south towards the target – though the navigation difficulties created by the effects of the then unknown 'jetstream' meant many were well off course. As they flew south, below them, the burning and twisted wreckage of nine bombers shot down formed an ominous track towards the city.

Then, almost perversely, as they approached Nuremburg, the longed-for cloud cover appeared. Ironically, it had been forecast to be clear over the target! The cloud, the unexpectedly fickle winds, and the enemy opposition had also affected the Pathfinders, so the

BELOW: In one of the most haunting images captured that night, anxious eyes are cast to the skies over Snaith awaiting the return of 51 Squadron's overdue aircraft.

target marking, and subsequent bombing accuracy was poor. To make matters worse, a near 15-mile-long creep back had developed into open country to the north of the target as crews progressively bombed the edge of the fire area as they saw it.

Nonetheless, at 0114hrs on March 31, Sgt Duckworth's bomb aimer, Flt Sgt Muir, released their warload — so beginning 51 Squadron's attack. It proved an eventful few minutes for the crew as at about the same time they were attacked by a Junkers Ju 88 after which both the gunners, Sgts O'Neill in the top turret and Stanton in the tail, fired

at and reported hits. The fighter turned away and wasn't seen again.

Sarjantson's crew bombed at the same time before both crews gratefully turned west for home. Over the coming ten minutes the Halifaxes, skippered by Flt Lt Pawell and Flt Sgts Davies, Pettifer, and Hall, all unleashed their loads, as did that of Flt Sgt Norton. The latter crew released their load of incendiaries from 19,000ft on seeing an intense glow of fires through the clouds. They later reported that "if the [bombing markers] were well placed, the attack should have been very successful". O'Loughlin's crew also bombed and set course for

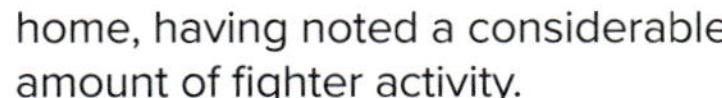

BELOW: Debrief — the strain of the previous eight hours is evident on the faces of Plt Off Mike O'Loughlin's crew — one of only three to return to Snaith that fateful night. In the centre is bomb aimer Flt Sgt Ian Craib, on his right, O'Loughlin, and on his left at the head of the table is navigator Sgt McCoss.

home, having noted a considerable amount of fighter activity.

While most of the crews that returned claimed they had bombed Nuremberg, subsequent analysis of the bombing photos revealed that around 120 aircraft had actually bombed the city of Schweinfurt — some 50 miles to the northwest; another 13 jettisoned their loads on realising they were lost.

Having survived the outbound leg, the extant 51 Squadron Halifaxes turned west for home on a route that avoided the heavily defended area of Stuttgart — about 100 miles to the southwest.

However, many aircraft uncertain of their position overflew it, including Sqn Ldr Hill in LV777. Shot down by flak near Bietigheim, just north of the city, at around 0230hrs, there were no survivors. O'Louglin's crew were luckier. Having strayed close to Stuttgart, they escaped with just damage to their port wing.

Die Abrechnung (the reckoning)

For the surviving ten crews, the flight back was uneventful and at just after 0530hrs, Sgt Duckworth eased LW364/MH-B down onto Snaith's runway. They were the first to return. It had been an anxious wait for Gp Capt Fresson — reports of heavy losses having already filtered down from HQ No. 4 Group at Heslington Hall in York. Fifteen minutes later, Flt Lt Pawell's crew arrived. At 0608hrs, O'Loughlin's navigator Sgt McCoss noted their ▶

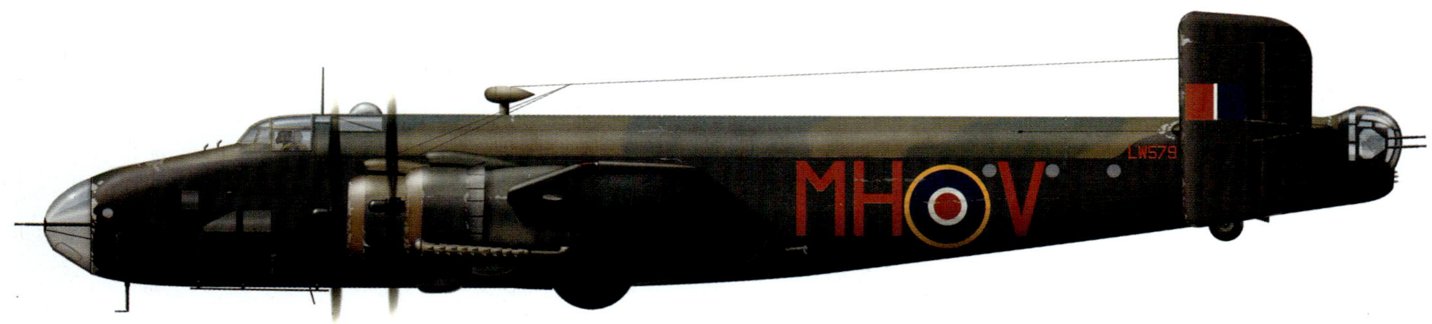

ABOVE: An English Electric built example, LW579/MH-V was the last of the 102 bombers lost that fateful night – the aircraft crashing into the Chilterns near Stokenchurch in Buckinghamshire while trying to land in deteriorating weather. There were no survivors. ANDY HAY-FLYINGART

BELOW: Today, this memorial lies in Cowleaze Wood, high in the Chiltern Hills, close to where the crew of LW579/MH-V tragically lost their lives.

landing time at Snaith in his log. They were the last to get back in – by then the base, covered with low cloud, was being battered by gusty winds and rain squalls. O'Loughlin recalled: "All was gloom as we entered the de-briefing room. Of the 18 aircraft detailed, 17 had taken off… but only three had so far returned."

Gradually reports came in that six others had landed elsewhere – including Flt Sgt Merv Hall's crew in LV880/MH-C. His navigator, Australian Fg Off Fred Kirkwood, noted in his logbook: "Ops Nuremburg. Petrol shortage. Landed Wing [Buckinghamshire]. 7hr 35min."

At their debrief, they noted the defences were very active and that fighters were encountered over the target. Tragically, there was one final twist in what was already a nightmare night for 51 Squadron. When trying to land in deteriorating weather, probably at Benson, LW579/MH-V flown by 21-year-old Plt Off Jim Brooks, crashed into the Chilterns, near Stokenchurch in Buckinghamshire. Theirs was the 102nd aircraft to come down. On board with Brooks was flight engineer Sgt Thomas Samuel, 20; navigator Flt Sgt Dennis Patrick McCormack, 21; bomb aimer Flt Sgt Stewart Glass, 23; wireless operator/air gunner Flt Sgt George Willam West, 22; mid upper gunner Flt Sgt Dennis Arthur Churchill, 20; and rear gunner Sgt Robert Frederick Kelly, 20. There were no survivors.

At Snaith, the journalists had remained at the Watch Office to await news of the raid. While waiting for '51' to return, they had witnessed – and experienced – the tension as the night wore on. Even after the heavy losses over Leipzig and Berlin just weeks before, no one really anticipated the scale of the disaster that had befallen them… over a third of the squadron, gone, in a single night.

> **66 I shall never forget the faces of two of them – both middle aged – when it was quietly put to them that six crews were unaccounted for 99**

Of their presence, one of the survivors, Sgt Philip Bailey, O'Loughlin's rear gunner, said: "They watched and waited so considerately whilst the lads were coming in but, as time went on, they too became aware that there were some losses. I shall never forget the faces of two of them – both middle aged – when it was quietly put to them that six crews were unaccounted for, 42 lads of the 119 they had watched set off into the night sky. The notebooks and cameras were put away and the owners quietly left, obviously not wishing to intrude on our feelings."

In all, 95 aircraft were missing and ten more were known to have crashed in England on return. In what would be Bomber Command's worst night, 537 men had been killed and 157 became POWs – although 11 evaded capture to return home. For '51', it had lost six Halifaxes from 17 – a staggering 35% of those despatched that night. Proportionately this was the biggest loss to any of the squadrons involved. It was the nadir of 51 Squadron's war. ■

Published in *Flight*, February 4, 1943. AVIATION ANCESTRY/WWW.AVIATIONANCESTRY.CO.UK

DON'T FEAR THE REAPER

It was said to be 'jinxed', yet flew more missions than any other Halifax, got three crews safely through their tours, and even survived Bomber Command's costliest raid. Jamie Ewan recounts the story of *Friday the 13th* – the Halifax that wouldn't be beaten

> **Losses were inevitable, HX342 was the seventh F-for-Freddy '158' had lost in just over 14 months**

When Handley Page Halifax III LV907 growled low over RAF Lissett on delivery to 158 Squadron, it looked almost identical to the others scattered around the East Yorkshire airfield. But those watching couldn't help but notice that it lacked any of the telltale scars of war – it was another replacement. They could not have known it at the time, but this Halifax was to become a legend.

Failed to return

Rolled out from Handley Page's Radlett factory in Hertfordshire during February 1944, LV907 was accepted for service that same month. Assigned to No. 4 Group Bomber Command and delivered to Leconfield, near Hull, soon after, it was initially held in reserve. At the time, the airfield was home to the Australian-manned No. 466 Squadron and recently formed No. 640 Squadron. It had been the intention to allocate LV907 to one of these. Instead, it transferred to '158' at Lissett, 17 miles northeast – a crew ferrying it there on March 10. On arrival, it was initially accepted

as a reserve. However, when HX342/NP-F *F-for-Freddy* "failed to return" from a strike against the German city of Frankfurt on the night of March 22-23, groundcrew were tasked with preparing LV907 for war.

Assigned to 20 mission veteran Flt Lt Kenneth Holmes that night, his luck ran out when HX342 fell to the guns of a German night-fighter over the Belgian village of Marbais. Of the crew, only Flt Sgt Leslie Morgan survived – the 21-year-old rear gunner escaping the stricken bomber to become a prisoner of war. By the time, the rest of HX342's crew were buried two days later, a cold shoulder had already been turned to the yet to be blooded LV907.

While loses were inevitable, HX342 was the seventh *F-for-Freddy* '158' had lost in just over 14 months – leading many to believe F-coded machines were 'jinxed'. So, when LV907 appeared as 'NP-F', it sent shivers across the station.

When lost, HX342 had flown 13 missions – nine with regular pilot Sgt Clifford Smith who'd arrived at Lisset the previous December. Thus, he had first claim on HX342's

replacement. However, as LV907 was readied, Smith and his crew were on leave. They still were, on March 30, when '158' received a Battle Order for a "maximum effort" raid that night. The target? Nuremburg.

Lucky for some

One of 16 aircraft allocated from '158', LV907 still needed a crew.

In the meantime, Flt Sgt Joe Hitchman thought he and his crew were finally heading off for a much-needed break when they got the call. He later

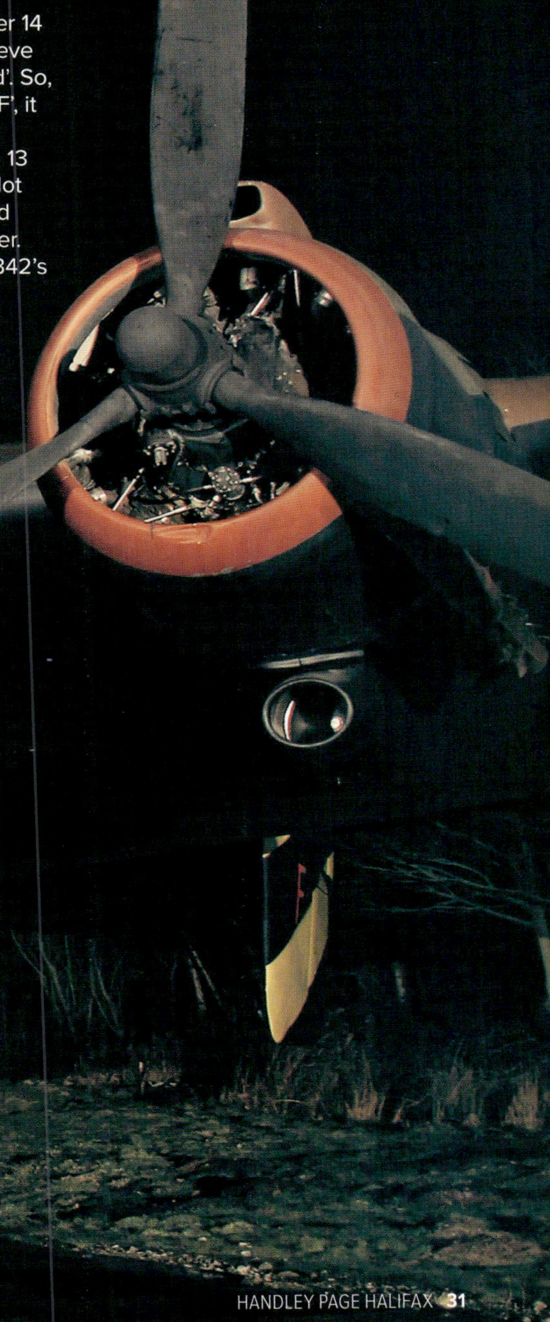

recounted: "We were supposed to be going on leave that day and had actually got to the main gate when we were recalled!" Dismayed, they made their way to the briefing, where they found out their regular aircraft, HX349/NP-G, had been assigned to the 'A Flight' commander, Sqn Ldr Sam Jones. Instead, they would crew *F-for-Freddy*. But they had a job to do.

Later that night, as Hitchman weaved LV907 towards the runway, he watched Jones guide *G-for-George* into the moonlit skies to join the 779-strong bomber stream bound for Germany. As he pushed open LV907's throttles at 2208hrs, little did he know that he had seen HX349 for the last time.

While much has been written about Bomber Command's worst night of the war, this 'jinxed' aeroplane proved lucky for its first crew.

By the time Hitchman eased LV907 back into Lissett, seven-and-a half hours later, news on the losses from what was expected to be a "typical raid" were filtering through – 105 bombers had been lost. While 95 fell to the enemy, ten had crashed in England trying to get home. Come dawn, the grim reality hit home. Some 800 men were missing, with fears more than 500 of them were likely dead. Although LV907 survived its baptism of fire, four of '158's bombers failed to return… including *G-for-George*. One of the few downed by anti-aircraft fire that night, it crashed near the Rhineland-Palatinate town of Hachenburg with the loss of Sqn Ldr Jones and his 23-year-old mid-upper gunner, Flt Sgt Kenneth Bray – the rest of the surviving crew being captured.

The stuff of nonsense

When compared to other squadrons, 158 Squadron lost just 25% of its attacking force (see *NUREMBURG NIGHTMARE*, p20). That said, it would be another nine days before it was back in action, by which

time Smith (then a pilot officer) had returned from leave to take charge of LV907 with his crew – New Zealand-born navigator Flt Sgt Harold King, flight engineer Sgt Rod Neary, bomb aimer Flt Sgt Keith 'Kiwi' Smith, another New Zealander, wireless operator/air gunner Flt Sgt Eric King, Australian mid-upper gunner Flt Sgt Ron Clarkson, and rear gunner Sgt Jack Goff.

With most of the crew having already flown nine missions together, four more than the average, bonds had been forged through an anvil of fear, freezing temperatures, deadly

> **66 *After five missions or so, the seriousness of the situation and the peril we faced began to sink in* 99**

flak, and prowling night-fighters. They knew their odds of survival were still slim – only one-in-six crews were expected to make it through their first tour of 30 operations. The chances of surviving a second tour didn't even bear thinking about. For some it was too much, as Eric King later revealed: "At first, we were just like kids, all enthusiastic and eager to get to work. But after five missions or so, the seriousness of the situation and the peril we faced began to sink in. The groundcrew had bets on which would be the first aircraft back. I heard someone say, 'it won't be a case of who is first back, but who is coming back.' I thought, 'God almighty!' Our first tail gunner found it harder than most. He only completed four operational missions with us before being overcome with fear and exhaustion."

With the uncertainty of life or death, superstitions were inevitable – unless you were Clifford Smith, who branded it the "stuff of nonsense". In fact, when he was asked by his grouns crew chief Jack Wicks what to name their newly

ABOVE: *Friday the 13th* – in just over a year of near-constant operations, this 'jinxed' aircraft proved to be lucky for 161 men from all corners of the globe.
ANDY HAY-FLYINGART

LEFT: The 'Smith crew' with 'Friday' at Lissett on August 1, 1944. From left, standing, they are: mid-upper gunner Ronnie Clarkson, flight engineer Rod Neary, bomb aimer 'Kiwi' Smith, pilot Clifford Smith (holding the crew's stuffed elephant mascot), wireless op/air gunner Eric King, navigator Harold King and rear gunner John Goff, while kneeling from left is engine fitter Mick Miller, Sgt Tom Daly, the NCO in charge of the airframe, and Flt Sgt Bill Cartwright.
ALL IMAGES KEY COLLECTION UNLESS STATED

ABOVE: A colour study of LV907's nose art and bomb markings taken on, or around, June 20, 1945. With yellow marks denoting night-time operations, the white examples tally those flown by day. Within months of this photograph being taken, 'Friday' was unceremoniously scrapped.

RIGHT: The 'Waterman crew' – from left, they are flight engineer Vincent Creane, mid-upper gunner Kenneth Cammack, wireless operator/ air gunner Brian Wilbraham, pilot Derek Waterman, bomb aimer Reginald Littlemore, rear gunner John Jackson, and navigator Wilfred Tyler. Kneeling are groundcrew Jack Wicks (left) and Tom Daly.

allocated Halifax, he replied: "Gosh! I don't care, I'm not superstitious… call it what you like, Jack!"

By early April 1944, LV907 had become *Friday the 13th*. On painting the name on the nose, Wicks also added a skull and cross bones, a scythe dripping blood, and the words "As Ye Sow… So Shall Ye Reap". It's thought the latter was in reference to comment made by Bomber Command's Commander-in-Chief, Air Marshal Arthur Harris during a speech about the strategic offensive against Germany on June 3, 1942, in which he said: "They sowed the wind and now they are going to reap the whirlwind…"

To prove Smith's point, Wicks even added an upside-down horseshoe, a broken mirror, and went as far as painting a morbid white tombstone with the crew's names on it, and an open ladder above the entry hatch. This, along with the tombstone, were later removed. While the tombstone shone brightly when the enemy's searchlights pinned the aircraft, the ladder was deemed as "taking things too far". The tombstone did, however, remain on the flag the crews would later fly from 'Friday' taxiing to and from the runway.

But not everyone was happy with the name. King recalled: "The squadron leader came along after we had named and painted it. He said, 'If I have to fly that thing, I'll need a gallon of thinners first!' I think we were all superstitious – I used to tap the side as I went in." But would giving *F-for-Freddy* an unlucky name break the so-called 'jinx'?

Luck of the draw

Although it isn't known when Smith's crew first flew LV907, it is known they climbed away from Lissett at 2040hrs on April 9 for their opening mission in 'her' – a strike against the marshalling yards (MY) at Villeneuve St George, near Pairs. With 'Kiwi' Smith releasing ▶

their warload just before midnight, Smith eased 'Friday' back onto Lissett's runway some two hours later. They were back in action later that day with the first of two trips against the MY at Tergnier in northern France – the other on April 18. While these proved uneventful for LV907, '158' lost five aircraft and 30 aircrew. Two days later, they again flirted with death. Shortly after dropping their bombs on the MY near the Belgian town of Ottignies, Goff spotted a Focke-Wulf Fw 190 night-fighter stalking them. Firing LV907's guns in anger for the first time, it quickly disappeared into the night skies. Two days later, they took part in a heavy attack that saw 2,150 tonnes of bombs dropped on the German city of Düsseldorf. Touching down at 0317hrs, Wicks met the aeroplane, and added a fifth mission mark. No matter the weather or time, he diligently added a new mark within hours of LV907's return.

With another four trips against rail and communication lines seeing out April, Hitchman's crew again climbed aboard 'Friday' for a strike against the MY at Malines in Belgium on the night of May 1-2. Departing at 2150hrs, they arrived home at 0140hrs.

As operations intensified in preparation for the Allied invasion of western Europe, 'Friday' went to war five times over the next two weeks – four times with Smith, and once with Flt Sgt John Evans. The latter for a raid against the MY at Lens, in France's Pas-de-Calais. Taking off at 2124hrs, and dropping their bombs from 9,500ft two hours later, LV907 landed at 0108hrs. Two days later, Evans and his crew were shot down in Halifax III HX334/NP-C by Luftwaffe night-fighting ace Oblt Heinz Wolfgang Schnaufer during a strike on the Belgian city of Hasselt. The crew managed to escape the stricken bomber; Evans, along with flight engineer Sgt Les E Board, navigator Fg Off Danny J B Daniels, Canadian air gunner/bomb aimer Fg Off Bill 'Robbie' Robertson, and wireless operator/air gunner

ABOVE: A wartime view of LV907's nose art and bomb tally shortly after January 23, 1945. The bomb flying into a football goal – used to mark the machine's 100th 'op' – was later changed as more symbols were added.

66 *Smith had all but finished his tour when the requisite was increased towards the 40 mark – it almost cost him his life… and 158 Squadron LV907* **99**

Sgt Doug A Lloyd, all managed to evade capture, while Australian air gunners Flt Sgt Dick V G Colledge and Sgt Frank J Tait saw out the war as prisoners in Poland's Stalag Luft VII.

That night, 'Friday' was back in the hands of Smith. Climbing away from Lissett at 2157hrs, they arrived back at 0217hrs. A week later, they were in the thick of it again – 'Kiwi' Smith dropping their bombs on the MY near the major fishing port of Boulogne-sur-Mer on the northern coast of France from 12,000ft. It was their 13th mission in LV907.

On May 24, 'Friday' was one of 20 aircraft '158' dispatched to the German city of Aachen. Departing at 2248hrs, mid-upper gunner Clarkson saw a Junkers Ju 88 homing in on their port quarter

BELOW: *Friday the 13th* at a snowy Lissett in early 1945. Note the yellow stripes visible on the port fin – these were added in mid-1944 to aid in unit identification during daylight operations.

some three hours later. Opening fire, the Australian noted sparks coming from the German machine as it broke away. Intact, Smith landed at 0252hrs to find out five 158 Squadron's machines were missing; records show 18 aircrew were killed that night, while 11 more were taken prisoner.

With a strike on Belgium's Bourg-Leopold three nights later, 'Friday' avoided two "single-engined night-fighters" while attacking a radar station near Cherbourg in Ferme d'Urville on June 2. Smith left Lissett at 0050hrs three nights later, with 22 others from '158' to hit the coastal battery at Maisy, near Grandcamp in Normandy's Calvados region. Dropping through 8/10th cloud cover, 'Friday' arrived home just after 0600hrs – it was LV907's 21st mission. To mark this "coming of age", Wicks added a 'key of the door' to 'her' tally.

With the intensity of operations increasing yet again, groundcrews worked almost non-stop around the clock as Battle Order after Battle Order was posted. Between June 6 and 30, 'Friday' flew 12 raids

across occupied Europe – including more than one in the same 24-hour period.

With Smith piloting four of these, Australian Flt Sgt Ralph Chilcott flew five, while Plt Off Roland New, Flt Sgt Edwin Pulsen, and New Zealander WO Leslie Fulker all flew one each – taking LV907's mission count to 33. Killed in action on September 12 that year during his 30th operation, a strike against the German town of Gelsenkirchen, Fulker was one of the few captains connected with 'Friday' who failed to finish their tour; he was just 23 years old.

With 31 missions to his credit, Smith had all but finished his tour when the requisite was increased towards the 40 mark – it almost cost him his life... and 158 Squadron LV907.

ABOVE: Armourers, fitters, and riggers pose with 'Friday' at Lissett in the days following 'her' unprecedented 128th operation. The success of any bomber unit depended on the efforts and determination of groundcrew, who often toiled around the clock in all weathers.

BELOW: Fg Off Norman Gordon peers down from LV907's cockpit moments after coming to a stop at Lissett in the early hours of January 23, 1945, following the bomber's 100th operation.

Close call

Returning to the fray on July 1 with a late afternoon strike against the V-1 site at Oisemont in northern France, Smith pulled 'Friday' into the air at 1529hrs. Running into the target at 13,000ft through spasmodic flak, an exploding shell hurled red hot shrapnel into LV907's forward fuselage – setting an ammunition container alight. It exploded and a blaze quickly spread. With the situation worsening by the second, Neary and Eric King jumped into action to get it under control. Unbeknown to them was the injury Harold King had suffered. Despite his discomfort, the Kiwi navigator refused any medical attention until he was sure they were clear of the target area. With Smith easing a damaged 'Friday' down at 1907hrs,

Wicks soon added a special bomb symbol to mark 'her' near demise. For their "coolness in the face of extreme danger", all three airman, as well as Smith, were awarded medals for gallantry – Clifford and Harold King the Distinguished Flying Cross, while Neary and Eric King received the Distinguished Flying Medal.

Of note, this incident is thought to have happened during LV907's 35th operation – however, 158 Squadron records suggest it was in fact during 'her' 34th. Interestingly, the aircraft's record card shows no entry indicating battle damage. While it's likely another operation involving LV907 prior to July 1, 1944, has been omitted, the total number of operations entered against *Friday the 13th* comes equal to her recognised 128, meaning it was likely credited with one more flown by another Halifax. That said, MZ337 was pressed into service as 'NP-F' for operations on July 6, while the records show 'Friday' operating to Caen with Canadian 'Skipper' Fg Off Gordon Montgomery the following day. A clerical error in the haze of war?

With 'Friday' flying eight operations through July – which included another brush with a Ju 88 night-fighter Goff claimed as 'damaged' on the 21st, and a near eight-and-a-half-hour trip to Stuttgart on the 24th – Smith's crew completed their tour with a trip against the V-1 facility in northern France's Chapelle Notre-Dame on August 1. With 10/10th cloud on the outbound leg, the raid was

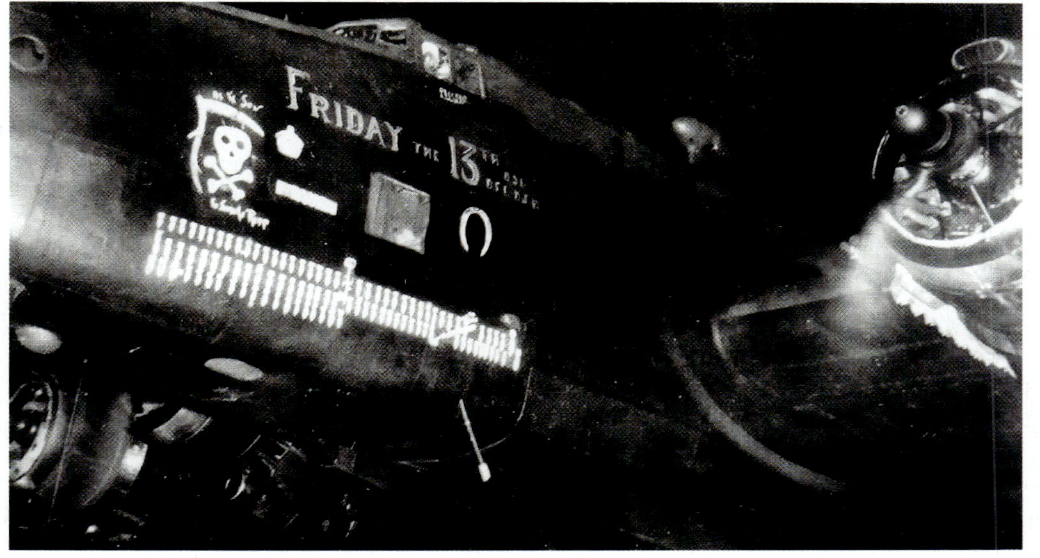

> **Turning for home, they touched down at Lissett an hour or so later – incredibly, this 'jinxed' machine had seen them safely through 29 operations**

abandoned at 2134hrs. Turning for home, they touched down at Lissett an hour or so later – incredibly, this 'jinxed' machine had seen them safely through 29 operations.

Half century... and more

Less than a day later, LV907's new regular pilot, Flt Sgt Derek Waterman (who had flown 'her' twice before) climbed for a strike against the V-1 launch/storage facility at Forêt de Nieppe in northern France. Joining '158' in June, Waterman's all sergeant crew comprised navigator Wilfred Tyler, flight engineer Vincent Creane, bomb aimer Reginald Littlemore, wireless operator/air gunner Brian Wilbraham, mid upper gunner Kenneth Cammack, and rear gunner John Jackson. Going on to fly 12 raids consecutively during the first 18 days of August, Waterman was in the cockpit when 'Friday' surpassed the 50-mission mark on the 9th with an uneventful trip to Bois-de-Haye in France's northeast. Departing just after 1100hrs, the weather was that good, Littlemore map read his way to the target, before releasing 'his' bombs visually from 12,000ft three hours later.

With another eight missions 'chalked up' by August 25 (six with Waterman, and one each with Fg Off Duncan MacAdam, and Flt Sgt Alfred Meaden), a change from strategic to offensive bombing, saw '158' allocate 23 bombers, including 'Friday', to Bomber Command's first daylight operation against the Ruhr two days later. Targeting the oil refinery at Homberg-Heerbeck, 'Friday' was assigned to New Zealander Flt Sgt Jack Harmer's crew – they were airborne for four-and-a-half hours. Harmer went on to pilot 'Friday' on 'her' 61st, 77th, and 79th missions to Soesterberg in the Netherlands, the north German

coastal town of Wilhelmshaven, and the Ruhr's second-largest city, Essen, on September 3, October 15, and October 23, respectively.

Although Meaden captained LV907's 60th and 62nd raids to La Pourchinte and Le Harve in northern France on August 30 and September 9, both strikes were abandoned due to cloud cover over the target.

By then, LV907 was beginning to show signs of near constant use since March 30. Assigned to Fg Off Stanley Rees on September 11 for another strike against Le Harve, a problem with the undercarriage meant 'she' flew the entire trip with it hanging partially down. While the mission was abandoned three hours after departing, due to the target becoming obscured, the extra drag caused LV907's fuel consumption to skyrocket – Rees ordered their bombs to be jettisoned as they turned for home.

With the problem fixed, Waterman (then a pilot officer) guided 'Friday' on the first of two successive daylight strikes against the synthetic oil plant in the German city of Gelsenkirchen on September 12 and 13. While LV907 returned from the first unscathed, 'she' was peppered by flak during the second – thankfully the damage was deemed minor and quickly repaired. With Waterman 'chalking up' LV907's 68th and 69th missions with strikes against targets in the German and French port cities of Kiel and Boulogne-sur-Mer on the 15th and 17th, respectively, he and his crew

needed just seven more to complete their tour. Two days later, Waterman eased 'Friday' back into Lissett on three engines after the port outer failed on route to the German city of Neuss. For the second time, Waterton ordered their bombs to be jettisoned into the sea.

ABOVE: *Friday the 13th* catches the eyes of Londoners while on display outside the bombed-out wreck of the John Lewis store on Oxford Street as part of the Victory in Europe celebrations in June 1945.

LEFT: The 'Gordon crew' pose with *Friday the 13th* following its 81st operation – a daylight strike on Domberg on October 28, 1944. From left are bomb aimer Fg Off William Peters, navigator Flt Sgt James Murray, flight engineer Sgt Arnold Hawthorn – the only non-Canadian – pilot Fg Off Norman Gordon, mid-upper gunner Sgt John Hyde, tail gunner WO Lawrence Pye, and wireless/air gunner Flt Sgt Thomas Little.

Soon back in the air, just two more missions were flown that September – both to Calais, the first with Sqn Ldr Arthur Salter, the other with Waterman.

But for how long?

As autumn approached, LV907's tally continued to increase – eight more being added between October 6 and 25, including strikes on the heavily defended industrial Ruhr cities of Bochum, Duisburg, and Essen, the latter in the hands of next regular pilot, Canadian Flt Lt Norman Gordan; on the 21st, 'Friday' was assigned to New Zealander Fg Off Thomas Sinclair for a raid against Hanover, however the attacking force was recalled in the air.

By the time Waterman, then a flying officer, and his crew flew their 26th and final mission in LV907 on October 28, 'Friday' boasted 80 missions marks. But many began to ask question: how long 'she' could continue?

The following day, Gordon with his crew – navigator Flt Sgt James Murray, flight engineer Sgt Arnold Hawthorn, bomb aimer Fg Off William Peters, wireless/air gunner Sgt Thomas Little, mid upper gunner

Sgt John Hyde; and tail gunner WO Lawrence Pye – took 'Friday' to Zoutelande in the Netherlands. Departing at 1014hrs, they dropped their bombs at 1201hrs. With Murray noting their arrival back at Lisset as 1345hrs, LV907 was grounded for major servicing – a rare occurrence in Bomber Command. At that time, most bombers averaged 40 operational hours... 'Friday' had flown more than that during that October alone.

Offline for a month, NR190 was put into service as 'NP-F', flying five sorties with Gordon. Repainted as 'NP-T' on LV907's re-entry to service, NR190 failed to return from a strike on Hanover on January 5, 1945, with all but one of the crew surviving.

On November 29, Gordon's crew resumed their association with 'Friday' during a near four-hour trip to Essen. With six raids flown between

November 30 and December 20 – one each with Sgt Robert Kaye to Duisburg, and Fg Off John Compton to Hagen, and four with Fg Off John Robinson, who guided 'Friday' to Soest where it narrowly avoided a burst of fire from a twin-engined night-fighter, Osnabruck, Essen, and Duisburg – Gordon racked up LV907's 90th mission with a late afternoon strike on Cologne on the 21st.

The unbeaten warrior

Three days later, 'Friday' was one of 21 aircraft '158' dispatched for a daylight attack against the airfield at Essen-Mülheim. However, while outbound, the port outer engine's boost dropped. Almost immediately 'Friday' began to lose height and speed. Turning for home, Robinson gave the order to jettison their bombs – they landed at 1519hrs. With three more trips seeing out the year, taking LV907's mission total to 94, Robinson was at 'her' controls on January 1, 1945, for a successful strike on the Dortmund-Ems Canal. On landing back at Lissett, many began to wonder if 'Friday' might be the first on the squadron to complete 100 missions?

That said, two '158' airframes could have clinched that title ahead of 'Friday'. HX356/NP-G *Goofy's Gift* with 73 and LV940/NP-J *Just Jake* with 82 had both been lost, ironically, in flying accidents on November 8 the previous year. But 'Friday' kept coming back – four strikes to the heart of the Ruhr between January 2 and 16 (three with Gordon, and one with Canadian Fg Off Norman Tilston) took 'her' mission tally to 99. Three days later, Gordon, then a flight lieutenant, pulled 'Friday' into the air at 1848hrs for a strike on the German city of Gelsenkirchen. Arriving over the target four hours later, 'Friday' dropped 'her' bombs through 10/10 cloud and turned for home. With Gordon easing LV907 down at 0032hrs, 'Friday', flag flying, taxied towards the waiting crowd. With scenes of celebration, an intensely proud Jack Wicks applied 'her' 100th bomb mark.

> **" Three days later, 'Friday' was one of 21 aircraft 158 dispatched for a daylight attack against the airfield at Essen-Mülheim "**

While some thought LV907 might be withdrawn, there was still a war on. With Germany almost on its knees and the Allies stranglehold on it increasing with each passing day, Bomber Command unleashed hell on what remained of its industrial centres. A week later, 'Friday' and Gordon were back at it with a six-and-a-half-hour trip to attack troop concentrations in the German city of Mainz. Then, between February 4-27, 'Friday' flew ten missions (six with Gordon, three with Salter and two with Kaye) – clocking up an incredible 62hrs 40mins.

A similar pattern followed in March with 'Friday' adding 13 missions to 'her' tally with trips to 13 different German cities – Cologne with Fg Off Arthur Elley on the 2nd, Kamen, Chemnitz, Essen, Dortmund, Wuppertal, Homberg, Hagen, Witten, Recklinghausen, Rheine with Gordon between the 3rd and 21st, while Fg Off Harold Wheeler flew 'her' to Gladbeck and Munster on the 24th and 25th, respectively.

With these, LV907 had flown an unprecedented 124 missions. And while they all proved relatively uneventful, Gordon was forced to divert 'Friday' into RAF Lavenham in Suffolk after losing the port outer engine returning from Chemnitz on March 5. 'Screened' later that same month, the Gordon crew became the third such to complete their tour in LV907. Flying their final raid on March 21, they had flown 'Friday' 24 times.

With the pace of operations slowing as the war in Europe entered its final phase, LV907 flew just three missions between April 4 and 18 – two with then regular pilot Wheeler and one with Canadian William Dargaval, a flight sergeant who joined the squadron the previous month. But peace was on the horizon.

On April 25, 'Friday' was back in action with Wheeler. Departing Lisset at 1447hrs for a strike against the coastal guns at Wangerooge (the most easterly of the East Frisian islands), 'Friday' battled through "considerable flak" and "swerving bombers" over the target, to arrive home at 1845hrs. With its 128th bomb mark added just hours later, both 'Friday' and '158' had flown their final missions – less than ten days later, the war in Europe ended.

In just over a year, this so-called 'jinxed' aeroplane had proved lucky for 161 men from all corners of the globe. For many at Lissett, when 'Friday' kept coming back, 'she' became a symbol of hope. For some it was a symbol of luck.

Officially struck off charge on May 18, 1945, 'Friday' was dismantled and taken to London where 'she' was displayed outside the bombed-out wreck of the John Lewis department store on Oxford Street as part of the Victory in Europe celebrations. Once finished with, 'Friday' was taken to the York Aircraft Repair Depot at RAF Clifton Moor, where despite 'her' distinction, she was unceremoniously scrapped during late 1945.

Today, the legacy of *Friday the 13th* lives on in the truly incredible Halifax reproduction at the Yorkshire Air Museum near York. How the museum came to boast a 'Halifax' is the stuff of legend and a story that includes 20 years of sheer determination, a hen house in Scotland, the French Air Force, British Aerospace apprentices, and a sprinkling of luck – with a truly magnificent result. ■

KEITH MEACHEM

> **66** *Unbeknown, with its 128th bomb mark added just hours later, both 'Friday' and 158 had flown their final missions* **99**

BELOW: While *Friday the 13th* was reduced to scrap in late 1945, 'her' nose art survives today as part of the RAF Museum's collection and is currently on display at its RAF Cosford site in Shropshire.

Published in *Flight*, February 5, 1942. AVIATION ANCESTRY/WWW.AVIATIONANCESTRY.CO.UK

YORKSHIRE'S OWN

When you consider some 6,176 Halifaxes were built between 1940 and 1945, it seems incredible that not one complete example was kept for prosterity. Now, compare that to the number of Avro Lancasters that survive today: 17 of the 7,377 built, two of which are airworthy.

That number – zero – is somewhat heart wrenching when one considers more than 40% of the 10,018 heavy bombers produced in Britain between 1940 and 1944 were Halifaxes. Even more so given that during its service with Bomber Command during World War Two, the Handley Page type flew some 82,773 operations and dropped 224,207 tons of bombs, while 2,083 aircraft were lost – some 2.5% – with countless more aircrew killed. For comparison's sake, the Lancaster's number is 156,192 sorties and 3,677 lost – representing 2.4%.

The forgotten backbone

It has to be said, the Lancaster was always considered Bomber Command's 'Golden Child' – even more so during the dark days of war. And yes, the Halifax had a troubled development and had issues that attracted a somewhat negative reputation, although many of these were blown out of all proportion. But mud sticks. It didn't help that countless official press releases seemed to disregard the considerable operational contribution of the Halifax and its crews, instead precedence was given to achievements of the Lancaster – which also had a troubled development. In one glaring case, a mission comprising 250 Lancasters and 250 Halifaxes, each bombing different targets, was reported in a newspaper as: "500 Lancasters attacked two targets in Germany last night" – a galling omission for the Halifax force.

It was a similar story following a near 800 aircraft raid on the German city of Hamburg across the night of July 27-28, 1943. The following day, one of the national daily newspapers reported: "Last night, a force of 800 four-engined Lancaster bombers attacked enemy targets in Germany." At the time, a young Halifax pilot is known to have said: "If they were all 'Lancs' on that trip, where the hell had we

Halifaxes been on the same raid?" The attacking force had been made up of Lancasters, Stirlings, Halifaxes, Wellingtons, and Mosquitos. In fact, 33% of the total force had been

LEFT: The sheer attention to detail across 'Friday the 13th' is more than evident in this view looking forward from the navigator's table towards the bomb aimer's couch. KEY-JAMIE EWAN

LEFT: 1945 or 2025? Forming the perfect backdrop for re-enactor Gerallt Wheeler, the Yorkshire Air Museum's masterpiece – 'Friday the 13th' – stands proud at its Elvington home on May 8, 2025. ALAMY-PA IAMGES

LEFT: 'The Founder Member' of YAM's Halifax project – the derelict fuselage section of Halifax II HR792 sat near Stornoway on the Isle of Lewis in April 1984, shortly before its journey south to Elvington. ALL IMAGE KEY COLLECTION UNLESS STATED OTHERWISE

When the Yorkshire Air Museum was established within the footprint of RAF Elvington, it was said that "such a museum without a Halifax would be like a frame without a picture". But with no examples left, it turned to building one. And that's what it did, as Jamie Ewan recounts

LEFT: Air- and groundcrew from No. 347 'Tunisie' Squadron crowd the watch office at Elvington to see their counterparts from No. 346 'Guyenne' depart home to France on October 20, 1945. In just 18 months of operations, both units lost some 50% of their aircrew.

LEFT: Perhaps one of the most iconic images of the Halifax is this one captured of JB911/KN-X of 77 Squadron RAF making a low pass over stablemate 'KN-M' (thought to be DT736) at Elvington at the end of a pre-op air test, circa early 1943 – much to the delight of the groundcrew.

LEFT: British Aerospace apprentices at work restoring HR792's fuselage at the firm's Brough facility in the East Riding of Yorkshire sometime in early 1987. Taking some 18 months to complete (which included remanufacturing and replacing most of the corroded aluminium), it was delivered to Elvington on May 20 that year and unveiled by The Right Honourable Charles Wood – the third Earl of Halifax. BAE SYSTEMS

made up of the Handley Page type. A contribution ignored, or an oversight in the haze of war?

None of this was helped by the quite open distrust and almost hatred for the type held by Air Officer Commanding-in-Chief Bomber Command, Arthur 'Bomber' Harris.

It could be said, this apparent antagonism towards the Halifax had a long lasting and detrimental effect – more so in the postwar years when aircrew had to put up with repeatedly being told that the Lancaster did this and it did that, completely ignoring the Handley Page machine's vast and significant contribution to the war. As such, a sad and unneeded atmosphere was created in which Halifax crews couldn't understand why their contribution had seemingly been brushed aside.

Little thought was given to preserving military aircraft after the war since the focus was on demobilising and transitioning back to peacetime economies. Redundant warplanes were seen as logistical burdens, not historic assets. Yet not one example of the type that helped form Bomber Command's backbone was saved. At one point it is said, some 400-odd Halifaxes sat at the Handley Page's York Aircraft Repair Depot at Clifton, just outside the city in 1945, awaiting scrapping. And what about those that ploughed the skies hauling passengers and cargo post war? Food for thought.

Readdressing the balance

Between 1935 and 1945, Yorkshire was home to 41 military airfields – most of them nestled in the flat and fertile agricultural land that makes up the Vale of York. There were so many, the county was often dubbed a land-based aircraft carrier. At the war's peak, more than 30 squadrons from across No. 4 and No. 6 Groups operated from these airfields – many of them using the Halifax. Today, the Book of Remembrance in York Minster records more than 18,000 names of those killed flying from these bases, both in training accidents and operationally.

In 1983, aggrieved there was very little commemorating these sacrifices, and barely anything left of the Handley Page type, a small group of aviation enthusiasts banded together to establish a museum on the site of RAF Elvington, southeast of York, to redress the balance. Elvington had been home to three Halifax squadrons during the war: 77 Squadron Royal Air Force between October 1942 and May 1944, and two squadrons from the Free French Air Forces – No. 346 'Guyenne' and No. 347 'Tunisie' between May 1944 and October 1945. While '77' suffered heavy casualties during its time at Elvington, with more than 500 aircrew killed or taken prisoner when 80 of its aircraft failed to return, some 50% of the Free French crews were lost in action during the 18 months they were stationed in York.

Today, some 40 years on from its opening, that museum is the Yorkshire Air Museum and Allied Air Forces Memorial – better known as 'YAM'. Incredibly, it boasts its own Halifax – 'Friday the 13th'. But how I hear you ask? The answer is dogged determination and unbeaten Yorkshire logic – the needed attributes necessary to see such an ambitious project led by Ian Robinson, who had been assigned to Clifton with Handley Page during World War Two, before becoming a civilian flight engineer with the manufacturer, through to its glorious finale.

"It's not real!"

The thinking was straightforward – there should be a Halifax on show at Elvington, where once Handley Page's under-praised stalwart took the war to the heart of the enemy. After all, "such a museum without a Halifax would be like a frame without a picture."

Of course, there was no chance of an original, so it was decided to recreate one, using as many genuine, or kindred, components as possible.

Starting with a derelict fuselage section of Halifax II HR792, which crashed on the Isle of Lewis near Stornoway, in Scotland, while on strength with RAF Coastal Command's 58 Squadron on January 13, 1945 (and used as a hen house thereafter for some 40 years) in 1984, the team behind its creation set about gathering the hundreds of pieces needed to complete it, while others set about making those parts that couldn't be found using original Handley Page drawings saved when the company ceased to exist in 1970. The front fuselage section was built from scratch. The undercarriage legs, manufactured from new, were mated with stock wheels and tyres. The tailplane was built using parts from LL505, a No. 1659 Heavy Conversion Unit machine that came to grief on Great Carrs in the Lake District during a night navigation exercise on October 22, 1944, all eight on board being killed – with others built by the team. The wing centre and intermediate sections came from Handley Page Hastings TG536, which ended its days on the fire dump at what was then RAF Catterick. The outer mainplanes, found in a scrapyard in the south of England, were Hastings 'new old stock'. The 'Covered Wagon' – the aircraft's fuselage centre section – was salvaged from

>

The number four engine – one of the Bristol Hercules gifted to the project by the French Air Force the previous decade – is lifted into position in June 1996.

Job done! Ian Robinson, who was instrumental in the creation of 'Friday the 13th', looks on at 13 years of work that gave the first true representation of a complete, restored Halifax, anywhere in the world, shortly after 'her' roll out, symbolically, on Friday, September 13, 1996.

Stepping into the aircraft's cockpit is like stepping back in time... KEY-JAMIE EWAN

ABOVE LEFT: Seen here shortly after completion in May 1989 is the restored fuselage section of HR792 mated with the rear fuselage built from new by British Aerospace apprentices, and the refurbished Boulton Paul 'Type E' rear turret – the latter coming from an unknown Halifax.

ABOVE RIGHT: Of note in this view of 'Friday' is the type's 'Covered Wagon' structure into which the wing front spar passes. A vital piece in YAM's Halifax jigsaw, it was salvaged from an unknown 'Hali' once based at RAF Linton-on-Ouse. Note 'she' carries the serial HR792 on the rear fuselage.

RIGHT: Seen here undergoing construction at Elvington, circa early 1995, in what is now appropriately named the Handley Page Workshop, the aircraft's forward fuselage was built from scratch by volunteers using original Handley Page drawings.

THE OTHER SURVIVORS

As well as 'Friday', two other examples now endure: Halifax II W1048/DY-S at the Royal Air Force Museum London and Halifax VII NA337/2P-X on display in the National Air Force Museum of Canada at Trenton in Ontario, Canada. Their individual stories can be found at www.rafmuseum.org.uk/documents/collections/73-A-1113-Halifax-II-W1048.pdf and www.airforcemuseum.ca/the-story-of-na-337, respectivley. I also encourage you to follow the progress of Halifax 57 Rescue (Canada) – an aircraft restoration group whose mandate is to save what it can of the Halifax. Its website can be found here: www.halifax57rescue.ca

ABOVE: While the aircraft's tailplane – seen here attached to the rear of the aircraft, circa early 1990 – was built at Elvington, with new parts being mated to those salvaged from LL505, the tail fins were manufactured new by British Aerospace at Brough and fitted with the rudders produced in-house using original Handley Page drawings. Note the 'NP-F' codes on the starboard side – these later being replaced by those of a No. 346 'Guyenne' Squadron aircraft in honour of Elvington's wartime past.

an unknown Halifax once based the other side of York at RAF Linton-on-Ouse. The fuselage rear bay and tail fins were manufactured from new using original drawings by apprentices from British Aerospace at its Brough facility in the East Riding of Yorkshire.

A gift from the French Air Force in 1987, the four Bristol Hercules radials were once used by that nation's then soon-to-be withdrawn Nord Noratlas fleet. The propellor hubs were salvaged from Halifax III LW687, a No. 432 Squadron Royal Canadian Air Force machine shot down during the disastrous Nuremberg raid of March 30-31, 1944. The 'props' were newly built by the team at Elvington, as were the rudders. The tailwheel was recovered from Halifax III

BELOW RIGHT: Today, 'Friday the 13th' – having redressed the balance – stands in silent salute to the 'Halifax Boys'.
KEY-JAMIE EWAN

HX271, a No. 466 Squadron Royal Australian Air Force airframe shot down on June 3, 1944 during a raid targeting the rail yards at Trappes in Northern France. The upper turret, discovered being used as a garden cloche, was mated with its needed fittings from a variety of sources, with the basic frame for the rear turret acquired from the Cotswold Aircraft Restoration Group.

It was a huge undertaking – a project that took 13 years to give the first true representation of a complete, restored Halifax, anywhere in the world. 'She' was unveiled to the world on September 13, 1996, with a dual identity. 'Her' starboard side bearing the markings of a Halifax B.VIII on strength with Elvington's own 'Guyenne' Squadron (NP763/H7-N) during 1944 that had also served with '77' – a reminder that the worldwide fight against darkness was shared by many nations, and that sacrifice spoke in many tongues. The port carries the name of the unbeaten bomber that defied superstition – 'Friday the 13th' (see, *DON'T FEAR THE REAPER*, p30). On the choice of the latter, Ian Robinson, in his book, *Home is the Halifax: An Extraordinary Account of Re-building a Classic WWII Bomber And Creating The Yorkshire Air Museum To House It*, published in 2010, said: "Bearing in mind that the YAM Halifax started its life when HR792 crashed near Stornoway

in 1945 and that the road to the stage now reached at Elvington in 1996 has been a long and rugged one, it is not inappropriate that our Halifax should carry the same proud name as one of its outstanding predecessors, one which kept going in spite of everything put in its way, through thick and thin, right to the end of the war. The name 'Friday the 13th' represents and symbolises *ALL* Halifaxes and *ALL* Halifax air and ground crews, from every unit, command and theatre in which they operated."

And while there are cries of "It's not real!", and the age old "Is it a replica or a reproduction?" – it is an example of the often-forgotten backbone of Bomber Command. When you consider that the aircraft boasts countless original parts, 'she' is just as real as some of the more modern-day examples of warbirds flying today.

For many who flew the type during those dark days of war, most of whom are now no longer with us, 'Friday the 13th' provided a final chance to be reunited with their old warhorse. It allowed them to share precious moments with those they were bound together with – not through want, but necessity. It helped them to remember those lost. For some it provided the opportunity to close a chapter in their own way.

While 'she' doesn't fly, or run, this very stillness carries a different kind of motion... the pull of remembrance, the weight of history, the breath of all those who never returned. 'She' is a promise kept that those who once filled its seats, navigated its stars, and trusted its wings will not be forgotten. 'She' is a symbol, a resurrected spirit of the thousands of Halifaxes and those who flew them. The aircraft is not only a machine – it is the vessel of a brotherhood that typified the 'Bomber Boys', and a reminder that courage was never carried alone. ■

"THIS CAN'T HAPPEN TO US!"

The late Tom Wingham recounted two 'dicey' occasions in the Handley Page heavy while serving as a bomb aimer with No. 102 (Ceylon) Squadron

"Most of the time, the main dangers facing Bomber Command's aircrew were the Germans, the weather, and, sometimes, inadequate aircraft to do the job.

At times, the Germans dropped to the bottom of the list, and, for us, the next trip was one such night.

"Having visited Berlin two nights before, it was a bit surprising that on March 29, 1943, we were heading back there once again... word was that Arthur 'Bomber' Harris [the Air Officer Commanding-in-Chief Bomber Command] wanted another crack at 'Big City' before the lighter evenings made it even

LEFT: 'The Hewlett Crew'. From left (standing) they are: Joe Holliday, Dave Hewlet, 'Blackie' Blackallar, Norman 'Chiefie' Beale, while kneeling, again left to right, are: Andy Reilly, Tom Wingham, 'Willi' Hall, and J Nightingale. The latter replaced 'Chiefie' after he had flown 20 'ops' with the crew to complete his second tour.

more difficult. The weather forecast was appalling and, unofficially, our two Met Officers at Pocklington (located at the foot of the Yorkshire Wolds) were backing to 'scrub' the mission.

"With ten aircraft detailed from '102', at the original time for take off, about 1830hrs, a postponement of two hours came through – there was an occluded front running north to south right through the Yorkshire and Lincolnshire airfields, with the cloud base sitting at just 800ft. Some two hours later, it was pouring with rain, with cloud all the way up to 16,000ft – the occlusion was moving far more slowly than forecast, leading to another delay.

"Having hung about the messes for nearly three hours awaiting a decision, no one really believed that we were going to face this weather, and a great deal of incredulity was expressed when we finally found ourselves committed. It was one of the few nights I can remember when 'Bomber' Harris's parentage was in doubt!

"After the postponements, the ten aircraft from Pocklington started to take off at 2146hrs, with the last leaving at 2206hrs. Our aircraft, HR663/DY-Q *Q-for-Queenie*, got airborne at 2147hrs. On board was me, pilot Sgt Dave Hewlet, flight engineer Sgt Joe Holliday, navigator

Sgt 'Blackie' Blackallar, wireless operator/air gunner Flt Sgt Norman 'Chiefie' Beale, air gunner Sgt Andy Reilly, and mid-upper gunner Sgt 'Willie' Hall."

Clapped-out

"When aircrews were tired, take-offs and landings could be extremely hazardous – even more so because most airfield's circuits usually overlapped with one, if not two other circuits. Pocklington was no exception, with our two satellites being Melbourne and Elvington – Melbourne was about four miles to the south, and Elvington, just seven to the west.

"On this night we lost JB848/DY-G *G-for-George* around a minute or so after it took off. It was being flown by William Comrie of the Royal Canadian Air Force and his crew. Getting airborne at 2158hrs with a full fuel and bomb load, it's thought JB848 got caught in the slipstream of another Halifax in the circuit at Melbourne, which flipped it over on its back, resulting in it diving straight into the ground, and exploding on

LEFT: A wartime study of Tom Wingham. A London-born Cockney, he joined the RAF in 1941 aged 18. Volunteering for aircrew, he went on to take part in some of Bomber Command's final raids against Germany in 1945 – but not before being shot down and evading capture. ALL IMAGES TED STOCKER UNLESS STATED OTHERWISE

BELOW: To war: RAF Pocklington's station commander, Gp Capt North Carter, waves off Handley Page Halifax II DT743/DY-O of No. 102 Squadron as it begins its take-off run for a night raid against the Schneider armaments factory and Breuil steelworks at Le Creusot in eastern France on June 19, 1943. One of 22 aircraft '102' dispatched that night (all of which returned safely), Tom Wingham was aboard JB894/DY-X *X-for-X-Ray* – which took off five minutes before this image was captured. Casualties among the local French civilians that night did little for the RAF's reputation... ALAMY-MILITARY-ARCHIVE-PIEMAGS

the edge of the town. Killing the crew, the youngest chap on board was just 20 – the same age as me."

Jack Merrick was walking back to Pocklington with his friend Peter Tranmere. Both R/T Operators in Flying Control, they were due to be on duty for the return from Berlin. Watching on as the Halifaxes circled the airfield, they saw the navigation lights of one of them turn over. His comment was: "Bloody hell! A Halifax can't do that!"

Tom Thackray, who was serving with 10 Squadron as a flight engineer at Melbourne said the story at the time was *G-for-George* "broke cloud and there was another aircraft very close, which made them take rapid evasive action and the aircraft stalled or some such action occurred, and they had not sufficient altitude to recover." Records simply state: "Attempting to avoid another aircraft, stalled and crashed soon after take-off". Just two nights before, the squadron 'boss', Wg Cdr George Holden, had taken *G-for-George* to Berlin. Setting off with eight other '102' Halifaxes from Pocklington at 2001hrs, it returned at 0240hrs, carrying minor flak damage.

"While *G-for-George* had only been with the squadron for a matter of weeks when it crashed having been delivered new on March 5, *Queenie* was one of the oldest, most clapped-out, Halifax IIs we had. From the moment we took off straight into the cloud at 700ft we were struggling. We were to take the northern route to Berlin across the widest part of the North Sea to Denmark, and then down over the Baltic. That's quite a lot of sea!

"The cloud was solid, and our rate of climb was abysmal. As we reached the Danish coast, we were just about breaking out the top of the cloud at a little over 15,000ft. We then realised that we had iced up and the rear ▶

gunner could not see out, while half the pilot's windscreen was also covered. With the throttles fully open we were just about able to get 135kts instead of the usual 160.

"At that moment, the guns around the German coastal town of Flensburg opened up, although the flak was bursting ahead of us – probably because the German gunners didn't believe anything could be flying so slowly! We decided to get rid of our bombs and turn back. I aimed them towards the centre of the gun flashes, and we turned back for the long haul back across the unforgiving waters of the North Sea... the graveyard of many aircraft.

"It proved to be fortunate that our wireless operator was very experienced, having completed a previous tour on Handley Page Hampdens. As a result, he established contact with Pocklington and periodically reported our progress.

"We eventually landed back at base at 0312hrs, and as we reached the end of the runway, had to cut the starboard outer engine for lack of oil pressure. As we proceeded to the dispersal, the groundcrew were signalling vigorously not to open the bomb doors – as was usual. Disembarking puzzled, we were led to first look at the port wing bomb bays where, due to icing, one of the small bomb containers had failed to

ABOVE: Myles Squiers, Douglas Harper, William Comrie, Frank Dorrington and William Jenkins pose together while serving with '102'. Like many that crewed together, they died together.
KEY COLLECTION

RIGHT: March 29, 1943: The Operations Record Book (ORB), for No. 102 Squadron tells its own story.
NATIONAL ARCHIVES

release. As we descended to lower temperatures, it had unfrozen – and as a result 96 4lb incendiary bombs, all live, were now pushing through the light bomb door... a rough landing could have set them off!

"On inspection, we also found our Identification Friend or Foe, or IFF, aerial had disappeared with the ice, while the two inners of our remaining three engines were literally pouring out their glycol coolant. Had we not turned back, it would have been impossible to get back home on one good engine... we would probably have ended up in the North Sea."

> **"** *Dortmund (some 250 miles southwest of the German capital) was to suffer the mightiest blow that the RAF could administer with 826 aircraft* **"**

It was a different story for 'Queenie' two weeks later on April 17 – the aircraft (then coded 'DY-T') being shot down by a Luftwaffe night-fighter [records attribute the 'kill' to a Messerschmitt Bf 110 flown by Hptm Wilhelm Herget of the Stab I./NJG 4 (Staff Unit, I Group Night Fighter Wing 4)] over northern France while returning from a raid on the Skoda factory at Plzeň in the Czech Republic – killing 22-year-old rear gunner FO Graham George Williams. While the pilot, Sqn Ldr Wallace Ivor Lashbrook, navigator FO Kenneth James Bolton, bomb aimer FO Alfred Martin, and wireless operator Sgt Robert William Laws evaded capture, flight engineer Flt Sgt Douglas Charles Knight and mid-upper gunner Sgt Lawrence Irving Neill weren't so lucky – spending the rest of the war as prisoners. Just over a month later, Tom had another scare...

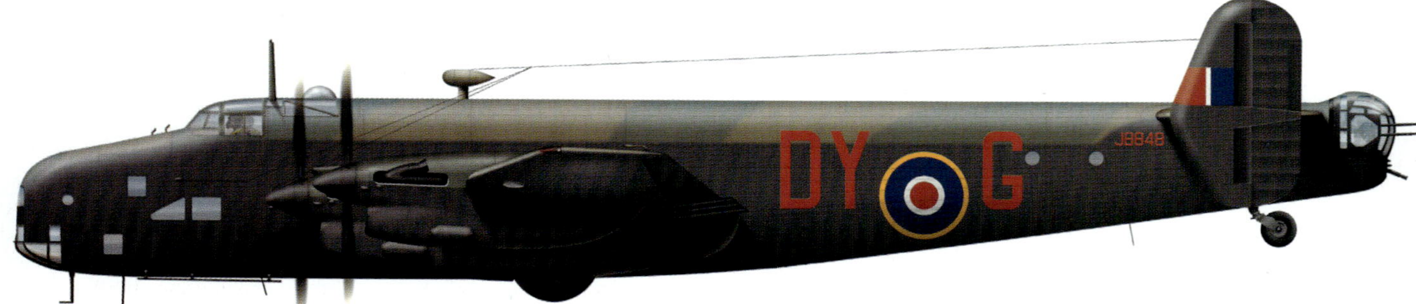

ABOVE: Rolled out by English Electric from its Samlesbury factory in Lancashire during late February 1943 as part of Contract No. ACFT/1808/C4 for 350 examples, Halifax II JB848 was taken on charge by No. 102 Squadron on March 5 that same year. Pressed into service, it was lost just three weeks later when it crashed at Pocklington almost immediately after taking off for a raid against the German city of Berlin on March 29. All on board were killed. They were pilot WO2 William Phelps Comrie, Royal Canadian Air Force, 27; Glasgow, Scottish-born flight engineer Sgt William McGrath, 23; navigator FO Douglas William Francis Harper, 22; bomb aimer FO William Hugh Jenkins, 34; wireless operator/air gunner Sgt Frank William Dorrington, 23; air gunner Sgt John King, 21; and South African air gunner Sgt Myles Christian Campbell Squiers – the latter just 20 years old. The aircraft was ultimately struck off charge on April 8, 1943, having amassed just over 28 of flying time. ANDY HAY-FLYINGART

Date	Aircraft Type & Number	Crew	Duty	Up	Down	Details of Sortie or Flight	References
	JB. 779	SGT. HALE R.R. SGT. MUIR A.C. SGT. HOBBIS W.A. SGT. LOWINGS J.L.SS. SGT. QUEVILLON R. SGT. GIBBS A.J. P/O. WILLCOCK E.D.	BERLIN	2156	0447	Attacked primary target at 18,000 feet heading 210°M Small amount of low cloud. Yellow markers seen enroute and the warning flares over the lake. Red T.I. markers at target were rather widely dispersed. Centre of concentration of seven T.I. markers in bomb sights. Own bursts seen. Few small fires burning. Fair number of T.I. markers going down. Holes in nose from heavy flak over target.	
	JB. 848	F/S. COMRIE W.P. P/O. HARPER D.W. SGT. DORRINGTON F.R SGT. KING SGT. SQUIRES M.C.C.C SGT. McGRATH W.J. P/O. JENKINS J.A.	As above	2158	-	Aircraft crashed one minute after take-off. Aircraft burnt out and all crew killed.	
	HR. 667	W/O. LEE J.L. SGT. JONES G.A. SGT. UNDERWOOD J.W. SGT. CURTIS R.L. SGT. RAYNOR F.M. SGT. MATHER R.A.M. P/S. MURPHY W.E.J. SGT. MARSHALL J.A.	As above	2205	0549	Attacked primary target at 18,000 feet heading 250°M No cloud ground haze. Yellow markers seen enroute and flares over lake. Red T.I. markers at target widely scattered but went for M.P.I. Centre of concentration in bomb sights. Six sticks of incendiaries seen burning on run in, believed dropped short of aiming point but many more sticks seen falling after own bombing. Small holes in both wings from heavy flak predicted between TEXEL and EGMOND at 14,000 feet.	
	JB. 867	S/L. MARSHALL J.E.H. P/O. McDONALD A.M. SGT. MITCHELL B.W. P/S. JONES D.M. P/O. McLOUGHLIN T. SGT. JOHNSON A.W. SGT. DUNSFORD P.R. F/S. WHITTLE P.	As above	2206	0604	Attacked primary target at 18,000 feet heading 250°M. No cloud ground haze. Yellow markers enroute and T.I. markers at target. M.P.I. of red markers in bomb sights. Only two sticks of bombs seen prior to own bombing. Several sticks seen falling as leaving and fires starting. Starboard elevator damaged and trimming tab controls severed, also TR9 aerial shot away from heavy flak vicinity of HANNOVER.	
	W.7934	F/S. McKINLEY T. SGT. SUTHERLAND F.A. SGT. MILLAR A. SGT. O'GRADY P. F/L. HOGG G.F. SGT. SHAW R. P/O. MOON D.G. SGT. RAGGETT S.	As above	2146	0109	Target not attacked. Returned owing to Constant Speed Unit going u/s. Bombs jettisoned safe in sea.	
	HR. 712	F/S. McCORMACK J.R. SGT. LAMBERT W.T. SGT. LEWIS J.A. SGT. LEE B. SGT. HOLDER T.M. SGT. BEALE N. SGT. FIELD D.A. SGT. NORRIS J.A.	As above	2150	0525	Attacked primary target at 18,000 feet heading 220° M 170 IAS Haze about 1000 feet. Red T.I. markers seen. Markers in bomb sights. Fires well alight when left, and a big explosion seen. The attack seemed well concentrated.	
	HR. 663	SGT. HEWLETT D.J. SGT. BLACKALLER H.A.S. P/S. HALL N.A. SGT. HALL D.W.V. SGT. REILLY A. SGT. HOLLIDAY E. SGT. WINGHAM S.T.	As above	2147	0309	Target not attacked, unable to get air speed of more than 135 IAS All perspex iced up aircraft attacked by heavy flak, so jettisoned to increase speed. Oil leaks in both inners and glycol in starboard outer discovered on landing.	
	JB. 868	W/C. COVENTRY H.R. SGT. REYNOLDS B.S. SGT. BROWN SGT. HARDY SGT. MOORE R.J. SGT. PINE-COFFIN G.T. P/O. ARMITAGE V.W.	As above	2202	0514	Attacked primary target at 19,000 feet heading 110°M. No cloud ground haze. Flares over lake and red T.I. over target. Markers in bomb sights. No evidence of any bombing prior to own, but many sticks seen falling later. Fires beginning to take hold. Small flak holes in port wing and fuselage from heavy flak believed over target. Starboard outer engine radiator damaged. Hit by cannon and machine gun fire from fighter on way home. Landed at HARDWICKE.	

In the lead

"When we got to the briefing room on May 23, 1943, and the target was revealed, there were the usual curses and trepidation at finding ourselves back on the 'Happy Valley' run. This was the March-July period, which was later to be known as the 'Battle of the Ruhr'.

"As the briefing commenced, we quickly found out that this was to be something different – the heaviest raid of the war. Up to this date, apart from the 'Thousand Bomber' raids of 1942, which pressed everything that could take off into service, without necessarily being able to carry much bomb load, Bomber Command had only been able to send between 300 and 580 aircraft on individual raids.

That night, Dortmund (some 250 miles southwest of the German capital) was to suffer the mightiest blow that the RAF could administer, with 826 aircraft bound to hit the city in a so called 'Maximum Effort'. While most of the aircraft being sent were 'heavies', Avro Lancasters, Halifaxes, and Short Stirlings, 151 Vickers Wellingtons and 13 de Havilland Mosquitos were to join them.

"The weather forecast was good, with no cloud cover over the target, and at the duly appointed time (2325hrs) we took off in JB894/ DY-X *X-for-X-Ray* – a Halifax II – and headed towards Holland.

LEFT: Wg Cdr George Holden at RAF Pocklington shortly after taking command of No.102 Squadron on October 26, 1942. He was at the controls of JB848/DY-G two nights before it was lost at Pocklington on March 28 the following year. Remaining with '102' until April 20, 1943, he was reassigned to take command of No. 617 Squadron after Wg Cdr Guy Gibson was retired from flying duties on August 2. Holden was killed the following month on September 16 during 'Operation Garlic' – a failed raid against the Dortmund-Ems Canal. ROYAL AIR FORCE

On board was me, pilot Sgt Dave Hewlet, second pilot Sgt T Sayer, flight engineer Sgt Joe Holliday, navigator Sgt 'Blackie' Blackallar, wireless operator/air gunner Flt Sgt J Nightingale, air gunner Sgt Andy Reilly, and mid-upper gunner Sgt 'Willie' Hall.

"That night, the Halifaxes of No. 4 Group were leading the attack, with us in '102' up front in the van. That said, we had had an uneventful trip, crossing the North Sea and Holland without problems – despite having observed aircraft falling either side of us. We continued across Germany, before we turned on our final leg, which would bring us to Dortmund from the north.

"As we started to run down to the Ruhr, the flak soon began to warm up and turned into the usual flashes and thumps so familiar to anyone who has experienced anti-aircraft fire – quite frightening in its own way. Taking the 'bomb tit' release button in my hand, I settled down in the prone position over the bombsight ready to carry out my task.

"Although it was a clear starry night with very good visibility, everything was still dark. As we neared our target, the flak intensified although, as I recollect, there were at this point no searchlights. Quite often the Germans would delay the use of these until the target had been marked, in case, one presumes, the searchlights would give them away.

"Being in the forefront of the attack, we kept on our course to Dortmund. Although we were only a couple of minutes from our ETA, no target markers were yet visible. Suddenly, a vivid splash of colour appeared ahead and below us – it was the primary marker! Relief quickly set in… we would not have to 'go round again'.

"Operating the controls, the 'skipper' called out, 'Bomb doors open.' I took over and guided him through my bombsight, 'Left… left… steady… steady… right… steady… steady… left, left… steady… bombs gone!' I pressed the 'tit' and the aircraft jumped with the release of the high explosives. At the same time the 4½-inch Photoflash 'bomb' left its chute at the rear, and we continued straight and level while I counted out the prescribed number of seconds.

"With the flak intensifying, it was a bumpy ride – almost to the point of realising the old-line: "The flak was so heavy you could get out and walk on it!""

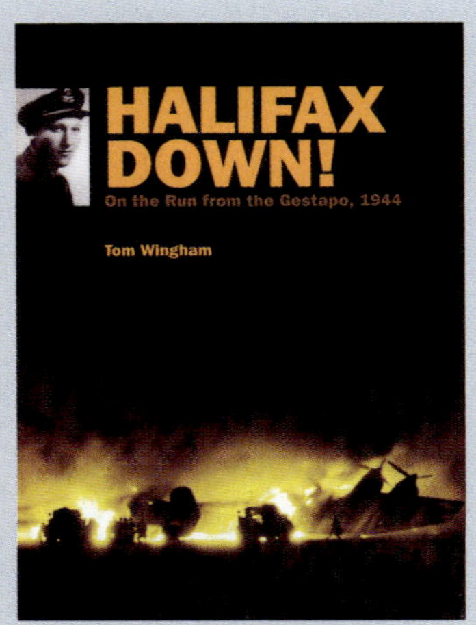

This feature is an adapted and abridged version of an extract from Tom's incredible book – *Halifax Down: On the Run from the Gestapo 1944*, published in 2009. Written in a frank and engaging style, it is the story of his flying career as a bomb aimer up to the night of April 22/23, 1944, when he was on board a 76 Squadron Halifax III MZ578, which failed to return from a raid on the German city of Dusseldorf. Tom managed to evade capture and the harrowing story of his time avoiding capture is an exceptional, edge-of-the-seat read. As well as Tom's story, the book uncovers the full story of that fateful night.

Prepare to bale out!

"We continued heading south across the target, and with the bomb doors closed, we were now free to 'jink' about and try to confuse the guns. Then there was an almighty bang – the aircraft almost shuddered to a stop, as we seemed to be dropping out of the sky.

"There was confusion over the intercom, which had gone extremely fuzzy with the loss of the generator, and, for a moment, there was a babble of voices as all the crew were enquiring about what had happened. The rear gunner's voice continued, and the pilot cut in to ask, 'Who's that?'… 'It's me, the rear gunner, what's up Dave?' The answer was very swift: 'Prepare to bale out!'

"With the loss of power, the aircraft had swung to starboard, and as we rapidly descended, we were heading west. Flying over the Ruhr Valley it felt as though every German gunner was turning their fire on us, while their searchlights probed the skies, seeking us out for the 'kill'. Meanwhile, in the

66 *Come on Dave, this can't happen to us, you can't let it happen to us. Get it flying again, it can't happen to us!* **99**

BELOW: Surviving the onslaught of German anti-aircraft fire and fighters was one thing, but simple human errors cost many Bomber Command crews their lives – including No. 102 Squadron's officer commanding, Wg Cdr Sydney Bintley, in Halifax II DT512/DY-O on October 24, 1942. Returning home following a raid on the Italian port city of Genoa with flak damage and on three engines, the aircraft was diverted to nearby RAF Holme-on-Spalding-Moor in poor visibility. With radio contact lost, Bintley received a green flare to land – which he did so safely, despite a burst tyre. However, unable to clear the runway, just seconds later his aircraft was hit by another '102' machine also diverting – W1181/DY-D. Unsighted and unaware DT512 was ahead of him, Flt Sgt Idris Lawton Berry, believing the green flare was for him, landed on top of DT512 – killing Bintley instantly, and fatally injuring his wireless operator/air gunner FLt Lt Arthur James Graham, Royal Canadian Air Force. Of note, the Officer Commanding RAF Pocklington, Gp Captain Edward Corbally, was acting as Second Pilot onboard DT512. The aftermath of the incident can be seen here, 'DY-O' on the left, and 'DT-D' on the right. No one onboard the latter was hurt. KEY COLLECTION

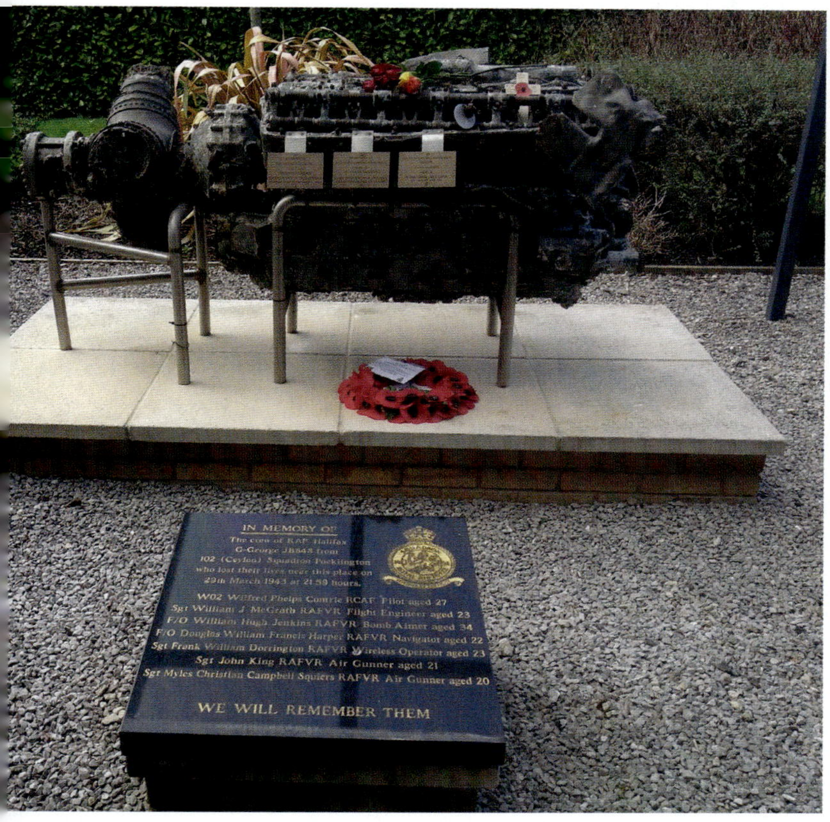

LEFT: In 2014, the battered remains of one of the JB484's Rolls-Royce Merlin engines were discovered during construction work in the area the aircraft fell that fateful night near Pocklington. Today, it forms the centrepiece of a memorial dedicated to the crew on May 9, 2015 – just a stone's throw from where they took their final flight. INTERNATIONAL BOMBER COMMAND MEMORIAL

been ripped off as he shot out of his turret. Running up to the cockpit, he then shouted in Dave's ear words to the effect of 'Come on Dave, this can't happen to us, you can't let it happen to us. Get it flying again, *it can't happen to us!*' But then, so many crews believed that it couldn't happen to them... only to other crews.

How many engines?

"At 7,000ft, a miracle occurred... the engines began to gradually splutter back into life again, and Dave began to stabilise the aircraft. With power to our elbow, as it were, we had a chance against the enemy – first weaving to get out of the searchlights and then, above all, climbing to get some height again. We had lost some 10,000ft in our fall. As we were in the middle of the Ruhr, we had no choice but to continue flying west through the best-defended area in Germany. But we eventually made our way out and had an uneventful trip back to base.

Arriving back at dispersal we finally had the chance to examine the aircraft and see what had happened – there were more than 20 holes across the aircraft. Apparently, we had been hit by shrapnel from a near miss. On looking, we found a large piece had sliced through the fire extinguisher buttons, setting three of them off in the engines, and thus giving them foam rather than fuel to digest. Not taking kindly to this, they gave up!" Of the 329 aircraft dispatched that night, 21 were lost – some 6.4% of the attacking force.

"The following morning, it was arranged for us to meet up with ▶

nose, 'Blackie' and I clipped on our 'chutes and started to clear the navigator's chair away from blocking the forward escape hatch.

"From the first time I had seen the Ruhr being bombed I had made up my mind that I would never bale out over a German target on the assumption that the populace would be quite likely to tear aircrew to bits – and in fact this did happen in many instances, sometimes observed by their fellow crew. During the Missing Research and Enquiry Service's post war investigations, many post-mortem examinations revealed aircrew had been killed by injuries inconsistent with those sustained in an air crash having parachuted to safety.

"However, Dave was still wrestling with the controls 'up front' and attempting to reduce our rate of descent. In the meantime, Joe – just behind him – had decided that maybe the fuel tanks had been holed and, although he had, as normal, changed to full tanks before going into the target, he hurriedly turned the cocks to switch to alternative tanks.

"By this time, we were 'coned' in the searchlights at just 7,000ft... everything that was within reach, was beginning to bear on us – including scores of light 'ack-ack'

with its frightening tracer... every one of which seemed to be heading towards the aircraft before it curled away.

"While all this was happening, I had looked back towards the cockpit and had been surprised to see a pair of white-socked feet dancing by the side of the pilot. At the time I did not question what they were doing there, and it was not until many years later, when talking to Dave, that I recalled the incident and asked for an explanation.

"Apparently, on the 'prepare to bale out' call, Andy's boots had

BELOW: An unknown crew pose with a Halifax III of No. 102 Squadron, circa 1944. The Halifaxes of '102' served exclusively with No. 4 Group until the end of hostilities. In 4,734 operational sorties flown with the Handley Page type, '102' lost 140 examples – some 3% of all those dispatched, the highest of all No. 4 Group's squadrons. INTERNATIONAL BOMBER COMMAND MEMORIAL

Date	Aircraft Type & Number	Crew	Duty	Time Up	Time Down	Details of Sortie or Flight	References
	Halifax II EB. 365 "E"	SGT. K.A.HEATON SGT. J.P.HAGUE SGT. K.DAVENPORT SGT. T.HESLOP F/S. D.D.EAR SGT. E.J.WILLIAMS SGT. M.D.E.SCOTT	PILOT. NAV W/O A/G A/G ENG BOMB	2254	0432	Attacked primary target at 20,000 feet heading 190°M IAS 180 No cloud, good visibility. Red and green T.Is. seen on aproach to target, greens combined with B.T.I. Red T.Is. in bomb sight. Concentrated incendiarie fires seen burning.	
	Halifax II JB. 834 "D"	SGT. D.W.WARD SGT. A.G.TOVEY SGT. P.BOSTLE SGT. R.G.SHAW SGT. J.B.POSKETT SGT. J.A.IRVING SGT. P.O'GRADY	PILOT NAV W/O A/G A/G ENG BOMB	2256	0426	Attacked primary target at 20,000 feet heading 213°M Clear good visibility. Red marker seen on run up. This burst out but was succedded by two greens. Centre of two green bushes in bomb sights. Concentration of fires in line running NW – SE Fires burning better than on previous attack and more concentrated.	
	Halifax II JD. 112 "H"	F/S. A.M.SARGENT SGT. A.CAMPBELL SGT. M.GALLOWAY SGT. A.G.NEWBERRY SGT. J.C.SMITH SGT. C.R.WEBB F/O. J.R.BULLOCK	PILOT. NAV W/O A/G A/G ENG BOMB	2258	–	Aircraft missing no news after take-off.	
	Halifax II W.7934 "J"	SGT. J.N.WHITEHOUSE F/O. D.S.SMITH SGT. F.C.BROWN SGT. J.C.WILKINSON SGT. H.TURNER SGT. M.SPENCER P/O. C.F.READ	PILOT. NAV W/O A/G A/G ENG BOMB	2243	0410	Attacked primary target at 19,000 feet heading 200°M 150 IAS No cloud good clear visibility. Yellow T.I. seen then timed run to target. Red T.I. seen also greens. Bombed centre of concentration of all T.Is. Well concentrated fires seen burning.	
	Halifax II HR.668 "K"	F/O. A.GIBSON F/O. D.L.MAYES SGT. G.F.POWELL P/O. W.T.CARROLL SGT. R.M.CURTIS SGT. D.J.VARNEY SGT. D.V.ATKINS	PILOT. NAV W/O A/G A/G ENG BOMB	2246	0359	Attacked primary target at 21,000 feet heading 217°M 160 IAS No cloud visibility moderate slight ground haze. Target identified by 3 red T.I. markers on run in, ETA correct. No ground detail v visible. 2 green T.Is. seen 5 miles N of HALTERN. Bombed on red T.I. marker. Incendiaries covered a wide area. Three fairly-in tense areas of fires near T.I. markers and one area of fires to NE of target.	
	Halifax II JB. 794	SGT. C.A.HYND SGT. B.S.DIXON SGT. P.WITT SGT. I.STORR SGT. J.K.JACKSON SGT. B.L.BALL SGT. J.D.MEEK	PILOT. NAV W/O A/G A/G ENG BOMB	2300	0437	Attacked primary target at 20,000 feet heading 191°M 214 IAS No cloud, slight ground haze, good visibility. Red markers on ETA following yellow track markers. Two reds in bomb sight. Several incendiaries seen burning. Lines of fires seemed to run Eastwards. Successful attack-opposition not excessive.	
	Halifax II DT. 705 "M"	SGT. R.A.WARD F/O. R.E.C.ALLEN SGT. J.MARTLAND SGT. R.L.HODDLE SGT. P.SMITH SGT. J.A.STEWART SGT. P.H.SHERMAN	PILOT. NAV W/O A/G A/G ENG BOMB	2247	0350	Attacked primary target at 20,500 feet heading 250°M 150 IAS Good visibility thin stratus cloud about 20,000 feet. Concentration of red and green T.I. markers seen. Bombed on green T.I. markers. Own bursts not seen. One big explosion seen in target area. Fires seemed to be taking hold. Starboard outer engine went u/s coming out of target area, also D.R. compass u/s. Attacked by E/A beleived JU88 from astern, who fired long burst of cannon shell and port wing was hit. Rear gunner got in two bursts and E/A last seen going down in steep dive.	

an engineering officer to inspect our aircraft. When we got to dispersal, we found him already wandering around, poking into holes at various places, as engineers are wont to do.

"For a few minutes we all drifted around, surveying the damage before we assembled in front of the Halifax – the engineer facing us… but keeping a few paces distance from us. Then began an encounter that would stay with me!

"The officer concerned had been a regular NCO during the inter-war years when all actions had to be governed by a book of rules. He first addressed the skipper by asking for an account of the events of the previous night. This Dave gave in full, answering questions as he went.

There was a brief pause before the following dialogue took place:

Eng Off: 'How far can a Halifax fly on one engine?'
Dave: 'Not very far.'
EO: 'Could you have flown back from the Ruhr on one?'
Dave: 'That would be impossible.'
EO: 'You would agree that three fire extinguishers have been operated?'
Dave: 'Yes.'
EO: 'What are the regulations about using an engine after the fire extinguisher has been used?'
Dave: 'Normally, shut down the engine, feather the propeller, and don't use again, but this was different. The engines had not been on fire.'
EO: 'The book says that an engine must not be used again after the fire extinguisher has been used.

Three of them have been operated, therefore you could not have used those engines again. A Halifax could not have flown back from the Ruhr on one engine. It just couldn't have happened, otherwise you wouldn't be here!'

"We stood there dumbfounded. Apparently, we weren't where we thought we were. There was not the slightest sign of a smile on his face or humour in the situation as he turned away and arranged for our aircraft to have three engines changed and the holes to be patched up.

"At the tender age of 20 I had learnt that, when using a rule book, always [to] make sure that it was up-to-date and applied to the current situation before using it!

"When later that morning I visited the photographic section, it was with great satisfaction that I found my developed photo showing a very clear picture of Dortmund with the aiming point right bang in the centre. At least I knew where I had *been*, even if I didn't know where I *was!*" ∎

> **66** *A Halifax could not have flown back from the Ruhr on one engine. It just couldn't have happened, otherwise you wouldn't be here!* **99**

Published in *Flight*, **December 24, 1942.**

OUTLOOK FROM 'THE ROCK'

Halifax crews routinely risked their lives to acquire vital weather information.
Ken Ellis describes the work of Gibraltar's last Halifax 'met ships'

I t was exacting work, maintaining an accurate flight profile, then pausing at regular intervals to collect and transmit vital data. Sorties were staged in all conditions, day and night – regular as clockwork. The information gathered could be crucial for operations and exercises, but more than that, it might save lives.

Until the advent of balloons with telemetry during the 1960s and high-flying commercial jetliners providing updates, and later still satellites, the Royal Air Force, Royal Navy, as well as countless civilian agencies, relied on meteorological flights to bring back the statistics upon which weather forecasts were based. The aircrew carrying out these sorties have always been

LEFT: Groundcrew assigned to No. 224 Squadron pose with one of the unit's Halifaxes, circa 1950-1951. ALL IMAGES AUTHOR'S COLLECTION UNLESS NOTED OTHERWISE

> **66 The information gathered could be crucial for operations and exercises, but more than that, it might save lives 99**

unsung – yet they risked their lives routinely.

The weather was a perpetual enemy, but during World War Two, so was the Luftwaffe. The importance of the job, and the hazards encountered, meant 'cloud hunting' was a frontline duty.

Of the countless roles undertaken by the Handley Page Halifax, 'met' reconnaissance is probably the least well known. But from the summer of 1943, this versatile four-engined 'heavy' took on the role. And it was that good, it was still carrying out

such sorties nine years later. Indeed, the last operational flight in the type's long and distinguished RAF career was a weather recce sortie on March 17, 1952.

Old sub hunters...

From March 1, 1941, collecting meteorological data became the task of RAF Coastal Command. Previously, it had been a Bomber Command responsibility, but diverting resources from the strategic war of attrition against

BELOW: A fine study of Handley Page Halifax Met.6 RG778/XB-B – the first example of the variant rolled out – of No. 224 Squadron overflying 'The Rock' in February 1950. NO. 224 SQUADRON RECORDS

ABOVE: One of 300 Halifax XIs rolled out by English Electric under Contract No. 3362/C4/C and delivered to the RAF in mid-1945, RG839 – later converted to a Met.6 – was severely damaged while 'circuit bashing' in the hands of a pilot new to the type on March 13, 1952, and scrapped soon after.
ANDY HAY-FLYINGART

Germany was vigorously opposed. With gathering weather information seen by many as mostly a maritime occupation, Coastal Command was seen as the 'natural' operator.

Eventually, five squadrons were devoted to the long-range role – each with an establishment of eight Halifaxes. First to convert was No. 518 Squadron at Stornoway in the Hebrides, with Mk.Vs in July 1943. This was followed by No. 517 in November 1943 at St Davids in Wales, No. 520 in February 1944 at Gibraltar, No. 519 at Tain in Scotland in August 1945, and No. 521 at Chivenor in Devon during December that same year.

Other than '518', which started off with Halifaxes, these squadrons had previously flown either Boeing Fortresses or Lockheed Hudsons for long-range weather hunting. By October 1946 four of the five units had disbanded.

At Aldergrove in Northern Ireland, '518' was renumbered as No. 202 Squadron, resurrecting the 'numberplate' of a famed U-boat killing unit. From the autumn of 1946 until March 1948, it maintained a detachment at Gibraltar to extend its data gathering. In March 1951, the

BELOW: Halifax Met.6 RG839/K-B of No. 224 Squadron rolling for take-off at North Front in early 1952.

Halifax Met.6s of '202' gave way to another Handley Page type – the four-engined Hastings transport, reconfigured for weather work under the designation Met.1.

Another veteran U-boat hunting squadron, '224' was re-formed at Aldergrove on March 1, 1948, with Halifax Met.6s to share the post-war weather task. This unit took up the Gibraltar detachment from '202' and, from October 18 that year, under Sqn Ldr F A B Tarns, '224' moved lock, stock and barrel to 'The Rock' – leaving just a detachment in Northern Ireland.

Weather ships, blind faith, and 'The Rock'

At first the Coastal Command 'met' squadrons were equipped with Halifax Vs – the Cunliffe-Owen Aircraft company at Eastleigh, Southampton, converting the bombers for their new role. But the programme suffered from delays, including initially getting Mk.Vs released to it from other units, and then in perfecting the equipment.

However, the Rolls-Royce Merlin XX-engined Vs proved to be a disappointment in the long-range,

over water, role, and from early 1945 the much more reliable Mk.III with Bristol Hercules XVI radials became the norm. The definitive Halifax 'weather ship' was another Hercules-powered variant, the Mk.VI – the first full conversion appeared in the summer of 1945.

Most Halifax VIs that went on to serve with met units were built by English Electric at its Samlesbury plant in Lancashire. The first was RG778 in June 1945, serving with No. 224 Squadron.

Even today, figures vary on how many Halifax VIs were converted to 'met ships', but it was between 35-40. In 1948 the RAF changed its designation system from Roman to Arabic numerals, the surviving Halifaxes hence becoming Met.6s.

Mounted on the starboard side of the nose of the Halifax, just behind what had originally been the bomb aimer's glazing, was a device called a psychrometer. This was a more sophisticated version of the hygrometer found in basic weather stations the world over.

The psychrometer was a rig holding two glass thermometer tubes. With the mercury bulb of one directly exposed to the airflow, ▶

LEFT: The sombre remains of Halifax Met.6 RG850…

RIGHT: Groundcrew from No. 224 Squadron prepare Halifax Met.6 RG836/XB-J for its next sortie at RAF North Front on Gibraltar. While the date this image was taken is not known, it is thought to be prior May 1, 1950, when the aircraft was struck off charge.

the other was surrounded in a muslin wick soaked in water. The difference in the reading between the 'dry' and 'wet' bulbs was used to calculate the atmospheric humidity.

Another thermometer would provide an accurate outside air temperature reading, while a drift meter was fitted to assess wind speed. The externally mounted instruments could be monitored through a glazing on the starboard side of the extreme nose.

For accurate low-level flying, a radio altimeter was essential. Crews would calibrate these instruments at every opportunity – descents through cloud to sea level would otherwise have been an act of blind faith.

An easy way to check out the altimeter was to fly alongside a spot height on a cliff, or a lighthouse, either of which would be of known elevation. This would provide a thrilling flypast for the aircrew, passers-by, and lighthouse keepers!

However, none of the data was recorded automatically, with the readings being taken visually by the crew. With the advent of the Halifax, a dedicated weather observer could, for the first time, be accommodated, cheek-by-jowl with the navigator in the nose.

> **"Crews would calibrate these instruments at every opportunity – descents through cloud to sea level would otherwise have been an act of blind faith"**

Apart from a dog-leg sector over the North Sea, and another out of Wick in northernmost Scotland, penetrating due north into Arctic waters, all of the Coastal Command met sorties headed west into the Atlantic.

A typical out-and-back profile would involve flying at the pressure altitude of 950 millibars – which would equate to around 1,800ft. With the temperature and humidity readings charted every 50nm, the cloud and sea state would also be noted. These figures, plus a sea level pressure reading and wind velocity, would be calculated at each 100-mile waypoint.

At the outermost point, the Halifax would begin a spiralling, monotonous climb to 18,000ft – to repeat the data-gathering exercise over a reciprocal heading for 500 miles. After that, the 'skipper' would make a brisk descent to sea level for another set of measurements, followed by a low-level return to base.

In the case of the Gibraltar 'run', codenamed 'Nocturnal', the sortie took the Halifax on a dead-straight course northwest towards the Azores for 1,100 miles. When this nominal point, deep in the Atlantic Ocean, was reached, the aircraft would begin its climb, ready to turn around and retrace its flightpath across lonely, inhospitable waters to 'The Rock'.

As the gateway and guardian of the western Mediterranean, Gibraltar naturally attracted the attentions of the Royal Naval Air Service and seaplanes were a common sight in the harbour from at least 1917. During the inter-war years, Gibraltar's extensive harbour played host to flocks of flying boats. The racecourse, located on the narrow isthmus just north of 'The Rock', served as a rudimentary airfield.

Pressures of war from 1939 meant that the racecourse, a stone's throw from the Spanish frontier, was inadequate. A 1,100m east-west runway was built – the western end extending, finger-like, into the Bay of Gibraltar. When the work was

completed in 1942, the airfield was named RAF North Front; today it is known as RAF Gibraltar.

However, the runway severed road communications in and out of the settlement. A traffic light system, still in use today, released vehicles to scurry across when there was a lull in flying.

When the Halifax Met.6s of No. 224 Squadron took up permanent residence at North Front in October 1948, they succeeded a detachment from '202'. Before '202', 'Gib' had been the domain of No. 520 Squadron, which boasted a wonderfully descriptive motto: 'Tomorrow's weather today'.

BELOW: This view looking across RAF North Front towards the Spanish border in early 1952, reveals Gibraltar's huge public cemetery. Visible to the left is a pair of Shackleton MR.1As, likely assigned to '224'. In the middle is a United States Navy Douglas C-117, and to the right is a '224' Halifax Met.6.

Rare for an RAF squadron, '520' spent its entire life based at Gibraltar – from its inception in September 1943 to its disbandment in April 1946. During that time, the unit operated an incredible variety of types, in sequence: Lockheed Hudson, Gloster Gladiator, Halifax V, Supermarine Spitfire V, Hawker Hurricane II, Miles Martinet I, Halifax III, and the Vickers Warwick.

Perilous sorties

From the spring of 1944 the round-the-clock arrivals and departures of lumbering, weather-hunting Halifaxes had become

commonplace to Gibraltarians. If the sorties seemed unremarkable, every so often the perilous nature of the task came to the fore. Many citizens could see the comings and goings on the airfield, so news spread quickly among the small, tight-knit community, across 'The Rock'.

On March 5, 1949, Met.6 RG850 – inbound from RAF Aldergrove – lost one of its starboard engines on approach. The pilot elected to go-around, but the Halifax lost speed, began to slip to starboard, and dived into the ground close to the base's eastern threshold. Five of the seven crew on board were killed. ▶

Less than two years later, on January 16, 1951, the crew of RG837 was making a three-engined approach during a regular pilot check out. As they did, one of the working Bristol Hercules failed. And although the pilot quickly went through the drills to bring the feathered example back to life, it was unsuccessful. Within sight of a large number of spectators, RG837 soon stalled and dropped into the water short of the threshold. Thankfully, none of the six crew on board were hurt, and they managed to scramble out of the partially submerged aircraft. With RG837 deemed as "damaged beyond repair", the cause of the engine failure is unknown.

ABOVE: With its upper forward fuselage overpainted white to help keep the cockpit area cool, No. 224 Squadron Halifax Met.6 ST804 shares the ramp at RAF North Front with an RAF St Mawgan-based School of Maritime Reconnaissance Avro Lancaster GR.3. Note the 'X' has been dropped from the unit code – the squadron having kept it until 1951.

LEFT: Two views of RG839 following its accident on March 13, 1952, after the port undercarriage hit the sea wall at the end of RAF North Front's westerly runway before collapsing as a result of the subsequent heavy touchdown.

ABOVE: An overview of RG850's wreck site – the crash claimed the lives of five of the seven people on board.

The final accident was another staged in full glare of the residents. While flying 'touch and goes' in a No. 224 Squadron Met.6 (RG839) on March 13, 1952, a pilot new to the Halifax came in very low on his third approach to Gibraltar's westerly runway. With the port undercarriage hitting the sea wall, it collapsed during the subsequent heavy touchdown. Broken, the Halifax slid to a halt. Nobody was hurt. With the unit all but through its conversion to the Avro Shackleton MR.1A, and the last-ever RAF Halifax operational sortie flown just four days later, not surprisingly, RG839 was not repaired. It was quickly scrapped.

In Northern Ireland, No. 224's colleagues on No. 202 Squadron suffered terrible losses for peacetime while operating Halifax Met.6s. Over 17 months, 23 of its airmen were killed in three separate accidents.

On July 9, 1950, Met.6 ST818 departed Aldergrove just after 0800hrs on a routine sortie out into the Atlantic using the callsign

BELOW: Today, the surviving wreck of RG843 lies on the slopes of Cruachán – a stark reminder of the challenges and dangers faced by the Halifax 'Met Men'.
KEY COLLECTION

'Demand Sugar'. On board was first pilot Eric Harold Tiller, second pilot Donald Alfred John William Britton Cross, navigator Charles Herbert Temple Broughton, flight engineer James Bell Dale, first signaller Percy McKenzie Graham, second signaller Thomas William Mawson, and meteorological observer Sgt Edward Clarance Cook. Records show that the weather was favourable, except for some patches of sea fog, and continuous non turbulent stratus cloud above 12,000ft. But at 1143hrs 'she' disappeared from radar. With a large air/sea rescue operation launched across a large area west of the Outer Hebrides islands, this was eventually suspended when no trace of the aircraft

nor the crew was found. With the crew maintaining radio contact, everything seemed normal – apart from, as reported in *Flight* magazine in October 1964 – that Tiller "had decided to carry out his climb 100 miles before his normal climb position, due to fuel transfer pump trouble". To this day, no trace of '818 or 'her' crew has ever been found.

The previous month, on June 16, eight crew were killed when RG843 flew into the south-facing slope of Cruachán, a mountain on Achill Island in Country Mayo, while returning from a met reconnaissance flight in widespread fog. Of note, the last position report received from the aircraft, immediately before impact, placed them southwest of Shannon. In reality, it was some 148nm ahead of the position calculated by the navigator. With Cruachán peaking at 2,257ft, orders issued to crews stated that "the third leg of the track above 51N, the approach to land, be flown under VFR [visual flight rules] or safety height, and not at the meteorological height of 950mb (1,800 ft)". All eight of the crew were killed. They were: pilot FO Ernest George Hopgood, co-pilot FO Michael William Horsley, navigator FO Joseph Kevin Brown, flight engineer Harold Shaw, first signaller, Cornelius Joseph Rogan, second signaller, Bernard Francis McKenna, second signaller Martin Gilmartin, and meteorological observer LAC James Charles Lister.

Finally, on December 29, 1950, ST798 failed to return from a 'met recce' with the following crew: pilot Sqn Ldr Terence Anthony Cox, second pilot Plt Off Donald Nattris, navigator Sgt Edward Arthur Keeble, ▶

> **❝ With the port undercarriage hitting the sea wall, it collapsed during the subsequent heavy touchdown ❞**

first signaller Flt Sgt John Henry Cobbold, second signaller Sgt John Frederick Stanley, flight engineer Sgt William Richard Martindale, and meteorological observers Sgt Stuart Gordon Purches and Sgt Gerald Walklate. The cause of ST798's loss has never been determined – although some reports from the time suggest the aircraft was on fire before impacting the sea just southeast of the Outer Hebrides. Despite a search and rescue effort, neither crew nor aircraft were found. On January 16 the following year, the trawler *Milford Countess* was working an area some 20 miles west of Castle Bay in Barra when they found the body of Sqn Ldr Cox in their nets with some debris. To this day, the rest of the crew has not been found.

New generation

On July 25, 1951, Shackleton MR.1 VP287 touched down at North Front – presaging the future for No. 224 Squadron. It had been with the unit for barely three months when it disgraced itself in a landing wheels-up on September 21. It was

LEFT: Still carrying weather instrumentation on the starboard side of the nose, former No. 224 Squadron Met.6 ST804 is seen here on the ground at St Mawgan in Cornwall during its final journey to No. 48 Maintenance Unit at Hawarden for scrapping in November 1951.

out of commission until the spring of the following year.

By the end of 1951 there were just three operational 'Shacks' on strength with '224'. As a result, the working life of its venerable Halifaxes was extended to cover the gap left by the slower than anticipated take over by the new generation machines.

Overseeing the transition from Handley Page to Avro was Sqn Ldr G L Mattey DFC. With little ceremony on 'The Rock', but considerable publicity in Britain, Flt Lt Finch carried out the last-ever sortie by

an RAF Halifax when he ferried No. 224 Squadron's final Met.6 to No. 48 Maintenance Unit at Hawarden, near Chester, on March 17, 1952.

However, there is some debate as to which Halifax took the honours. It is officially recorded as RG841, but the press photo released at the time showed RG778. Whichever machine it was, it drew a line under the exceptional service the type had rendered the RAF. Starting off as a frontline bomber in November 1940, a dozen years later, the Halifax was still putting itself in harm's way. ∎

BELOW: With the extensive seawall of Gibraltar's huge harbour and the hills of Spain visible, a No. 224 Squadron Halifax Met.6 carrying the codes 'BX-H' patrols over 'The Rock' sometime in 1950.

66 *The cause of ST798's loss has never been determined – although some reports from the time suggest the aircraft was on fire before impacting the sea* **99**

Published in *Aeroplane*, October 17, 1941. AVIATION ANCESTRY/WWW.AVIATIONANCESTRY.CO.UK

Steve Snelling tells the story of how Bomber Command's most costly operation of World War Two was redeemed, in part, by the faith and determination of one young pilot

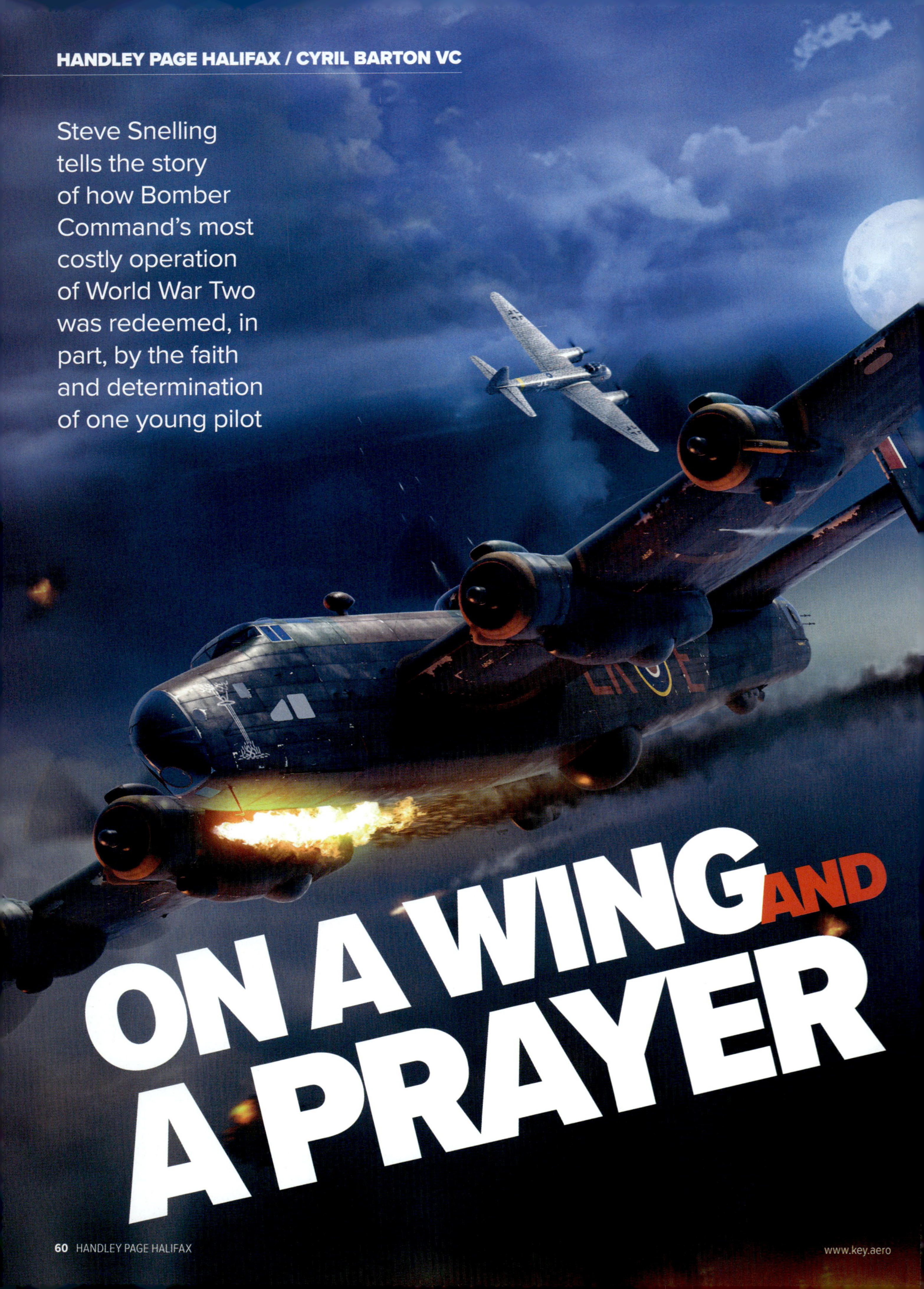

ON A WING AND A PRAYER

RIGHT: Sergeant pilot Cyril Barton proudly displaying his 'wings' in 1943 while on leave at his home in Surrey. ALL IMAGES COURTESY OF THE AUTHOR UNLESS OTHERWISE NOTED

LEFT: 'ON A WING AND A PRAYER': Fg Off Cyril Barton fights for control of his Halifax III, LK797/LK-E *Excalibur*, after a devastating head-on attack by a Luftwaffe Junkers Ju 88 night-fighter during Bomber Command's disastrous raid on the German city of Nuremburg during the night of March 30-31, 1944. ANTONIS KARIDIS

FAR RIGHT: The face of a boy who dreamed of learning to fly – the war gave him his opportunity. Cyril Barton, the aeroplane-mad teenager, poses with a balsa wood model he made in 1937.

BELOW: A Halifax II assigned to 78 Squadron runs up on its dispersal at RAF Breighton in 1943. Cyril Barton amassed some 67 hours – 40 of which in combat across ten operations – with '78' between September 15 and December 29 that same year. KEY COLLECTION

The attack was shattering. In the cockpit, Cyril Barton – just 22 years old – wrestled with the controls in a frantic but futile attempt to evade the deadly darts of fire peppering his bomber.

For several minutes during the spectacularly backfiring raid, his Halifax weaved through the night as streams of white tracer raked its fuselage – puncturing fuel tanks, severing the intercom, wrecking the radio, and setting the starboard inner engine on fire.

From the now useless rear turret, Freddie Brice heard bullets "thudding" into the aircraft and saw sparks "shoot" past him as the bomber began to "vibrate badly". Moments later came a second night-fighter attack, which Barton successfully dodged. And then another which he did not, before a fourth and final attack was at last beaten off.

Suddenly the sky fell quiet. There was no flak, no searchlights, nor sign of any night-fighters. What appeared once again to be a 'normal' flight quickly proved anything but. As Barton took stock, he made the startling discovery that he was three men short of his crew of seven.

It marked the beginning of an epic flight on a harrowing March 1944 night, destined to be remembered as the bloodiest and most contentious raid mounted ▶

during Bomber Command's offensive against Nazi Germany.

Noisy extrovert

Cyril Joe Barton was an unlikely hero. 'Cy' to his friends and crewmates, he was a teetotaller and non-smoker who had endured prolonged spells of hospitalisation for meningitis and peritonitis as a youngster. A devout Christian, he helped run regular Bible classes.

Born on June 5, 1921, in Elveden, Suffolk, his father worked as an electrical engineer for the wealthy Guinness family on the Earl of Iveagh's Breckland estate nearby. He was a bubbly, good-natured boy whose strong faith was perhaps matched only by his passion for aviation. Lovingly remembered by his sisters as "a noisy extrovert" and "a great tease", he was mad about flying. Family legend had it that a five-year-old Cyril filled his sleeves with freshly plucked chicken feathers, climbed onto a coal shed and leapt off, flapping his arms in a vain attempt to take flight!

Growing older, he settled for watching displays and building models until the exigencies of war gave him the opportunity to leave his reserved occupation as a draughtsman at the Parnall Aircraft Factory in Tolworth, Greater London, to join the Royal Air Force Volunteer Reserve. By then, his family, who had settled in New Malden, Surrey, had returned to Suffolk to escape the German bombing, while he moved in with his Bible class teacher and his young family in Surbiton in southwest London.

According to a friend and fellow churchgoer, it was Barton's experience of the winter Blitz of 1940-41 that prompted his enlistment, having come to believe that "unless the power of Nazi Germany was broken, the whole world would be in danger of being submerged by the forces of the Antichrist and the work of the gospel be brought to a standstill".

A veteran of World War One, Cyril's father grudgingly acceded to his son's request for permission to join up, even though he felt certain Cyril could have been exempted due to prior poor health. In his letter, he promised to write to the Air Ministry, and added: "I wish you every success and a happy ending to your enthusiasm. Stick to your principles and have faith... 'Happy Landings', Dad." On April 16, 1941, Barton joined the RAF, completing his basic training with the rank of leading aircraftsman on November 1 that same year.

Determined

Pilot training in the United States followed. There, after another bout of illness, Cyril found himself sharing accommodation with Bertie Boulter, who recalled his effervescent personality and enquiring mind. "He was always happy – even when upset," Boulter recalled.

ABOVE: Cyril Barton's logbook shows he first flew Halifax III LK797 as 'LK-E' during an operation against Stuttgart on March 18, 1944 – shortly after the aircraft had been delivered to No. 578 Squadron at RAF Burn. Christened *Excalibur* by Barton and his crew, it was one of 104 Halifax IIIs rolled out by Fairey Aviation from its Heaton Chapel factory near Stockport under Contract No. ACFT/891.
ANDY HAY-FLYINGART

BELOW: Canadian Flt Lt Maxi Baer 'beats up' Burn in MZ527/LK-W on his return from his tour concluding operation against the German airfield in the Belgian city of Tirlemont on August 14, 1944 – something Cyril Barton never had the chance to do...
N FRANKLIN

Cyril never hid his beliefs. "He'd read his Bible," said Boulter, "And, at night, he'd kneel down and say his prayers... he'd be kneeling down for quite a while, but he never tried to impose his beliefs on me – that was simply what he believed; he didn't try to push it onto anyone."

Arriving at Darr Aero Technical School in Georgia on January 17, 1942, he made his first-ever flight two days later in a Boeing PT-17 Kaydet. Some three weeks later, on February 12, he went solo for the first time.

While at Cochran Army Airfield in Georgia, flying Vultee BT-13 Valiants and North American AT-6 Texans from Napier Army Airfield in Alabama, Boulter came to regard Barton as "a cheerful soul" who, perhaps as a result of his engineering background, was "more inclined to analyse

RIGHT: A beaming Cyril Barton after soloing for the first time on February 12, 1942, while undergoing his flying training with Darr-Aero-Tech in Albany, Georgia, as part of the Arnold Scheme established in June the previous year to train RAF pilots in the US during World War Two.

FAR RIGHT: A light-hearted Cyril points out his promotion to flight sergeant. Promoted on September 5, 1943, he and his crew were listed on a Battle Order for the first time just ten days later with 78 Squadron.

LEFT: Bertie Boulter, who roomed with Cyril while training in the US, remembered him as cheerful and full of determination.

BELOW: Cyril, then a flight sergeant, centre, poses with his crew at Breighton in September 1943. They are, back row from left: Sgt Jack Kay, Plt Off Wally Crate, Sgt Len Lambert and Sgt Maurice Trousdale. Front row from left are Sgts Freddie Brice and Harry Wood.

things" than most. He also had another striking attribute – an unwillingness to accept defeat.

"One occasion we went roller-skating," Boulter recalled. "I'd skated a little bit as a youngster and, though I wasn't good at it, I didn't find it difficult. But Cyril had never roller-skated and as soon as we started that became clear. He couldn't stand. He kept falling down. He'd stand again, have another go, and fall down again, until there was a big wet patch on the floor because he was soaking with sweat. He wouldn't stop. He was determined to carry on until he could go round without falling."

Returning to Britain at the end of 1942, the two, Barton by then a sergeant, were billeted in the North Yorkshire town of Harrogate before going their separate ways – Boulter to RAF Desford in Leicestershire enroute to a successful career as a de Havilland Mosquito pilot and Pathfinder, Cyril ultimately to No. 19 Operational Training Unit at RAF Kinloss on the Moray Firth in the north east of Scotland to become a bomber pilot.

> **I wish you every success and a happy ending to your enthusiasm. Stick to your principles and have faith... 'Happy Landings', Dad**

Arriving on May 4, 1943, his two-month stint in Morayshire saw him introduced not only to the necessary techniques, but also to those who formed the basis of his crew. His navigator was Len Lambert, his wireless operator Jack Kay, his rear-gunner Freddie Brice and Canadian Wally Crate his bomb-aimer.

Transferred to No. 1663 Heavy Conversion Unit at RAF Rufforth, near York, it was there, while in the process of converting from the twin-engine Armstrong Whitworth Whitley to the four-engine Handley Page Halifax, two more men joined the crew: flight engineer Maurice Trousdale, and mid-upper gunner Harry 'Timber' Wood. As Lambert put it: "Cyril – 'Cy' as we called him –

LEFT: Ground personnel 'bomb up' Halifax III MZ527/LK-W at Burn sometime during 1944. Delivered to No. 578 Squadron in February that same year, MZ527 flew 105 operations with the unit before being struck of charge in April 1945. Cyril Barton's logbook shows he flew three flights in MZ527 during early 1944: a "Night Cross Country" on January 28, 1944, a "Bomb Load Climb" the following day, and an "Air/Sea Firing" sortie on February 1.

> **The blood-covered Lambert, who had helped guide the aircraft back, required hospital treatment that kept him grounded for a little over two months**

had chosen well. We were a good crew and worked well together".

Untested though they were, they swiftly bonded under Cyril's calm, occasionally high-spirited, command. And despite having been rated as no more than "average" as a pilot, his crew had complete faith in him. Brice drew comfort from the fact that no matter how bad things were, he never showed "any panic", while Lambert was impressed by his quiet authority. "[Cy] was a very confident pilot," he recalled. "He was strict in his ideas as to how things should be done but he had a nice easy-going way of putting it over."

The goal was greater efficiency, and though open-minded and fun on

the ground, in the air Cyril was utterly focused. According to historian Chaz Bowyer in his commanding 1978 title *For Valour – The Air VCs*, "he had no place for slackers", nor was he prepared to tolerate idle chit-chat. He wouldn't allow any swearing while flying. And, as Lambert recalled: "We always had to use the absolute minimum of words when we were speaking over the intercom. It had to be pilot to navigator, navigator to pilot, just what we had to say, no chatter or anything else. We had to concentrate. There was a lot of hard work required, and our lives depended on it."

An awkward hush

Having flown as a second pilot on two raids against the German city of Hamburg that July, with 76 Squadron out of RAF Holme-on-Spalding Moor, in the East Riding of Yorkshire – the first on the 24th in Halifax V DK203/MP-A, the other three nights later in DK241/MP-Q – a newly promoted Flt Sgt Cyril Barton was ready to lead his own crew. Assigned to 78 Squadron at RAF Breighton in North Yorkshire, they were listed on the Battle Order for the first time on September 15 – a night sortie against a tyre plant in the central French commune of Montluçon. It was a lucky break.

By Lambert's own admission, Montluçon was an easy target and

was the ideal confidence builder. Still, as he remarked, "...it was surprising the number of people that didn't return from their first trip".

The tension lifted, they got into their stride and completed

BELOW: A No. 578 Squadron Halifax III passes over its target during a daylight raid over France, circa July 1944.
VIA ANDREW THOMAS

RIGHT: A Halifax III on strength with No. 578 Squadron gets airborne for an operation from Burn, circa 1944. Through its 14-month existence, '578' flew some 2,722 missions against 107 targets. During that time, 46 Halifaxes failed to return from operations or crashed, resulting in 219 airmen being killed, and at least 60 others becoming prisoners of war. In that time, operational personnel from '578' earnt 143 Distinguished Flying Crosses (DFC), 82 Distinguished Flying Medals (DFM), two Distinguished Service Orders (DSO), and a one Victoria Cross.
B O DAVIES

four missions to more heavily defended industrial centres in Germany, including Hannover, Manheim, and Bochum, before October. By then, Cyril had been promoted to pilot officer. Following a pause, they resumed their tour on November 19 with near disastrous consequences. While attacking a chemical plant in the German city of Leverkusen, on the eastern banks of the Rhine, they ran into heavy anti-aircraft fire. With fragments tearing through the fuselage floor, Lambert was hit in the head, fracturing his skull, while Crate's leg was wounded.

Despite suffering what Lambert described as "serious flak damage", Cyril retained control and flew the battle-scarred Halifax across the North Sea to land at the huge Emergency Landing Ground at Woodbridge, near Ipswich in Suffolk. The blood-covered Lambert, who had helped guide the aircraft back, required hospital treatment that kept him grounded for a little over two months.

For Cyril and the rest of the crew there was no let-up. Just 11 days later, they were back in action with a replacement navigator and bomb-aimer over Berlin – this operation marking the beginning of a series of big raids mounted against the big cities, including Frankfurt and Stuttgart. Conversion to a new variant of the Halifax, the III, after the New Year was soon followed by a transfer to the newly established No. 578 Squadron (itself formed at RAF Snaith in the East Riding of Yorkshire on January 14, 1944, from 'C' flight of 51 Squadron) at Burn, near Selby in North Yorkshire, resuming their tour with a third trip to Berlin at the end of January.

Shortly after, Cyril took charge of Halifax III LK797/LK-E, which was christened *Excalibur,* after the legendary sword of King Arthur, and decorated with appropriate nose art. This would become his regular aircraft – although their association did not get off to the best start.

> **66 As we continued on our way, the sky remained almost cloudless... we realised it was a night for the night-fighter 99**

On its first sortie with Cyril at the controls, the oxygen supply to the mid-upper turret failed over Stuttgart. Two nights later, during a raid on Frankfurt, the bomb doors failed, and when they eventually did open – enabling the jettisoning of bombs over Darmstadt, about 80 miles to the north – they refused to close and remained parted for the rest of the way home.

This fraught journey paralleled another more personal struggle that had troubled Cyril since returning to the UK. Writing in March 1944, he told of his decision not to "openly kneel in my bed in prayer every night – something I have funked since my first days in the RAF". A few days later, he plucked up the courage to do so, while his gently spoken Canadian bomb-aimer and wireless operator were listening to the radio in the room they shared. What he called "an awkward hush" followed when they "very reverently" turned down the volume. "The Lord was very real to me for a few minutes, and I was very thankful to him for bringing me through," wrote Cyril, "whatever the consequences might be."

He had just completed his 18th mission and was "looking forward to finishing" his tour "within a reasonably short time". Next up was a first mission against Nuremberg, a city synonymous with Nazism and the hate-fuelled orchestrated ▶

rallies that had helped propel Germany to war.

Flared into flames

Codenamed Operation Grayling, the raid was controversial. Intended to strike a damaging blow to German morale, the city deemed of great symbolic significance to the warring nation's leadership, it was risky, involving a perilous flight plan that included a 265-mile straight leg south of the Ruhr followed by a 79-mile run-in to the target — made all the worse by an unfavourable weather forecast.

Lambert was among a host of aircrew and senior officers with misgivings, and he expected the mission to be cancelled once aerial reconnaissance reported little prospect of much-needed cloud cover on the way out and overcast skies over Nuremberg. Even without the weather conspiring against them, the idea of directing hundreds of bombers along what Lambert called a "tremendously long" leg "without any deviation" appeared particularly bad.

> **66** *One of these was Excalibur – in it, 'her' 22-year-old pilot was faced with a major dilemma: jettison his bombs and instruct his remaining crew to bale out, or press on...* **99**

But, for reasons never satisfactorily explained, the mission was not aborted and 'Barton's Barmy Bomber Boys', as *Excalibur*'s crew had been dubbed by a local family who had befriended them, were among a 795-strong force — 12 of them Halifaxes from '578' — climbing skyward a little after 2200hrs on March 30, 1944.

Rear gunner Freddie Brice remembered "a night of little cloud and a brightly lit moon". Climbing steadily, they passed through "what little cloud there was, up into a sky almost as light as day". It was an ominous portent. Brice noted: "As we continued on our way, the sky remained almost cloudless... we realised it was a night for the night-fighter..."

And so, it proved. In the hour between crossing the Belgian border and the final run-in to Nuremberg, almost 60 bombers were shot down. Barton's mid-upper gunner, Wood, later recalled "the usual evidence of German fighter activity, the unequal contest between bullets and cannon, told its own

vivid story as a bright but brief flash lit up the cloud carpet, signalling the end of a bomber."

It was a slaughter without parallel — and *Excalibur* was in the thick of it.

Hardly had they crossed the enemy coast than they registered the first signs of trouble. "Two searchlights snapped on... either side of the route we were flying," wrote Brice. "We passed between them, and they did not move. Then ahead again fighter flares began to appear..."

Designed to guide night-fighters onto their targets, these descended in a garish red pattern either side of the bomber stream until *Excalibur*'s flight path was "almost like a runway lit up". In a steady voice to calm fraying nerves, Cyril spoke over the intercom, reminding everyone to keep their eyes peeled.

Any lingering doubts about the threat were swiftly shattered. "The bomb aimer reported an aircraft was being attacked ahead," recalled Brice, "and then yet another." From the mid-upper turret Wood watched as "coloured tracer" drew a deadly line towards a hapless bomber until it "flared into flames" and fell away in "a fiery curve". "The blazing path through the clouds, followed by a brief but bright flash lighting up the cloud carpet, told its all too vivid story," he wrote.

"Frozen fast"

More by luck than judgment, *Excalibur* survived unmolested to

BELOW: The sombre and battered remains of *Excalibur* at Ryhope Colliery. Three crew were pulled out of the wreck alive thanks to the sheer will, skill, strength, and sacrifice of Cyril Barton that fateful night.

the turning point, some 70 miles short of Nuremburg. Cyril had just begun "a steep turn to port" when their fortune deserted them. "We were halfway round when there was a shout," recalled Brice. "The next thing was a series of bangs up front."

One of two marauding Luftwaffe Junkers Ju 88 night-fighters had launched the first in a series of attacks, raking the nose, both flanks, and the starboard wing with vicious fire in a harrowing head-on pass. Amid the mayhem, Wood heard a voice call for evasive action an instant before the intercom died. He felt *Excalibur* shudder and enter a dive as Cyril attempted to corkscrew out of trouble. At the same time, he rotated his turret, elevating his four .303 Browning machine guns, and opened fire "blindly to the rear" to find that only one of his guns worked – the rest had "frozen fast".

Brice glimpsed their attacker rushing in from the starboard quarter. "I reached for the emergency call light button and waited a while... then as he began closing in, I sent a series of dashes on the call light for evasive action at the same time as trying to bring my guns to bear. Cy immediately threw

the aircraft to starboard. I pressed my firing button, but nothing happened... my guns, for some reason or other, were out of action."

Almost as suddenly as it began, it was over. Chased by a long burst from Wood's solitary gun, their assailant vanished, leaving *Excalibur*'s captain to take stock of the damage wrought. The starboard inner engine all but knocked out, two wing tanks ruptured with the loss of some 400 imp gals of fuel, the entire communications system wrecked, and the rear turret useless.

The bad news didn't end there. Checks revealed that they were now a crew of four, the bomb aimer, wireless operator and navigator having abandoned the aircraft – although quite how was unclear. The most likely explanation was that in the confusion, and with the intercom knocked out, they had mistaken one of the light signals calling for evasive action for orders to bale out.

The truth only emerged after the war. Lambert, who, with Crate and Kay, had spent the rest of the war in captivity (Lambert in Stalag luft VI near the town of Hydekrug, Memelland – now Šilute in Lithuania – Crate and Kay, in

ABOVE: Bombs fall from a Halifax silhouetted against the glare of target indicators during a raid on Germany. Known for its consistent bombing accuracy, No. 578 Squadron were granted the motto 'Accuracy'.

Stalag Luft I near Barth in Germany's extreme north) told how mischance as much as mishap had contrived to catapult him from *Excalibur*, prompting the others follow.

Blind to what was happening outside his blacked-out compartment, the navigator recalled being shaken by "a terrific clatter" as cannon shells tore through the nose in "a brilliant display of blue flashes and then flames from the electrical circuits". Aware that he might only have mere seconds to react, he reached for his parachute pack, but with the aircraft lurching one way and then the other, he inadvertently grabbed hold of the metal D-ring handle – leading the parachute to burst open.

Despite a mass of silk billowing ahead of him, he somehow contrived to fasten the pack onto his harness while holding the rest of the material in his arms. At this point, with *Excalibur* still being thrown around, and with no idea what was going on elsewhere in the aircraft, he decided to open the escape hatch beneath his chart table in case he had to make a sharp exit. But it was jammed – probably by enemy fire. With his hands full, he resorted to trying to kick it open. "I don't know whether someone pushed ▶

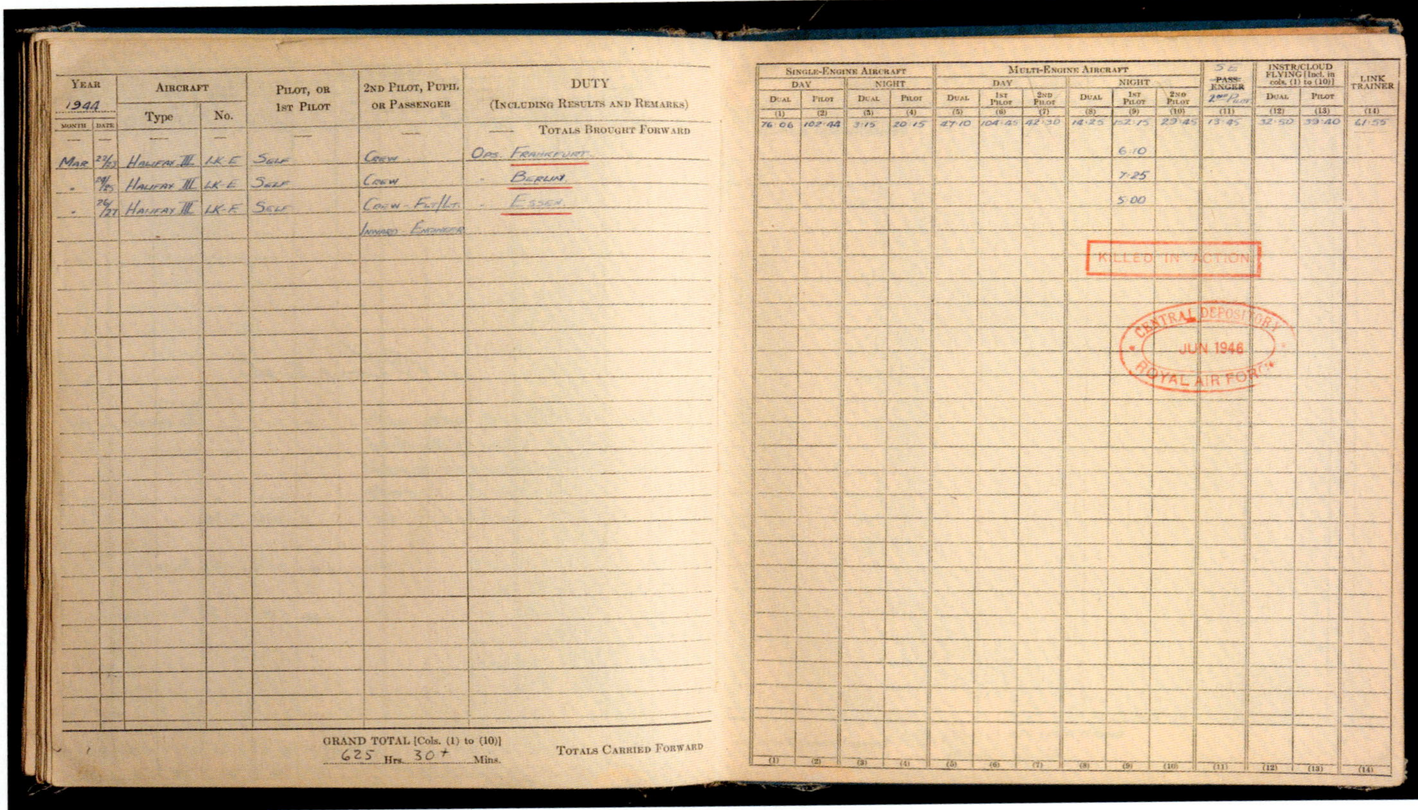

Year 1944		Aircraft		Pilot, or 1st Pilot	2nd Pilot, Pupil or Passenger	Duty (Including Results and Remarks)
Month	Date	Type	No.			Totals Brought Forward
Mar	22/23	Halifax III	LK-E	Self	Crew	Ops. Frankfurt
"	24/25	Halifax III	LK-E	Self	Crew	Berlin
"	26/27	Halifax III	LK-E	Self	Crew – Fkr/Lt.	Essen
					Inward – Engineer	

Single-Engine Aircraft				Multi-Engine Aircraft						S.E. Passenger	Instr/Cloud Flying [Incl. in cols. (1) to (10)]		Link Trainer
Day		Night		Day			Night			2nd Pilot			
Dual	Pilot	Dual	Pilot	Dual	1st Pilot	2nd Pilot	Dual	1st Pilot	2nd Pilot		Dual	Pilot	
(1)	(2)	(3)	(4)	(5)	(6)	(7)	(8)	(9)	(10)	(11)	(12)	(13)	(14)
76·06	102·44	3·15	20·15	47·10	104·45	42·30	14·25	102·15	29·45	13·45	32·50	39·40	61·55
								6·10					
								7·25					
								5·00					

KILLED IN ACTION

CENTRAL DEPOSITORY · ROYAL AIR FORCE · JUN 1946

GRAND TOTAL [Cols. (1) to (10)] 625 Hrs 30+ Mins.   Totals Carried Forward

me or whether it was the aircraft, but the next thing I knew I was in mid-air," he said. "I didn't jump as such and the other two obviously followed me because they were in the nose of the aircraft."

Incredibly, as he floated away, his 'chute deployed. "The roar of battle suddenly ended," he recalled. "There was only the gentle flapping of a piece of the pilot 'chute… and the strangely distant sound of aircraft."

One of these was *Excalibur* – in it, 'her' 22-year-old pilot was faced with a major dilemma: jettison his bombs and instruct his remaining crew to bale out, or press on in a badly damaged bomber without the means to communicate, navigate or to defend itself?

Stab in the dark

No one could have blamed Barton had he chosen the former, but he elected to take undoubtedly the more dangerous course. He did so, Commander in Chief No. 4 Group, AVM Roderick Carr, observed, despite knowing that "by continuing on his mission he would be almost at the mercy of hostile fighters when silhouetted against the fires in the target area and would, if he survived, still be faced at best with the prospect

of a four-and-a-half hour journey across heavily defended territory on three engines".

It was a stab in the dark. Not knowing his actual location, Cyril had to make an educated guess, steering for the red glow of what he imagined were target indicator flares lighting up what he took to be Nuremburg. According to

37.

Secretary of State

This was a splendid display of gallantry in the highest tradition of Bomber Command.

As P.U.S rightly points out, operational factors must determine whether the V.C. was earned. In my opinion the pilot added enormously to the risk to his own life by going on to the target and I agree with the Awards Cttee that a posthumous award of the V.C. should be recommended.

I see no reason why the citation should not be amended in the sense suggested by P.U.S. All that need be said is that the inter communication set was destroyed and that the 3 members left the aircraft as the result of a misunderstanding in the heat of the battle.

P. 6/6

> **Excalibur had made landfall at Ryhope Colliery, near Sunderland, some 90 miles north of its base**

Fear of fire spreading across the wing with its ruptured fuel tanks proved short-lived, as sparks erupting from the shattered mounting flickered only briefly before dying, leaving Cyril to fly on. Having taken soundings from his flight engineer and mid-upper gunner, he scorned the idea of diverting to neutral Switzerland and began the gruelling 800 mile flight home – most of it over enemy territory – with only the stars, a compass, and the map strapped to his knee to guide him.

It was a daunting prospect but, against all odds, he very nearly made it. Avoiding searchlights and the worst flak hot-spots, the stricken bomber passed low over the enemy-held coast at which point Brice, who had been called forward, saw Cyril "with a big grin on his face [giving] the thumbs-up sign".

They might have diverted once again to Woodbridge, but instead turned for their home base – staying clear of the shore for fear of inviting friendly fire from anti-aircraft batteries. Attempts to send mayday calls came to nothing, as did the sighting of a Bristol Beaufighter that passed them, despite Trousdale's efforts to flash an 'SOS' via torch.

Eventually, with fuel running short, a light was spotted through the murk of a grey dawn. Believing it "must be land", as Brice put it, they made for it, and as they passed over it saw that "it was indeed land". He said: "We didn't care where, and I think we all said a silent prayer…".

A burst of fire greeted their first approach until an SOS, flashed from the nose, silenced it. Undaunted, Barton was "grinning all over his face" as he shouted to Brice to tell the engineer "to change tanks". Barely had he turned to go back to the cockpit than he saw the mid-upper gunner racing towards him calling out "crash positions".

ABOVE: Chief of the Air Staff Charles Portal's handwritten note to the Secretary of State appended to the recommendation for Cyril's VC, in which he described the pilot's act as "a splendid display of gallantry in the highest traditions of Bomber Command". THE NATIONAL ARCHIVES

LEFT: Cyril Barton – June 5, 1921 – March 31, 1944. ROYAL AIR FORCE MUSEUM

subsequent analysis, it was most likely Schweinfurt, some 55 miles to the northwest.

There, together with other bombers that had lost their way, he aimed for the shining glare of the markers before jettisoning his bombload by using the cockpit release toggle. The young pilot's difficulties, however, were far from over. Having flown well past the 'target' area before turning on what his mid-upper gunner called "a direct heading for home", *Excalibur*'s badly shot-up starboard inner engine began "vibrating furiously".

"Eventually," Wood later wrote, "its propeller, which was red hot, tore loose and flew up and away into the night like an enormous Catherine Wheel."

Into the arms of God

Moments later, with his back against the rear spar and hands behind his head, Brice felt "a bump", as the aircraft lurched followed by "a blue flash". "The next thing I remember was silence. I thought, 'this is it'." Blacking out briefly, he recovered to hear voices calling. "I became conscious of faces looking down on me and I raised myself up and soon willing hands were pulling me out over the wreckage."

Excalibur had made landfall at Ryhope Colliery, near Sunderland, some 90 miles north of its base. It was the last of 95 aircraft lost – 11.9% of the force sent out that disastrous night, the highest of any raid.

During its final descent, with just one engine fully functioning, Cyril succeeded in avoiding all but one house before plunging to earth on the edge of a railway cutting, killing a miner on his way to work. That man was Geroge Heads. He had been cycling to the pit when the air raid sirens sounded. Knowing that his wife was a hard of hearing he decided to double back and make sure she was safe and in doing so he was struck by debris from the aircraft and killed. He was greatly missed in the community, being remembered as a kind and gentle man.

In devoting himself to his mission and then to saving his crew, Cyril paid the ultimate price. Barely alive when lifted from the shattered remains of his cockpit, he succumbed to his injuries before he reached hospital. His three remaining crew escaped. Barton's mid-upper gunner, Wood, later recalled the 22-year-old's final words were of concern for his crew.

A few days later, his younger brother delivered a letter to his mother that Cyril had written almost a year earlier. He had fully anticipated that he would not survive the war: "I hope you never receive this," it began, "but I quite expect you will. I'm expecting to do my first operation trip in a few days. I know what 'Ops' over Germany means and I have no illusions about it. By my own calculations, the average life of a crew is 20 'Ops' and we have 30 to do in our first 'tour'… All I can say about this is that I'm quite prepared to die, it holds no terror for me. I know I shall survive the judgement because I have trusted in Christ as my own saviour. I've done nothing to merit glory, but because he died for me it's God's free gift… I commend my saviour to you."

Three months later, on June 27, 1944, the *London Gazette* announced the posthumous award of a Victoria Cross to the aircraft-mad boy from New Malden for an act of "unsurpassed courage and devotion to duty".

In a letter to Cyril's parents offering his sympathies and to commend his gallantry, Air Officer Commanding-in-Chief Bomber Command, Arthur 'Bomber' Harris, wrote: "Your boy set an example of high courage and, finally, of extreme devotion to duty toward his crew, which will go down in history in the annals of his service and shine as an inspiration for all who come after him."

What Charles Portal, the Chief of the Air Staff, described as "a splendid display of gallantry in the highest traditions of Bomber Command" made headlines not just for the manner of his death, but for the Christian values Barton upheld. As well as accomplishing his final earthly mission in the face of what the citation for his VC – the sole such award bestowed on a Halifax pilot – called "dire peril" and "almost impossible odds", Cyril had also, in the words of the nation's so-called Radio Padre, shown "the meaning of life eternal".

Laid to rest with full military honours in Kingston-upon-Thames Cemetery in Surrey on April 6, his friend and fellow Christian, Frank Colquhoun declared at his funeral: "Cyril's last flight was not downward but upward. While his plane crashed to earth, his spirit flew straight into the arms of God…" ■

> **❝ Cyril's last flight was not downward but upward. While his plane crashed to earth, his spirit flew straight into the arms of God… ❞**

LEFT: The shattered remains of Nuremberg following its capture by the US Seventh Army on April 7, 1945. Both a symbolic and military target, between August 1940 and April 1945 Nuremberg and its surrounds were bombed some 28 times by both the RAF and United States Army Air Force destroying much of its Old Town and damaging other areas. Of the 795 bombers sent to attack the city on the night of March 30-31, 1944, 95 never returned – 537 aircrew lost their lives, while another 157 became prisoners. US DEPARTMENT OF DEFENSE

Published in *Flight*, November 5, 1942. AVIATION ANCESTRY/WWW.AVIATIONANCESTRY.CO.UK

ONE WAY TICKET

Ken Ellis pays tribute to the crews of the Brindisi-based 'Special Duties' Halifax units and their unsung 'passengers'

Normally, 'special duties' personnel were ferociously camera-shy. Their work involved dropping agents deep into enemy-occupied territory or supplying resistance fighters with the means to sabotage the Axis war machine. Such clandestine tasks were best kept under wraps.

At Brindisi in southern Italy during March 1944, the boss of No. 334 Wing was told to open the doors – it was to host a publicity 'splash' showcasing its work. By then the tide of the war was changing. On September 3 the previous year, Italy had signed an armistice with the Allies, effectively ending its participation in hostilities as part of the Axis powers. As such, the process of ridding southern Europe of German troops was gaining traction. It was time to reveal to the world what the Allies were doing to realise Prime Minister Winston Churchill's long-held command to

ABOVE: Aircrew from No. 148 Squadron pose with one of the unit's Halifaxes at Brindisi during the height of its involvement in supply operations to Warsaw in August 1944. That month alone, '148' lost five aircraft during such operations – resulting in 25 aircrew being killed. Another nine were taken prisoner, while seven more evaded capture. How many of those seen here made it back? ALL IMAGES KEN ELLIS COLLECTION UNLESS STATED OTHERWISE

LEFT: A wartime study of Wg Cdr Alfred Basil 'Woody' Woodhall captured while serving as the officer commanding No. 334 Wing at Brindisi in 1944. A Royal Air Force legend, this was to be his final post before he was demobbed.

"set Europe ablaze". So, flash bulbs popped and quotes were dished out, to prove that, on many fronts, Hitler was on the run!

At that time, the officer commanding No. 334 Wing was the charismatic 47-year-old Wg Cdr Alfred Basil 'Woody' Woodhall. Then in his last posting before being demobbed, Woodhall's career had been glittering. Among his many exploits, he'd served with the Royal Marines on the Western Front during World War One, flown Blackburn Dart torpedo bombers from the carriers HMS *Furious* and *Eagle* through the 1920s, tested new types with the Aeroplane and Armament Experimental Establishment during the late 1930s, become one of the most widely respected fighter controllers during the Battle of Britain, and had a stint as station commander of RAF Duxford in Cambridge in 1940.

To spearhead creating mayhem throughout occupied Europe, the Special Operations Executive (SOE) had been established in June 1940. Following its entry into the war on December 7, 1941, the United States soon emulated the SOE, setting up its own Office of Strategic Services (OSS) in June

ABOVE: A very rare view of the No. 334 Wing 'ops' board at Brindisi. While how much of the information on it was for the benefit of the photographer is unknown, of note is the sheer number of sorties being directed to Yugoslavia – 37 of the 67 detailed, more than 50%.

ABOVE RIGHT: Pensive crews at Brindisi – believed to have been taken during a briefing before they headed to the besieged and aflame Polish city of Warsaw.

1942 to "co-ordinate espionage activities behind enemy lines for all branches of its armed forces". Of note, the experience gained by OSS ultimately led to the creation of the Central Intelligence Agency, better known as the CIA, on September 18, 1947.

With broadly the same objectives, the SOE and OSS worked behind the lines to disrupt and undermine the enemy by any means. Covert reconnaissance, intelligence gathering, disinformation, and inserting saboteurs were important activities, but the greatest effort involved fostering, training and co-ordinating national resistance groups – especially across the Balkans in southeastern Europe.

As the Allies consolidated their hold on southern Italy during the autumn of 1943, the thrust was mainly directed towards Rome and beyond. That said, the so-called 'heel' of Italy – including the strategically important port of Brindisi – was another vital objective.

Prior to its landings in Italy, Allied support of underground forces in southern Europe involved gruelling round trips of more than 1,400 miles out of bases across Egypt and Libya. Just 50 miles across the Adriatic Sea from Brindisi lay Tirana, the capital of Albania, while the coasts of Greece and Yugoslavia were not much further away. As such, ▶

ABOVE: Framed by the nose of another '148' Halifax, Mk.II JP246/FS-B undergoes maintenance at Brindisi before another supply drop during the summer of 1944. One of 40 examples rolled out of the London Passenger Transport Board's factory at Leavesden in Hertfordshire, under Contract No. B124357/40 delivered to the RAF between February 2 and March 12, 1944, records show this aircraft was struck off charge on November 18 that same year following a landing accident at Brindisi the previous month. There are no further details.

> **❝ Some 30 days after '1586' touched down, No. 148 (Special Duties) Squadron completed the transition from Tocra in Libya ❞**

Brindisi was the perfect staging post for SOE and OSS campaigns.

Multinational 'Ops'

Overseeing the special duties units at Brindisi, No. 334 Wing was deemed operational on December 23, 1943, with the arrival of the Handley Page Halifax Vs of No. 624 Squadron – then under the command of Wg Cdr Clive Stanley George – from Libya. However, the unit did not stay long, redeploying to North Africa in February the following year. By then, the Halifax IIs and Consolidated Liberator IIIs of Polish-manned No. 1586 Special Duties Flight had settled in, having worked up at Sidi Amor in Tunisia – the first of its aircraft touching down at Brindisi on New Year's Day 1944.

> **66** *By the spring of 1944, Brindisi was a major special duties hub – hence Woodhall's instructions to stage a press junket* **99**

Almost immediately, the crews were principally engaged in aiding compatriots across their homeland. With the flight redesignated as No. 301 'Pomeranian' Squadron in November 1944, it remained at Brindisi until April 1945.

Some 30 days after '1586' touched down, No. 148 (Special Duties) Squadron completed the transition from Tocra in Libya. Under Wg Cdr D L Pitt, personnel of '148' began to familiarise themselves with the area, as well as phasing out the small handful of Liberator IIs it had on strength to standardise on the Halifax II as its main equipment.

Whenever 'special duties' are mentioned, the Westland Lysander IIIA springs to mind and '148' had need of the type's short field capabilities. Seasoned 'agent dropper' Flt Lt Peter Vaughan-Fowler ran '148's Lysander flight, with 'ops' across the Adriatic and to northern Italy. During July and August 1944, the Lysanders were also detached to Calvi on Corsica, flying into southern France. In the last two months of

1944, a handful of Short Stirling IVs supplemented the unit's Halifax IIs and Vs. The squadron moved up Italy's Adriatic coast to Foggia in June 1945 and converted exclusively to Liberator VIs. The unit disbanded in Egypt during January 1946.

Joining forces

While there was some collaboration between the SOE and OSS, both organisations mostly kept to their own agendas – although there was at least one exception to this, at Brindisi. Part of the United States Army Air Forces' (USAAF) 62nd Troop Carrier Group (TCG), the 7th and 51st Troop Carrier Squadrons (TCS) were detached there from Sicily with Douglas C-47 Skytrains and C-53 Skytroopers – the aircraft arriving on February 9, 1944. These two units were replaced in mid-March by the similarly equipped 60th TCG, comprising the 10th, 11th, 12th and 28th TCSs. In a most unusual arrangement, the Americans were placed under the control of

No. 334 Wing. While the US assets were there primarily in support of Operation Bunghole – the OSS' mission to establish a weather station in German-occupied Yugoslavia to help improve the effectiveness of USAAF bombing raids against targets in Central and Eastern Europe, as well as support efforts to supply the Partisans in the Balkans – the C-47s and C-53s also took part in parachute resupply missions, while the Halifaxes provided long-range heavy lift capability in return. At that time, the situation in Yugoslavia was so fluid that occasionally freedom fighters held control of airstrips and even airfields, allowing the USAAF to land, deliver cargo, and repatriate personnel. The 60th TCG stood down in July 1945.

By the spring of 1944, Brindisi was a major special duties hub – hence Woodhall's instructions to stage a press junket. Once the propaganda people had finished, 'Woody' and his men returned to their most exacting and dangerous operations.

LEFT: Putting faces to the names. No. 148 Squadron's leaders pose for the press in their flying gear at Brindisi. From right: Sqn Ldr Richard Pryor, OC 'A' Flight; Wg Cdr Douglas Hayward, OC '148'; and Flt Lt K C Dobbin, OC 'B' Flight.

LEFT: Groundcrew, with the help of two Yugoslav partisans wearing Titovkas (the distinctive green side cap worn by these resistance fighters), transfer parachute containers and bundles of supplies from a lorry to Halifax II BB338/FS-M' of No. 148 Squadron at Brindisi. A London Passenger Transport Board-built example, '338 was lost ditching in the Adriatic Sea while returning from a similar operation on December 5, 1944 – the crew being safely rescued.

Ousted from Bomber Command's order of battle, the Rolls-Royce Merlin-engined Halifax II found a new role in special duties.

The standard crew was seven, but to increase range, the 'Poles' flew sorties with just five – and often, even fewer when needed. With the nose armament and dorsal turret removed, the rear turret provided the only means of self-defence.

Cylinders and jeeps

The bulk of supplies were packed into CLE Canisters, which could carry up to 250lb of freight – be it, food, clothes, ammunition, medicines, weapons or other equipment. For example, a single CLE could carry 12 rifles and 1,000 rounds of ammunition. A cylindrical fuel can was also developed to fit the CLE Canister, with a canister able to accommodate three of them.

These cylindrical containers received their designation from the Central Landing Establishment at Ringway, near Manchester, home of parachute training and equipment development for airborne warfare.

Made from a metal framework faced with plywood, weighing just over 100lb, and 5ft 6in-long, each CLE had a parachute at one end, while the opposite end boasted a frangible percussion head or "crash dome" designed to collapse upon landing to absorb the impact.

With a quick release trigger that opened a hatch, allowing hasty stripping of the cylinder's contents, each had attachment points that worked with the standard bomb

RIGHT: Officer Command No.148 Squadron Wg Cdr Douglas Hayward (third from right), shares a moment with one of his crews at Brindisi sometime during August 1944. From left: Flt Sgt Victor Murphy (rear-gunner), WO Charles Hall (pilot), Sgt Ray 'George' Ward (wireless operator), Flt Sgt Harry Wild (navigator/observer); Hayward; Flt Sgt Jim Leeming (flight engineer), and WO William 'Taff' Nicholas (bomb-aimer). Hayward and the 'Hall Crew' had both served and flown operations with No. 614 Squadron before joining '148'.

BELOW: This view of a 'Packing & Assembly Station' container storage 'dump' in the south of Italy reveals the sheer scale of the operation needed to keep the various resistance groups supplied for their activities against, for the most part, the common enemy. It's likely many of the containers seen here were bound for Brindisi. ALAMY-PIEMAGS-WW2ARCHIVE

A briefing in full swing. Note the target maps and data boards are suitably out of focus...

shackles within the Halifax's weapons bays. While nine CLEs could be fitted in the Handley Page's main bomb bay, another three could be carried in each of the wing centre section 'cellules'. Additional containers could also be loaded into the aircraft's slab-sided fuselage – although they were difficult to drop through the belly hatch in the fleeting moments over the drop zone (DZ). All parachutes were initiated by a static line, this deploying a pilot 'chute, which in turn opened the main canopy.

That said, other loads carried within the fuselage, mostly bags, were hurled out without a 'chute – the contents either being robust enough, or had extensive 'packing', to help cushion their 'arrival'. With packages raining down, personnel at the DZ needed to keep their wits about them. Jeeps were dropped into northern Italy as the Allies advanced beyond Rome, northwest towards Milan – the latter being liberated in April 1945. Mounted to metal beams under each axle, the Jeep was attached to the bomb bay shackles, while the bomb doors were kept open. Twin parachutes deployed as the vehicle was jettisoned. The maximum payload of a special duties Halifax could be up to 7,500lb.

> ❝ *Ousted from Bomber Command's order of battle, the Rolls-Royce Merlin-engined Halifax II found a new role in special duties* ❞

ABOVE: A very rare inflight view of a No. 148 Squadron Halifax low-level during a daylight air drop. It is thought the high ground visible in the background is that of the French Alps.

LEFT: Personnel load a CLE Canister into the port centre section 'cellules' of a Halifax II at Brindisi. In all, the Handley Page type could carry 15 such canisters.

The 'Joes'

Then there was human 'cargo'. While it was usually a single parachutist, aircraft were known to have carried up to five. For runs to the Balkans these might be agents, couriers, or what today would be called 'special forces' raiding parties. Mostly it was instructors with CLEs full of weapons. Traditionally, these anonymous 'passengers' were referred to as 'Joes' by both air and groundcrews – be they male or female. The aircrew were never to know their real names.

While some had previously jumped into the void through the round aperture in the rear fuselage floor – branded the 'Joe Hole' –

many were doing so for the first time. Initially drops were made at night, requiring precise navigation and clear DZ marking by the recipients. But by summer 1944, with the threat of the Luftwaffe diminishing, the Halifaxes shifted to daylight 'ops'.

In the nose, the bomb aimer took charge of timing the drops while looking for the pre-arranged Morse code letter being flashed by the reception party below.

In the rear fuselage was the dispatcher – usually the mid-upper gunner reroled. Assisting him was the wireless operator or, depending on the consignment, another dispatcher. Often working in complete darkness to ensure that no light showed from the aircraft when the bomb bay was open, they were attached to the aeroplane via static lines.

Further back, the rear gunner watched for enemy fighters and monitored proceedings – if possible, reporting whether the containers had overshot or undershot the DZ, taking photographs if he could.

Dispatchers and 'Joes' had their eyes glued to the 'traffic light' – green, yellow, and red – close the 'Joe Hole'. As the DZ came up, the bomb aimer toggled a yellow light for 'standby', then a green for 'go'. There was a red light if the drop had to be aborted. As one 'special duties' Halifax pilot said: "Once the signal had been seen, the lights would appear, and you circled around, opened your bomb bays, got to green, flew down, dropped everything off and shot off. That was

> **With packages raining down, personnel at the DZ needed to keep their wits about them!**

LEFT: This image, captured by one of the waiting partisans, shows a Halifax II of No. 148 Squadron dropping supplies over a DZ in Yugoslavia. Note the smaller 'packages' visible leaving the 'Joe Hole' – just behind the open bomb bay doors.

ALAMY-PIEMAGS- WW2ARCHIVE

ABOVE: This photograph, captured by Sgt Charles James Dawson of the British Army's No. 2 Army Film & Photographic Unit, shows personnel packing a consignment of shirts and battledress bound for partisans into CLE Canisters somewhere in northern Italy as the war in Europe entered its final throes in 1945. KEY COLLECTION

LEFT: This view looking forward through the glazed nose of a Halifax running into a DZ shows countless 'chutes on the ground. KEY COLLECTION

RIGHT: Yugoslav Partisans, wearing Titovkas, help prepare a '148' Halifax II for a supply drop at Brindisi during 1944. Note the so-called 'Joe Hole' chute is visible under the fuselage directly below the 'S' of the unit's 'FS' code.

the briefing… never hang about!" It was said a good dispatcher, assisted by the wireless operator, could drop half a ton of supplies in just three seconds.

Depending on the conditions locally, the first run over the DZ — bomb doors open, the flaps partly down, and the engine throttled back — was a 'prover' followed by up to four more until all the cargo was jettisoned. 'Joes' were always the first out. The drop height would be somewhere between 400 and 800ft — below 400ft the 'chutes would have insufficient time to open. Above 800ft dropping accuracy would suffer.

Such was the clandestine nature of the work, only the pilot and navigator would know where drops were to take place — although the dispatcher would be told the number and gender of the agents they would be taking, and the contents of any containers. Often, the squadron's Operations Record Book didn't list a destination.

Yugoslavia itself had grown out of the ashes of the collapse of the Austro-Hungarian Empire at the end of World War One. As such it was an uneasy gathering of Croats, Serbs, Slovenes and others. When the Axis forces — Germans and Italians — invaded in April 1941,

Yugoslavia was already mired in civil strife. The occupying troops found themselves in the middle of a many-sided conflict.

Paths of resistance

When not engaged in fighting one another, there were two main elements of Yugoslavian resistance. By far the most organised and largest was led by Marshal Josip Broz Tito. Labelled variously as both socialist and communist, his forces were referred to as the 'Partisans' by the Allies and were backed by SOE.

Active from 1941 were the Serbian-centred Četniks, with royalist or even nationalist/fascist loyalties, led by Gen Dragoljub 'Draža' Mihailović. Hating Tito's men as much as the Germans, the Četniks were assisted by OSS, but by the autumn of 1944 were virtually a spent force.

The crews of No. 334 Wing and its 'Joes' were thrown into this convoluted turmoil — it was a war within a war. A regular 'client' for '334' was member of parliament and former Special Air Service commando Fitzroy Maclean, who was appointed Winston Churchill's emissary to the Yugoslav underground. Perturbed by Tito's communist leanings and concerned that OSS was siding with Mihailović, Maclean sought clarification from the British PM in December 1943. Ever pragmatic, Churchill declared that Maclean was to "find out who was killing the most Germans" and work with them. Tito was the obvious choice. By the middle of 1944, Tito's army was estimated to be 800,000 strong and, side by side with the Soviet Red Army, liberated Belgrade that November. Tito was destined to rule Yugoslavia until 1963. ▶

The stuff of nightmares

From April 1944 the Polish aircrews of No. 1586 Flight, led by Sqn Ldr Stanislaw Król, began long-range sorties in support of their fellow countrymen. Even from the relative proximity of Italy's 'heel', such trips were around 1,640 miles out and back – most of which was through hotly contested airspace. Flying in total darkness, without communications for fear of being overheard, in an atmosphere of fear, sweat, terror, and the ever-present threat of attack, it was five or six hours in a noisy, shuddering, vibrating, uncomfortable aircraft that stank of fuel, with a cargo of ammunition or explosives and occasionally, a 'Joe'.

One veteran said: "If you want to know what it was like, try getting into a steel rubbish bin, and have yourself rolled around the floor, with someone beating on the bin with a hammer, and blowing a whistle in your ear!" He added: "It was the stuff that nightmares were made from!"

Polish resistance forces had unified under the banner of the Polish Home Army (PHA) and, in July 1944, the armed forces of the Soviet Union – the Workers' and Peasants' Red Army, often shortened to the Red Army – was fighting its way towards the eastern outskirts of Poland's capital, Warsaw. This was the trigger for the PHA to strike at German assets. The Warsaw Uprising began on August 1, 1944. Despite being involved in bitter fighting with the Red Army, the Germans gave no quarter to the insurrectionists. As well as No. 1586 Flight, the Polish exiled government

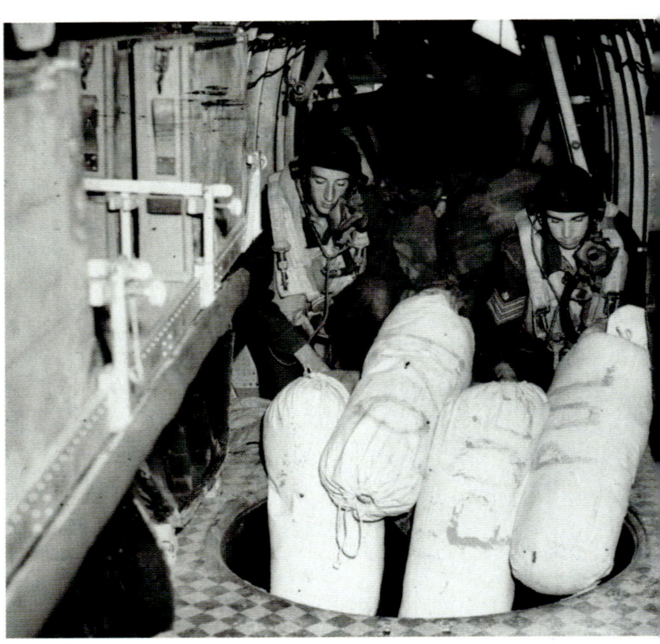

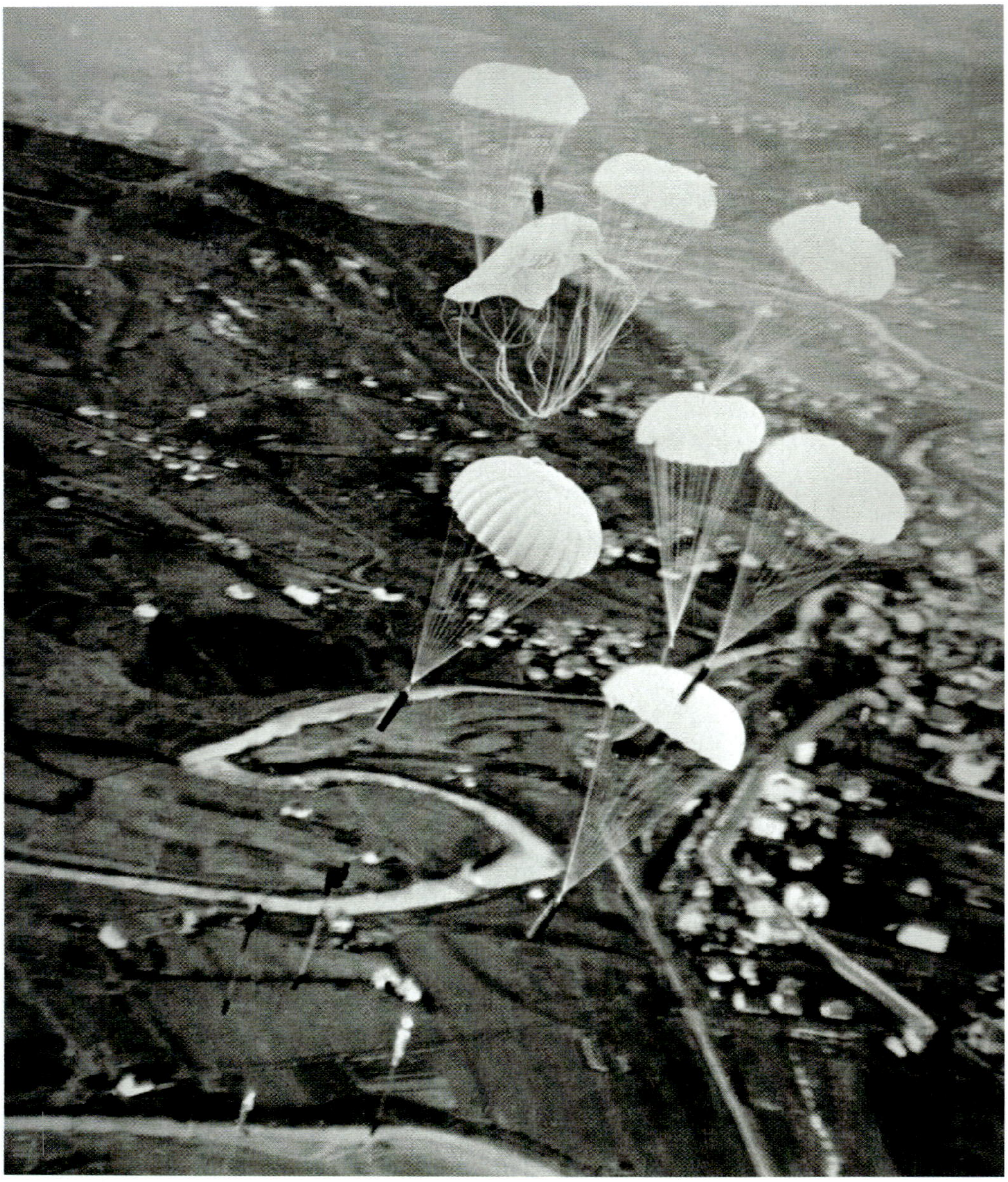

in London demanded a maximum effort to keep the rebellion supplied.

By September 1944, Wg Cdr Douglas Hayward – whose devotion to duty across three operational tours was later described as "unfailing" – was in command of No. 148 Squadron. Posted to '148' as a squadron leader from No. 614 Squadron on August 22, Hayward assumed command of the unit on the 28th – being promoted to acting wing commander that same day. At that time, '148' were suffering increasing losses.

While the squadron had lost eight Halifaxes on operations between January 10 and June 24 that year, with the loss of 32 personnel (one of those was JP327, lost over northern Italy on June 24, see *FINDING THE FALLEN*, p82), 11 more had failed to return by the end of August – resulting in another 60 aircrew dead. In July alone, '148' flew 137 supply drops. Of those 19, ten were lost on missions to Poland. In comparison, '1586' lost six aircraft and 28 men during the same period – three of them on August 27. Five of those six were lost over Poland.

As it was, between September 1 and February 3, 1945, another 18 Brindisi-based Halifaxes would be lost – ten from '148' (33 dead, including four 'Joes'); seven from '1586' (32 dead) and a single machine from '301' with the loss of eight crew.

On the ground, the fighting was urban, meaning considerable accuracy was needed when conducting drops – German troops could be just streets away. Michael

R D Foot's exceptional history of SOE – *SOE: The Special Operations Executive 1940-1946* published in 1984 – records a pilot's quip at a briefing: "Finding a particular square in the city was better done from a taxi than a Halifax!" To make matters worse, to avoid the gauntlet of enemy fighters and withering anti-aircraft fire, pilots forced their Halifaxes down as low as 100ft. In fact, they flew so low that crews reported they could smell Warsaw burning from inside their Halifaxes – one noting how it looked like "…the ground and the sky were mingling in one blinding eruption of flame."

It was rare for an aircraft to come back unscathed – many often-required extensive repairs. According to records, at least 13 Halifaxes were documented as written off at Brindisi between February 1944 and April 1945. And while some were in accidents, many were as a result of battle damage; another three airframes were written off in "unconfirmed circumstances". Of note, when a Special Duties squadron like '148' suffered a loss, it usually meant that the operation had been a failure.

As a result, '148' and '1586' were often sorely depleted. By the middle of August, Mediterranean Allied Air Forces commanders wanted to withdraw from Warsaw 'ops' – but political pressure prevailed. In August, crews from No. 31 and No. 34 Squadrons of the South African Air Force were ordered to Brindisi to join the effort dropping supplies to the encircled Polish resistance.

After negotiations with the Soviets, more than a 100 USAAF Boeing B-17 Flying Fortresses dropped much-needed supplies into Warsaw on September 18. With the B-17s remaining cautiously high, it is estimated that about 1,000 of the more than 1,200 containers dropped fell into German hands – the small size of the area held by the resistance and strong prevailing winds did not help. The armada landed at bases in the Ukraine; they then refuelled and rearmed, before hitting the strategically important rail yard at Szolnok in Hungary on the return leg the following day, landing at bases across southern Italy.

> **66 *You circled around, opened your bomb bays, got to green, flew down, dropped everything off and shot off. That was the briefing… never hang about* 99**

Flights to Warsaw stopped in late September and the PHA, facing the inevitable, capitulated on October 2. Approximately 16,000 Polish fighters died and upwards of 200,000 civilians were killed during the conflict and in the reprisals that followed. The people of Warsaw, attempting to create a 'free' Poland, had fought to the last bullet. The Red Army 'liberated' the city on January 17, 1945, and the country remained under Soviet tutelage until 1989. At Brindisi, No. 334 Wing licked its wounds as 77 personnel had been killed in 192 supply drops to Warsaw. A further 125 had been lost on sorties across Albania, Hungary, Italy and Yugoslavia between the beginning of 1944 and February 1945. The entire toll will probably never be determined – especially when it comes to 'Joes'. While such statistics pale against those of Bomber Command, they are a salutary reminder that special duties crews were putting their lives on the line with each 'op'. Even today, the crews are yet to be fully recognised for the service they gave, since they and their missions were secret. Their sacrifice often went unnoticed, and largely unrecorded; many of those lost have no known grave.

With Halifax IIs and Vs sourced from Britain and North Africa, the first attrition replacements arrived at Brindisi on August 30. However, they required extensive modifications for the special duties' role, and it was the end of October before No. 148 Squadron was back to strength.

A Brindisi 'Joe'

Many of No. 148 Squadron's 'passengers' would not regard their assignments as heroic despite the fact their method of 'delivery' was senselessly dangerous. After their 'insertion' they spent a harrowing time behind enemy lines. On top of this, they faced the terrifying prospect of not being extracted.

Let's now examine the experiences of a Brindisi 'Joe', a humble weapons instructor. Among the equipment released to Tito's partisans by the SOE was ▶

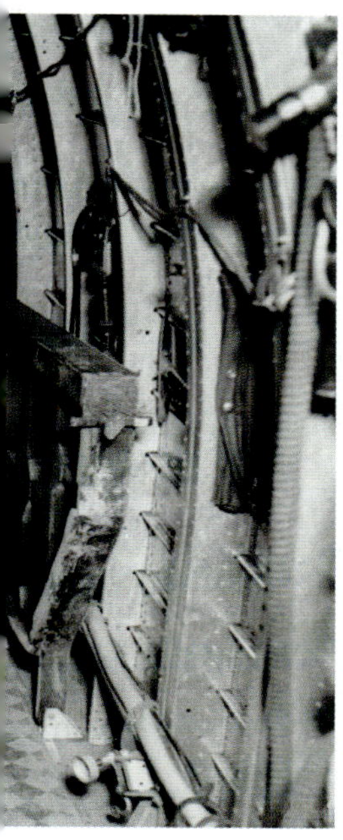

ABOVE: A posed shot for the press at Brindisi, despatcher Flt Sgt J Stewart (right), assisted by wireless operator, Flt Sgt R Short – both of No. 148 Squadron – demonstrate how supply bags are dropped through the 'Joe Hole'. Note neither man has secured his parachute static line to the aircraft.
ALAMY-PIEMAGS- WW2ARCHIVE

LEFT: Supplies from above: a swathe of CLE Cannisters fall to earth…
ALAMY-PIEMAGS- WW2ARCHIVE

RIGHT: …to the waiting Yugoslav partisans below. Here, Partisans watch on as much-needed supplies arrive by air to a field just outside the Italian city of Cuneo.
ALAMY-PIEMAGS- WW2ARCHIVE

the Projector, Infantry, Anti-Tank, universally known as the PIAT. This British-developed man-portable anti-tank weapon had become increasingly ineffective against armoured vehicles – but it came into its own when the target was lorries or buildings. At 32lb, the PIAT was considered heavy, but it was robust and practical – and therefore ideal for resistance forces. After dropping into central Yugoslavia with CLEs full of PIATs and warheads, there were anxious moments for our 'Joe' at the DZ. Would the 'reception committee' be as intended? Or a rival band? Or even German? If nobody spoke English, instruction on how to handle a PIAT was conducted with annotated cards, plus lots of 'hands on' demonstrations.

By the summer of 1944, Tito's men openly decried PIATs. The partisans wanted US-built M1A1 Bazookas. Half the weight of the PIAT, they were far more potent. However, even that famous tool was sub-standard in the eyes of the freedom fighters. What they really coveted was the deadly German Panzerfaust anti-tank weapon – a much-prized piece of war 'booty'.

While disappointed with PIATs, the partisans were welcoming and protective of their guests. On our instructor's third and final drop into Yugoslavia, this was not the case. In the dark confines of the Halifax's rear fuselage, while waiting for the 'traffic lights', the 'Joe' ran through

LEFT: A Partisan, Sten gun slung over his shoulder, folds up a parachute following a supply drop close to the Italian/French border.
ALAMY-PIEMAGS- WW2ARCHIVE

BELOW: This aerial recce image of Warsaw's Old Town, captured around the time of the uprising, reveals not only the devastation wreaked but gives meaning to the pilot quip: "Finding a particular square in the city was better done from a taxi than a Halifax!"
KEY COLLECTION

the drill. A 'clean' drop through the hole was vital, otherwise a bang on the head when exiting could render them unconscious. Of course, the static line would deploy their parachute, but landing in a dazed state – or worse – could be fatal.

Touch and go

Waking up in a barn, remembering nothing about the jump, the PIAT instructor was surrounded by suspicion and loathing. The paperwork he had been carrying made it obvious that he was destined for Tito's men... but it dawned on him that he was in the hands of the 'opposition' – the dwindling Četnik forces. Left to its own devices, the parachute had drifted way beyond the DZ. He was lucky to be alive. As for the cargo of PIATs, they were nowhere to be found. Picked up by the renegades, it was obvious he was not welcome... not only did he have nothing to offer, but he was

RIGHT: Members of the Polish Resistance pose with PIAT anti-tank weapons dropped to them by the gallant men of No. 334 Wing during the Warsaw Uprising. Between April 24 and September 11, 1944, '148' Squadron lost 11 aircraft on such missions to Poland, with 42 crew killed. While another 22 became prisoners of war, six successfully evaded capture. KEY COLLECTION

also impeding their progress and consuming already scarce rations. Nevertheless, patched up and given back the documents outlining the exfiltration procedure, he was

> **66 Finding a particular square in the city was better done from a taxi than a Halifax! 99**

escorted to the Adriatic coast with a warning from his so-called reluctant 'allies' to never return as they considered him to be a 'collaborator'.

From there, the Četniks turned inland, plotting to ambush not Germans, but Tito's followers. Only 'high value' assets, such as Fitzroy Maclean, were given a trip home by Lysander, the rest, including our 'Joe' returned by sea. Such extraction was carried out courtesy of a corvette or submarine. That said, the further north up the Adriatic the rendezvous point, the more likely it was to be the latter.

Long days followed as our 'Joe' nervously awaited the sanctuary promised by a flashing light off the coast. Wrapped in blankets and warmed with several tots of rum, the PIAT specialist enjoyed a submerged passage back to the 'heel' of Italy and reassignment, back in Britain.

● Dedicated to the author's uncle Bert and others who took one-way tickets from Brindisi, including the gallant personnel of No. 334 Wing. ■

FINDING THE FALLEN

A personal connection to the loss of a Handley Page Halifax in June 1944 prompted artist Loz Atkinson to create a thought-provoking memorial. Jamie Ewan reveals the story behind it

ABOVE: Battered and broken: this Bristol Hercules engine, recovered from the wreck site of Halifax II NR203/AL-P near Haddocks Farm, in Myton-on-Swale during the early 2000s, form a key part in telling the story of the tragic loss of Sgt Arthur Pinder and JP237/FS-F, as well as artist Loz Atkinson's own journey of discovery. Could it have been this engine that failed, resulting in the loss of '203'? ZOE CHILDERLEY VIA LOZ ATKINSON

I t's August 2020 and the UK is still coming to terms with the COVID-19 and its implications on daily life. At Leicester Museum & Art Gallery the imposing sight of a battered Bristol Hercules radial engine from a Handley Page Halifax greets visitors in the lobby. I make my way towards Gallery 7 – the muted, yet steady, drone sound made by a heavy bomber drawing me towards it.

There I am met by the award-winning, multi-disciplinary artist Loz Atkinson – the driving force behind what she calls *Finding the Fallen*. Looking slightly nervous, she comments: "This is more than five years of work". Peering into the room, I can see several display cabinets and the twisted remains of a propeller…

The roots of this exhibition stem from the tragic demise of a No. 148 (Special Duties) Squadron Halifax II – JP237/FS-F – and its crew in Northern Italy during the early hours of June 24, 1944. Taking off from Brindisi in the south of the country just after 2010hrs the previous evening, on a mission dubbed 'SOUND 1', instead of a landing time the Operations Record Book (ORB) states: "Nothing was heard from the aircraft after take-off, and it is presumed lost." In the squadron's event log, it simply reads: "The loss of such an excellent crew is a sad blow to the squadron." It was their 31st operation.

One of those on board that fateful night was 41-year-old flight engineer Sgt Arthur Pinder – Loz's great grandfather. She revealed: "My grandad, Roy, was just 11 years old when his father was killed… he always remembered the telegram arriving at the door. When I was growing up, he would tell me the stories about him – apparently, he was a typical Yorkshireman! But as I got older, he admitted he didn't really know much about what actually happened, his role as a flight engineer, or what he in fact did during the war. So, I took it upon myself to find out… "

Why did he do it?

Born in Doncaster in 1903, Arthur moved to York and joined the British Army's West Yorkshire Regiment, before marrying Freda Slights in 1923. Eventually fathering seven children, Arthur worked as a railway porter before taking a position with the Royal Mail as a postmaster.

LEFT: Arthur Pinder proudly poses in his uniform, shortly after joining the Royal Air Force in July 1941 – this is the only other known image of him while serving. Note he is yet to receive his rank chevrons. LOZ ATKINSON

BOTTOM: A band of brothers: having crewed together at No. 1663 Heavy Conversion Unit during early 1944, JP237's crew would go on to fly and die together. From left to right (rear): Sgts Dixon Finlayson (air gunner), James Robertson (bombardier), Nicholas Holyk (navigator) and John Sumner (air gunner). And (front) Sgt Arthur Pinder (flight engineer), Flt Lt Donald Hillman (pilot) and Sgt Edward Chapman (wireless operator). LOZ ATKINSON

ABOVE: Handley Page Halifax II JP237/FS-F – one of 710 examples built by the London Aircraft Production Group, which was headed by the London Passenger Transport Board, between January 1942 and April 1945.
ANDY HAY-FLYING ART

RIGHT: Francesco Sabini – a wild boar running by behind him – inspects a piece of JP237, shortly after discovering the wreck on Mount Zatta during the spring of 2009.
FRANCESCO SABINI VIA LOZ ATKINSON

In 1941, with World War Two raging across Europe, Arthur joined the Royal Air Force – despite holding a reserved occupation. But to do so, he had to turn to deception, as Loz explained: "The cut-off age was 33, and while most of those lying about their age made themselves older, Arthur said he was younger – he was actually 38! While we will never know if he did this purposefully, or if the RAF possibly turned a blind eye amid the so-called 'aircrew shortage', it begs the question... what made a man with seven children gamble it all? Especially when he didn't have to...", as Loz's words faded away, she pointed to a picture of Arthur and added: "...but it always intrigued me. And the more I found out, the more it drew me in. He joined No. 148 Squadron in March 1944. But just three months later, he was killed."

With nothing more to go on than a few family stories, Arthur's service number, and the aircraft's serial number, Loz set out on what she calls her "own journey of discovery".

First, she contacted the Ministry of Defence and National Archives to get information about Arthur's service records. Among her discoveries were the names of his crewmates. On completing his training during early 1944, Arthur was sent to No. 1663 Heavy Conversion Unit at RAF Rufforth in

North Yorkshire. There he joined the crew, a band of brothers if you will, he would fly and ultimately die with. Led by Canadian pilot Flt Lt Donald Hillman, they were Sgt Nicholas Holyk – another Canadian – navigator, Sgt James Robertson – again, another Canadian – bomb aimer, Sgt Edward Chapman, wireless operator/air gunner, Sgt Dixon Finlayson, air gunner, and Sgt John Sumner, air gunner. Just seven ordinary young men, drawn from all walks of life, and from different nations, that a most 'extraordinary' set of circumstances threw together in the war-torn skies over Europe.

Around the same time that Arthur 'crewed up', a brand-new

> **❝ The roots of this exhibition stem from the tragic demise of a No. 148 (Special Duties) Squadron Halifax II – JP237/FS-F – and its crew ❞**

Halifax II sat at RAF Leavesden in Hertfordshire ready for collection. Built by the London Aircraft Production Group, which was headed by the London Passenger Transport Board, the factory fresh aeroplane – adorned in the Bomber Command's Temperate Land Scheme of Dark Earth and Dark Green over Night Black – carried the serial JP237. Inside, it carried a data plate with 'TYPE HALIFAX II L.A.P SERIAL NO L.A.P./84789' stamped on it. Picked up by an Air Transport Auxiliary crew (typically a pilot and a flight engineer) in mid-February, they delivered the bomber to No. 1 Overseas Aircraft Preparation Unit at RAF Kemble in Gloucestershire. By then assigned to '148' at Brindisi, a crew from No. 1 Ferry Unit (headquartered at nearby RAF Lyneham in Wiltshire) were ▶

RIGHT: With the last of its load being prepared 'down the back', a '148' Halifax II sits ready to go at RAF Brindisi in 1944.
KEY COLLECTION

ABOVE: Just some of the parts Francesco Sabini found at the wreck site of JP237 – including, from the middle, an Air Ministry stamped data plate, a parachute 'D' ring, the remains of a watch, part of the aircraft structure, and a Mk.IV generator for a rev counter. FRANCESCO SABINI VIA LOZ ATKINSON

ABOVE: It is possible these instrument dials – a BOOST indicator, top, two RPM gauges, bottom – discovered within JP237's wreck site came from Arthur Pinder's flight engineer panel... FRANCESCO SABINI VIA LOZ ATKINSON

tasked with ferrying 'her' out there soon after.

One of the biggest discoveries was that Arthur was flying with the then secretive RAF Special Duties Service.

RIGHT: The all-important data plate discovered on Mount Zatta that confirmed the crash site was indeed that of a Halifax. FRANCESCO SABINI VIA LOZ ATKINSON

Its third and final incarnation, No. 148 Squadron was re-formed as a 'special duties' outfit equipped with both Halifax and Consolidated Liberators at Gambut in Libya on March 14, 1943. Thrown into action almost immediately, it was primarily tasked with dropping desperately needed supplies to partisans across southern France, Italy, and further afield into the Balkans. Loz commented: "It was always believed that Arthur was serving with Bomber Command when he was killed. Instead, he was in fact dropping Allied agents, supplies... weapons, ammunition, clothing, food, tobacco, medicine, money and the like... packages, and propaganda leaflets to the resistance groups behind enemy lines – it was incredibly dangerous."

Even today, very little is known about No. 148 Squadron's operations. Even less is known about these brave men who flew them, and even less about their duties. When you consider a lone bomber, flying over hostile territory, on a straight and level course, with the bomb bay doors open, perhaps in moonlight, under fire, then you may come to realise the risks they took.

Often flying at low level and in challenging conditions, the crews navigated by dead reckoning, hoping to catch a glimpse of any kind of landmark through the darkness. As one No. 148 Squadron veteran of such operations disclosed: "The life expectancy on '148' was just one month. Most of us weren't coming back. You knew your odds were slim to none... but we just did our job."

Loz explained: "No one knows what caused the aeroplane to crash – and probably never will. There were some reports at the time that it had been shot down."

A helping hand

Turning to the internet, Loz got a 'hit' almost immediately: "I came across Francesco Sabini of Archaeologi dell'Aria [a volunteer, non-profit aviation archaeology society founded in early 2009], which had discovered JP237's wreck on Monte Zatta, about 13 miles east of the coastal city of Genoa, in 2009. What followed was a whirlwind of emails and messages."

Francesco recalled: "One evening, I was immersed in a book (the title of which translates to 'On the ground

RIGHT: Believing they had been forgotten with not even a flower or a plaque to remember them, Francesco and Alessandro built a small memorial for the crew of JP237. FRANCESCO SABINI VIA LOZ ATKINSON

RIGHT: Just seven ordinary young men, drawn from all walks of life, and from different nations, that a most 'extraordinary' set of circumstances threw together in the skies over Europe, the crew of JP237 were laid to rest in Genoa's Monumental Cemetery of Staglieno following Italy's liberation in April 1945. FRANCESCO SABINI VIA LOZ ATKINSON

BELOW RIGHT: In this piece named *Record Of Service*, Loz inscribed text from her great grandfather's service record embossed with 24ct gold into the landing gear strut recovered from Halifax II NR203's wreck site. ZOE CHILDERLEY VIA LOZ ATKINSON

BELOW: Loz engraved the mud-coated prop she acquired from Halifax II NR203 with a 24ct gold line representing the GPS data collected while exploring JP237's crash site in Italy. ZOE CHILDERLEY VIA LOZ ATKINSON

shall go down to the battle') on local history that told the story of the partisans in our area, written by Ferruccio Ferrari. And while many of the stories nowadays seem more like fables, my eyes were quickly drawn to the words describing an aeroplane crashing into a mountain between the towns of Tornolo and Liguria in 1944 – killing all on board."

As well as the Hillman crew, JP237 carried an eighth crewmen that night, records showing that Drago Karol Bozeglav, a member of the Royal Yugoslav Air Force, was on board undergoing instruction as a despatcher.

"As a lover of history and aviation, I was very curious and wanted to know more about this tragedy that happened in our mountains. So, the next day, I contacted my friend and researcher Alessandro Sabini – we are both part of the GRRS Montegroppo – Recovery Historical Research Group. I told him what I had read, and we agreed that we'd head to the crash site for a look as soon as the weather permitted." In the meantime, Francesco went on the hunt for any information he could glean. "The clues were very few..." he said, adding: "The answers to where the aircraft had come down were vague, and didn't lead to anything really concrete. But, as a veteran of the industry, we knew that when things are a little tough, you should never give up! And I didn't.

"Incredibly, through some acquaintances, I met a man who had so much to tell... he was there when it crashed! On meeting him, I made a leap back in time, precisely to the night of June 24, 1944."

Recalling that fateful night, he spoke of the silence being broken

> **" The scene was said to be both "terrifying and blood curdling"... a hand still wrapped in a glove clutching a photograph of his loved ones "**

around 0200hrs by a dull roar that echoed through the valley, before flames, "ascending to heaven", could be seen reaching into the sky. "It was clear that a plane of some kind had crashed, but no one had the courage to force their way through the dense bush in the darkness of night..."

As dawn drew, several rescue teams and countless onlookers picked their way to the crash site. Francesco said: "When they arrived, they came upon an horrific scene... dozens of uprooted, broken and burnt beech trees in and among a huge, then still-smoking crater. It was said an acrid smell of burning and death enveloped the surrounding area – it was clear that no one had survived."

With aircraft parts and the bodies of the crew strewn across the area, the scene was said to be both "terrifying and blood curdling", a hand still wrapped in a glove clutching a photograph of his loved ones being found among the chaos.

With their bodies recovered, the crew were carried down the mountain, where they were carefully placed in coffins and buried together in the civil cemetery at Santa Maria Del Toro. Loz explained: "It is said that the entire village was in attendance and covered their coffins with flowers, while a group of armed partisans provided a guard of honour."

In the book that inspired Francesco, it notes that "this choral and spontaneous demonstration of the people [did] not go unnoticed by the dense network of fascist spies, causing subsequent threats and intimidation to the parish priest who fulfilled this specific duty. But he could not deny the funeral to poor innocent victims". While Arthur was 41 when he was killed, air gunner John Sumner was the youngest at just 19.

Angels on the mountain

And so it was, on a cool spring morning, Francesco and Alessandro, armed with as much information as possible, set off in search of the fallen aircraft. "While we knew roughly where the aeroplane had crashed, it would be like finding a needle in a haystack!" recalled Francesco. "We couldn't but admire the beauty of this pretty inaccessible place, a stream nearby trickling slowly toward the mountain ridge. A long-awaited moment, we turned on our metal detectors and started sweeping side to side. After about an hour, we hadn't found anything. The disappointment was setting in – were we in the right area? Suddenly, the silence of the forest was broken by a shout from Alessandro: 'I've found something!' Running over to him, just below the leaves, was a piece of molten aluminum. ▶

Within minutes, my detector picks up something – brushing away the leaves, it was a 'D' ring from a parachute. If only the crew had the chance to use them that fateful night. Heading along the stream, we find dozens more small fragments of the aeroplane, instruments dials, engine parts, and even the battered remains of a watch."

On inspection many of the parts carried the Air Ministry's crown and 'A.M' mark. "On seeing this, we knew this was a Royal Air Force aeroplane," commented Francesco, adding: "While Alessandro was busy searching, I sat on a rock near the stream to watch the water running down the valley, while listening to the sound of the wind breaking against the surrounding trees. My mood suddenly changes as my mind jumps back to that dark night when those men died in this place. For a moment I think I see their faces looking at me – angels watching over the mountain where their lives were shattered. Looking on, who knew this mountain had taken [eight] lives? Those poor boys. Years had passed. Not a flower, or a plaque to remember them. Had they been forgotten?

"Before long it's time to head home – but the beep of the metal detector draws our attention to the most important of our discoveries. It's a small plate with the words 'TYPE HALIFAX II L.A.P SERIAL NO L.A.P./84789' on it. Knowing aeroplanes, I knew the Halifax was a four-engine bomber used by the RAF.

"The day had almost come to an end – the rays of sunset stretched our shadows across the ground. We were tired but satisfied. I couldn't believe our luck, finding a fragment with the aircraft's type on it... knowing that was fundamental for our research."

Returning home, Francesco took to the internet in search of any information on those "poor boys" he could find. Before long, he found their names. And, as they say, the rest is history.

"Sometime later," explained Francesco. "Alessandro and I went back to the site and made a stone altar – laying on it a few pieces of the aeroplane, and a bouquet of flowers in memory of those young lives cut short so tragically and seemingly forgotten. After a few minutes of silence, a few drops of rain began to bathe our faces – we knew it was time to go home. While heading down the mountain, a dense fog began to descend. And when I looked back to the altar one last time, for a moment, I seemed to see seven angels smiling and watching us, before the fog engulfed them and hid them from sight."

> **" Years had passed. Not a flower, or a plaque to remember them. Had they been forgotten? "**

'Expedition JP237'

After corresponding with Francesco, Loz travelled to Italy in early July 2019 to visit JP237's crash site with noted photographer Zoe Childerley. Her aim was to create art in her great grandfather's memory.

Dubbed 'Expedition JP237', the trio explored the site and uncovered fragments of the wreckage that had survived some 75 years of freezing winters and sweltering summers. With aluminum a valuable material at that time, in the days following the crash, locals scavenged what material they

ABOVE: Just some of the surviving pieces from JP237 that form *Finding the Fallen*, including the chilling sight of the battered remains of a flying boot (third from left, bottom row). The use of a model Halifax helps show what most of these twisted remnants once were... ZOE CHILDERLEY VIA LOZ ATKINSON

LEFT: Loz has adopted techniques from the Japanese practice of Kintsugi on the engine recovered from NR203's wreck site. This is a method of repairing pottery with precious metals to show the breakage and repair of an object as part of its history. KEY-JAMIE EWAN

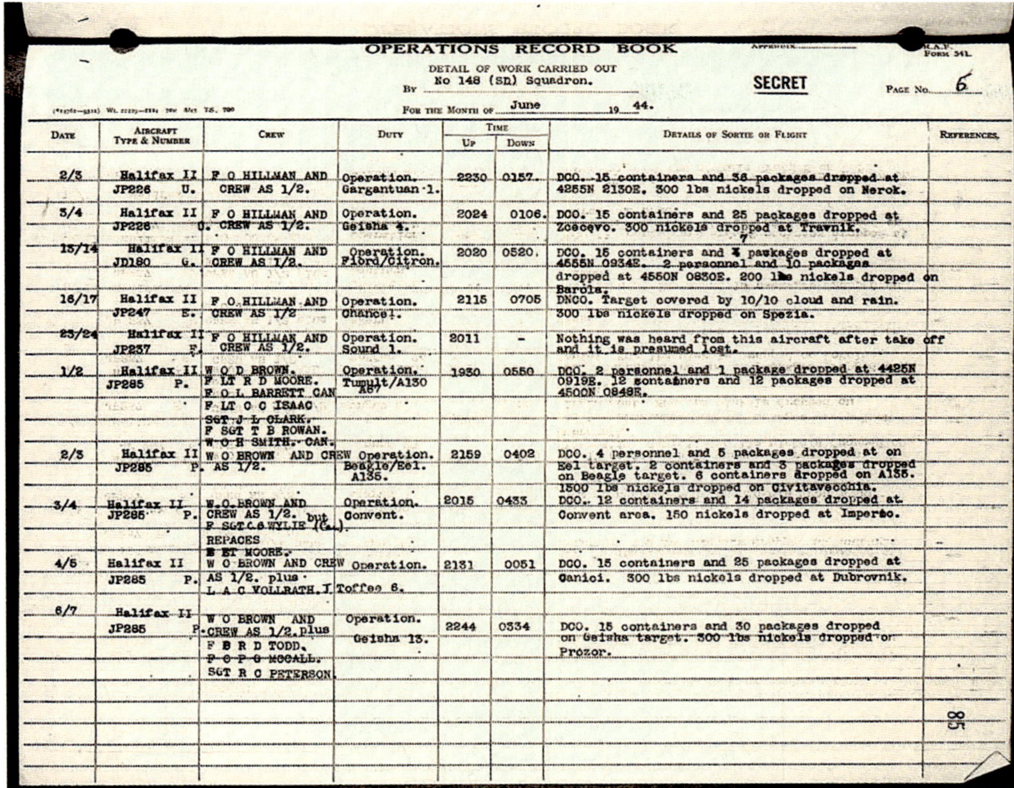

OPERATIONS RECORD BOOK

DETAIL OF WORK CARRIED OUT

By No 148 (SD) Squadron.

SECRET

Page No. 6

For the Month of June 19 44.

Date	Aircraft Type & Number	Crew	Duty	Time Up	Time Down	Details of Sortie or Flight	References
2/3	Halifax II JP226 U.	F O HILLMAN AND CREW AS 1/2.	Operation. Gargantuan 1.	2230	0157.	DCO. 15 containers and 36 packages dropped at 4255N 2130E. 300 lbs nickels dropped on Nerok.	
3/4	Halifax II JP226 U.	F O HILLMAN AND CREW AS 1/2.	Operation. Geisha 4.	2024	0106.	DCO. 15 containers and 25 packages dropped at Zcecevo. 300 nickels dropped at Travnik.	
13/14	Halifax II JD180 G.	F O HILLMAN AND CREW AS 1/2.	Operation. Fiord/Citron.	2020	0520.	DCO. 15 containers and 3 packages dropped at 4555N 0934E. 2 personnel and 10 packages dropped at 4550N 0830E. 200 lbs nickels dropped on Barola.	
16/17	Halifax II JP247 E.	F O HILLMAN AND CREW AS 1/2	Operation. Chancel.	2115	0705	DNCO. Target covered by 10/10 cloud and rain. 300 lbs nickels dropped on Spezia.	
23/24	Halifax II JP237 F.	F O HILLMAN AND CREW AS 1/2.	Operation. Sound 1.	2011	–	Nothing was heard from this aircraft after take off and it is presumed lost.	
1/2	Halifax II JP285 P.	W O D BROWN. F LT R D MOORE. F O L BARRETT CAN F LT O C ISAAC SGT J L CLARK. F SGT T B ROWAN. W O H SMITH. CAN.	Operation. Tumult/A130 A57	1930	0550	DCO. 2 personnel and 1 package dropped at 4425N 0919E. 12 containers and 12 packages dropped at 4500N 0849E.	
2/3	Halifax II JP285 P.	W O BROWN AND CREW AS 1/2.	Operation. Beagle/Eel. A135.	2159	0402	DCO. 4 personnel and 5 packages dropped at on Eel target. 2 containers and 3 packages dropped on Beagle target. 6 containers dropped on A135. 1500 lbs nickels dropped on Civitavecchia.	
3/4	Halifax II JP285 P.	W O BROWN AND CREW AS 1/2. but F SGT C G WYLIE (Can). REPACES B ET MOORE.	Operation. Convent.	2015	0433	DCO. 12 containers and 14 packages dropped at Convent area. 150 nickels dropped at Imperio.	
4/5	Halifax II JP285 P.	W O BROWN AND CREW AS 1/2. plus L A C VOLLRATH. I	Operation. Toffee 6.	2131	0051	DCO. 15 containers and 25 packages dropped at Canici. 300 lbs nickels dropped at Dubrovnik.	
6/7	Halifax II JP285 P.	W O BROWN AND CREW AS 1/2. plus F B R D TODD. P O P G McCALL. SGT R C PETERSON	Operation. Geisha 13.	2244	0334	DCO. 15 containers and 30 packages dropped on Geisha target. 300 lbs nickels dropped or Prozor.	

could, while some was sold to a wrecker in nearby Liguria.

Loz commented: "We found bits of the fuselage, part of a seat with a piece of the leather still attached, fuel and hydraulic lines, along with bits of Plexiglass from the cockpit and gun turrets, and even uniform buttons — that was incredibly heart wrenching. But these bits of twisted and broken metal capture the violence of a truly devastating event. The parts on show are exactly how they were found on the mountain."

While in Italy, Loz also had the chance to visit Genoa's Monumental Cemetery of Staglieno to see Arthur's grave. "Following Italy's liberation in April 1945, the crew were exhumed on the order of the Allies and buried side by side in the British section at Staglieno. Although my granddad made plans to visit Arthur there, it never happened for one reason or another — which is something I think haunted him." That said, Loz was able to record a final message from Roy for his dad that she played at the JP237's final resting place. Loz said: "I listened to it just once when I edited it, and while I won't repeat what was said, it was very matter of fact yet heartfelt at the same time.

"Before I started the project, I asked Roy what he thought about it — having his permission to dig up

ABOVE: With no 'down' time against the entry for JP237 on "23/24" the Operations Record Book for '148' simply states: "Nothing was heard from the aircraft after take-off, and it is presumed lost." NATIONAL ARCHIVES

the past was incredibly important to me. And although he never got to see the exhibition, he did see what we managed to recover from the crash site. The tables had turned... I was then telling him the story."

Having been hugely moved by the project, Francesco explained: "It was very exciting to be involved. When I found the remains of JP237 back in 2009, I felt the presence of those guys killed doing their duty, thousands of miles from home. Never would I have thought that fate would one day let me meet Loz, with whom a splendid friendship was born. I hope that our work will be remembered for years to come, so not to forget the many men who made history."

A room in Leicester

Supported by the Arts Council, *Finding the Fallen* itself is a dynamic display that combines both contemporary art and history — something which Loz admits was a difficult balance to strike: "There was a lot of correspondence and double-checking with relevant organisations to make sure everything we were doing was above board. I've come at this from an artistic angle, but I have done the research to make sure the balance is there."

Held in a single, light, airy room, the story of Arthur and JP237's crew is chronologically laid out with images of the expedition covering the walls. Loz's layered approach explores the ideas of sacrifice and remembrance — as well as the universal need to connect with your own personal heritage.

At the centre of the exhibition is the engine, propeller, and part of the undercarriage from Halifax III NR203/AL-P, which crashed near the North Yorkshire village of Myton-on-Swale on November 21, 1944. An English Electric built example on strength with No. 429 (Bison) Squadron Royal Canadian Air Force, the all-Canadian crew were forced to abandon 'her' after the starboard outer engine failed during a training flight out of nearby RAF Leeming.

The pilot later reported that they were unable to feather the prop, before aileron control became difficult. Fearing he would eventually lose control, the pilot ordered the crew to bale out. Loz commented: "These parts were discovered close to where Arthur used to live in York. Even as found objects they are seen as art... so I didn't really have to do anything to them, but I wanted ▶

RIGHT: Loz Atkinson's 'layered' approach means visitors can take in as much of the information as they want and still gain a true understanding of the exhibition. As she commented: "I hope this will inspire people to delve into their heritage and discover incredible stories within their own past." KEY-JAMIE EWAN

LEFT: This overview of *Finding The Fallen* shows the remains of Halifax II NR203, along with some of the images that aim to immerse you in 'Expedition JP237'
KEY-JAMIE EWAN

LEFT: Arthur's diary, which offers just a glimpse at the dark world of a Special Duties Squadron, uncovers how he spent some of his off time – his last entry being made on just two days before he was killed…
KEY-JAMIE EWAN

BELOW: While in Italy, Loz left a small memorial plaque for the crew of JP237 close to where they lost their lives on June 24, 1944. ZOE CHILDERLEY VIA LOZ ATKINSON

is open on his last entry), a set of his flight engineer wings, his posthumously awarded medals, photographs and documents, plus the shells he collected on an African beach just before arriving in Italy. Loz explained: "The diary helps paint a picture of how Arthur spent his days – both on and off ops – and reveals a glimpse into the dark world of a Special Duties Squadron."

The addition of a near-ten-minute-long video relating to the Halifax in general and the work Loz undertook on a loop, quietly in the background, adds another dimension. Perhaps the most hard-hitting exhibit of all is the twisted and mangled heel from one of the crew's flying boots… no words can describe it.

As I thanked Loz for her time, she explained: "It means a lot to share the story of what was ultimately Arthur's final adventure – I hope it might inspire people to do the same and dig into their past. This is definitely my greatest adventure in life, so far."

● This is an updated version of the feature that first appeared December 2020 edition of *FlyPast*. At the time of producing *Halifax* in September 2025, Loz was looking to get *Finding the Fallen* back on show. If you can help, she can be reached through the Contact page on her website. To find out more about the artist and her work visit: www.lozatkinson.co.uk

My thanks to Loz and Francesco for their help in producing this feature. ■

to add something to link them to Arthur's story."

Still covered in the residue of mud, the prop has been engraved with a 24ct gold line representing GPS data collected while exploring JP237's crash site. Similarly, Loz has adopted techniques from the Japanese practice of Kintsugi – a method of repairing pottery with precious metals to show the breakage and repair of an object as part of its history – on the engine.

Some of Arthur's personal effects on display include a diary (which

> **66** *When I found the remains of JP237 back in 2009, I felt the presence of those guys killed doing their duty, thousands of miles from home* **99**

Published in *Flight*, **March 4, 1943.** AVIATION ANCESTRY/WWW.AVIATIONANCESTRY.CO.UK

HALIFAX VERSUS LANCASTER
A PERSONAL PERSEPCTIVE

Flight Engineer Humphrey Phillips recalled his experiences with both the Avro and Handley Page heavies to Sean Feast

While Bomber Command was thankful for the introduction of its four-engined 'heavies' – the Short Stirling, Handley Page Halifax, and Avro Lancaster – into its armoury, these mammoths presented two major challenges, among many smaller ones, for the powers that be at the Air Ministry, and the aircrew bound to fly them operationally. The first was how to convert both experienced and novice pilots from two engines to four, without taking them away from frontline duties for longer than was necessary and with only a limited number of new aircraft at their disposal? The second was how to monitor and manage the additional engines and complex systems that were now clearly beyond the scope of the man responsible for flying the aircraft?

Of the 'Big' three, it was the Stirling that reached an operational squadron first – the initial production machine being delivered to 7 Squadron at RAF Leeming in North Yorkshire on August 2, 1940. And while the first operational Halifax joined 35 Squadron, also at Leeming, just over two months later, on November 13, it would be another year before the initial Lancasters arrived at RAF Waddington in Lincolnshire to join 44 Squadron – the first three examples touching down on Christmas Eve 1941.

Initially, conversion training was achieved through the creation of dedicated Conversion Flights within each operational squadron. These were designated accordingly, for example 44 Conversion Flight was a part of 44 Squadron, No. 103 Conversion Flight (CF) was based at Elsham Wolds, Lincolnshire, working up on Halifaxes for No. 103 Squadron.

Instructors who had already trained on the type were then tasked with converting their colleagues to the new aircraft – each pilot having to wait patiently

LEFT: A wartime study of Humphrey Phillips. Originally joining the war effort as a flight mechanic, he became one of the very first of the new breed of flight engineers – pioneering the role.

ALL IMAGES VIA THE AUTHOR UNLESS STATED OTHERWISE

for his turn. However, as more aircraft became available, the Conversion Flights were merged into homogenous Conversion Units (CU, later designated Heavy Conversion Units, or HCUs – one being formed per Group), to which pilots and crews were sent immediately after their Operational Training Unit. From the HCU, they would be posted to their operational squadron. While this solved the issue of converting pilots, solving that of the increased complexity of the heavies was one more convoluted in its gestation and confused in its birth. Ultimately it led to the creation of a new aircrew category: the flight engineer.

A new breed

The primary role of the flight engineer was essentially to "act as the link between aircrew and groundcrew

Humphrey Phillips poses precariously atop the number three Bristol Hercules of a Halifax during his time instructing on the Handley Page type.

for the care and maintenance of the aircraft, to carry out engineering checks before, during and post flight and to assist the pilot during take-off and landing, especially when there was no 2nd Pilot".

In Air Ministry Order A.538/1943, the 'FLIGHT ENGINEER'S DUTIES' were noted as follows:

"(i) To operate certain controls at the engineer's station and watch appropriate gauges as indicated in the relevant publications.

(ii) In certain types of aircraft, to act as pilot's assistant to the extent of being able to fly straight and level. and on a course.

(iii) To advise the captain of the aircraft as to the functioning of the engines and the fuel, oil and coolant systems, both before and during flight.

(iv) To ensure effective liaison between the captain of the aircraft and the maintenance staff by communicating to the latter such technical notes regarding the performance and maintenance of the aircraft in flight as may be required.

(v) To carry out practicable emergency repairs during flight.

(vi) To act as stand-by air gunner.

Initially, flight engineers were taken from the ranks of existing airmen considered to have the needed skills. With volunteers from among a pool of highly

RIGHT: The introduction of the four-engined 'heavies' – the Short Stirling (top), Handley Page Halifax (middle), and Avro Lancaster (bottom) – into Bomber Command's armoury ultimately led to the creation of a new aircrew category – the flight engineer.
ALL KEY COLLECTION

BELOW: The sergeant on flying control duty reports the landing of a Halifax V of No. 1663 Heavy Conversion Unit at RAF Holme-on-Spalding Moor in the East Riding of Yorkshire on October 21, 1943. While students passed through such units in a matter of weeks with courses typically comprising some 40 hours of instruction, it must have been somewhat terrifying for the instructors flying in often war weary, barely serviceable aircraft with novice aircrew day in day out wondering which would try and kill you first – the aircraft or the rookies?
ALAMY-PIEMAGS

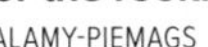

skilled flight mechanics recruited, their talents were supplemented with a six-week gunnery course after which they were considered qualified. While the training evolved considerably throughout World War Two, in the beginning it was at best ad hoc – with a little invention along the way."

Humphrey Phillips was one of this new 'breed' of aircrew. An apprentice motor mechanic before the war having left school aged 15, not surprisingly, he volunteered first for training as a flight mechanic when he was called up to join the war effort in June 1940. On qualifying near the top of his course, he was given further instruction to become a more exalted Fitter II E – the 'E' standing for 'engines'. He was just 20 years old.

Humphrey was retained as an instructor with No. 4 School of Technical Training at RAF St Athan ▶

in South Wales, before seeing the Air Ministry Order calling for further volunteers to become flight engineer aircrew in April 1942. After some additional gunnery training, he was posted to the Halifax equipped No. 102 Squadron at RAF Dalton (the satellite of nearby RAF Topcliffe in North Yorkshire) and immediately attached to the unit's CF – then commanded by New Zealander Sqn Ldr Peter Robinson DFC. It was the start of a near two-year stint there as an instructor on the Halifax. This being before the days that all aircrew held the minimum rank of sergeant, he rose from the rank of corporal in charge of flight engineers, before being commissioned, and appointed flight engineer leader.

With a series of short attachments, often less than a fortnight, to the CFs of Nos. 102 and 103 RAF, and 460 (Royal Australian Air Force) Squadrons, his early career reflects the transitional period for training at that time.

Humphrey's instruction included a brief attachment to No. 1652 CU, just up the road at RAF Marston Moor, to take part in the first two 'Thousand Bomber' raids against the German cities of Cologne and Essen across the nights of May 30/31 and June 1/2, 1942, respectively, as part of a scratch crew of tour-expired instructors.

It also included a ten-day spell with Avro at its Woodford facility near Manchester to train specifically on the Lancaster – and complement his existing knowledge on the Halifax gained during a similar visit to English Electric (also responsible for series production of the type) at Samlesbury, near Preston.

From there, he became a founding member of No. 1656 CU. Headquartered at RAF Lindholme, near Doncaster, in South Yorkshire, the

LEFT: Humphrey noted the flight engineer's position in a Halifax (left) was just as uncomfortable as it was in the Lancaster (right) – "Ergonomics had not been uppermost in the designer's mind!" BOTH KEY COLLECTION

LEFT: A Halifax flight engineer (left) and Lancaster flight engineer (right) monitor their respective panels while pre-flighting their bombers. BOTH KEY COLLECTION

unit was formed in October that same year by amalgamating 103 and 460 CFs under the command of Australian Wg Cdr Arthur Hubbard DFC.

Scrounge and adapt

Humphrey had something of a privileged view of the four-engined heavies of that time – particularly the Halifax and the Lancaster. He also had first-hand knowledge of the dangers of converting to them – not only for the novice crews, but also the experienced instructor pilots and flight engineers obliged to go along for the ride!

His logbook is populated by such names as 'Harry' Drummond, 'Daddy' Lashbrook, 'Shorty' Fahey, 'Willie' Caldow, 'Bluey' Graham and other such notable pilots of their time. It would be fair to say that their contribution in transitioning new crews has perhaps not yet been fully recognised.

Humphrey recalled: "The task of training at HCU was divided into ground instruction and instruction in the air. Ground instruction was primarily lectures for all the crew, sometimes together, and sometimes split into their individual specialisms, on such things as day and night landings, three-engined flying procedures, and emergency drill. As well as the lecture halls, we had rooms equipped with different

BOTTOM LEFT: Many of the aircraft assigned to Bomber Command's Heavy Conversion Units were often war weary and already beat up airframes. One such example was Halifax II HR868/MH-B. Delivered new to 51 Squadron sometime between May 9 and June 16, 1943, the aircraft is seen here at RAF Snaith in East Riding of Yorkshire showing the aftermath of a night fighter attack while tasked with attacking the German city of Frankfurt during the night of December 20-21, 1943. Repaired, it was later handed over to No. 1656 HCU – remaining with them until being struck off charge on January 1, 1945. KEY COLLECTION

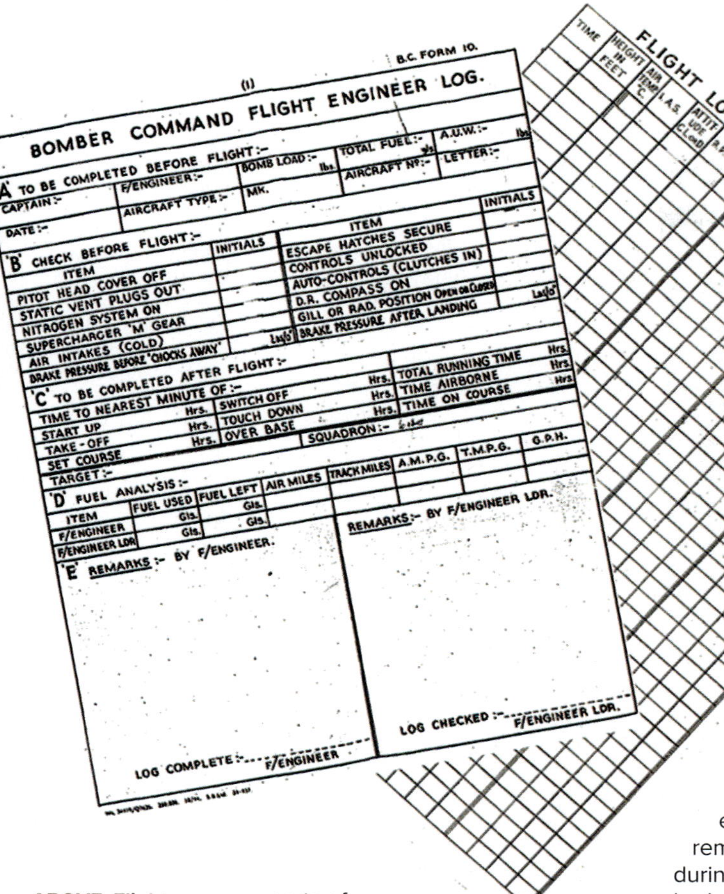

ABOVE: Flight engineers were required to log their readings pre-flight, then every 30 minutes in flight airborne, or each change of flight or engine conditions, until completing their after-flight checks.
INTERNATIONAL BOMBER COMMAND CENTRE

parts of the aircraft so we could better illustrate how systems worked."

Left to their own devices, section leaders got somewhat inventive when it came to training aids. "We would scrounge parts from crashed aircraft before the official 'salvage' teams moved in!" commented Humphrey, adding: "This enabled me, with the help of our chief ground instructor, to commission the construction of a working, diagrammatical fuel system and a fully working undercarriage mechanism so that I could demonstrate the functions of the locking mechanism."

It was in the air, however, that the fun really began. Humphrey said: "After a familiarisation flight, the pilots were trained in take-offs and landings referred to as 'circuits and bumps' two at a time, until both pilots were safe to perform solo. Their dual training also included learning how to handle the aircraft on three engines.

"When it came to the solo, the flying instructor retired to the control tower, while the staff engineer, which could be me, remained with the aircraft. It was during some of these solos that I had my hairiest moments.

"One night I was with two trainee pilots practising circuits and bumps and after the first circuit we landed and taxied to the end of the runway for a second take-off. The pilot began running up the engines against the brakes while I kept an eye on the instrument panel.

"To my horror I could see that there was no oil pressure on the starboard inner engine. Neither pilot had noticed that the engine had, in fact, stalled! The pilot is supposed to check these instruments as he opens the throttles… they were about to try to take off on three engines!

"On another solo, as the second pilot responded to the instruction 'undercarriage down', we had a Red light to show that the starboard wheel was not down and locked.

"We went through the various emergency routines, but the wheel remained obstinately stuck. As we circled at 1,000ft, the pilot called the control tower, and the instructor 'Daddy' Lashbrook, asked whether we had checked the 'up locks'. Making my way aft, I was rather surprised to find one of our staff wireless 'ops' on the rest bed, making up his monthly hours!

"The up-lock control emerges from the fuselage side at the foot of the bed, and on this particular aircraft, it had been fitted with an extension bar to make it accessible if overload fuel tanks were fitted. Our 'intruder' had pulled the bar out on which to rest his feet! No sooner had he taken his feet away and I was able to push the bar to the 'unlocked' position, the Green light blinked to tell as the undercarriage was down."

"Tired old crates"

From their early days, many of the aircraft that equipped the Halifax training units were early war-weary Mark I, IIs and Vs that had been withdrawn from the front line. If learning to fly these four-engined giants wasn't hard enough, flying these old war horses was a trial in itself! A Halifax in inexperienced hands was a perilous machine… it was difficult to taxi, it had an undercarriage-straining swing on take-off, and demanded special care on landing. The airframes the novices were to train on had been bashed around, heavy hands had pushed them to their limits as they fought the night war over Germany, and it showed as the fledgling pilots climbed into the cockpit. Bill Webb, who converted onto the Handley Page type with No. 1652 HCU, recalled: "All the aircraft had done several tours of operations and were really 'clapped out'. To fly a cross-country, it was ►

> **Initially, conversion training was achieved through the creation of dedicated Conversion Flights within each operational squadron**

RIGHT: The flight engineer's panel in a Halifax (left) was said to be well laid out, with the fuel tank gauges, oil temperature gauges, engine temperature gauges etc all logically displayed, while the Lancaster's (right) seemed to be rather more 'Heath Robinson' in its approach.
BOTH KEY COLLECTION

necessary to start at one end of a long line of Halifaxes, and try to find one that responded to the pre-flight checks… and actually started! Few were fully serviceable, but if most of the systems worked, you considered it was worth taking, and out we taxied."

Other problems included leaking fuel tanks, weakened undercarriages from earlier squadron use, and the ever-present fear of rudder overbalance – the latter occurred when the rudders induced a large sideslip angle, which was enough to stall, or almost stall, the fins. Not the best of idiosyncrasies when flying tight turns in the circuit where there was no height to correct the problem! Discovered during the type's early testing, it was a fatal flaw that followed it into service and claimed the lives of many crews – both in training, and operationally alike.

The aeroplane's rudders had to be aerodynamically balanced to reduce operating loads at the rudder pedals. When the rudder area forms a fairly large proportion of the whole fin and rudder area, a large sideslip can be generated. Under such conditions the airflow over the fin broke down,

reducing the effectiveness of the balance, with the downwind rudder overcoming the pilot's effort such that it could "self-lock" hard over when the sideslip reached about 20°. Eventually a complete cure was found when fin area was increased, the original kidney-shaped fin giving way to a rectangular fin. This restricted the sideslip angle that could be reached with full rudder. It was fitted in production from the Halifax III onwards, but many IIs were retrofitted.

While both incidents Humphrey previously mentioned occurred when flying a Halifax, it was during a routine air test in a Lancaster that Humphrey came the closest to coming to grief. He recalled: "A well-known danger among trainee pilots and instructors throughout the war was the quality and reliability of aircraft in which we flew. Seldom did we get our hands on anything 'new'… more usually they were second-hand, tired old crates, the airframes and engines of which had been flogged beyond endurance. Serviceability was an issue – despite the heroic efforts of the groundcrews who, it seemed, were fighting a daily battle they could rarely win!

"*A-for-Apple* was a 'rogue' Lancaster that had all the hallmarks of being a squadron cast-off. My pilot, 'Willie' Caldow, and I received instruction to fly the initial air test prior to putting the aircraft into service.

"We had been told that 'she' had some 'gremlin' in the ailerons – that made us understandably cautious. It was, therefore, in a thoughtful mood that we made our way out to dispersal via the flight office, where Willie signed the aircraft's Form 700.

LEFT: An electrical fitter adjusts the automatic pilot system onboard a Handley Page Halifax. Nicknamed 'George', a similar system in a Lancaster almost cost Humphrey and his pilot their lives during an air test… GETTY IMAGES-PIEMAGS

LEFT: Engine fitters work on a Halifax II's Rolls-Royce Merlin XXs at RAF Linton-on-Ouse in North Yorkshire, circa June 1942. Powering both the Halifax and the Lancaster during their early days of service, the 'XX' suffered its fair share of problems. ROYAL AIR FORCE

BOTTOM LEFT: The Halifax tended to 'swing' – both when taking off and landing. While it was difficult to train new pilots to land the Handley Page type as a result, 'veteran' hands were sometimes caught out by this foible – as the 'special duties' crew of No. 138 Squadron Halifax II Halifax DT727/NF-K found out on their return from an air test on June 22, 1943. 'Swinging' on landing at RAF Tempsford in Bedfordshire and hitting a hangar, the aftermath is seen here. While the aircraft was deemed a write off, the three crew onboard were unhurt. ROYAL AIR FORCE

ABOVE: Group Captain Terence John Arbuthnot, the station commander at RAF Fiskerton in Nottinghamshire, removes a belt of .303 ammunition from the burning wreck of Avro Lancaster III JB228/J9-R – the No. 1668 Heavy Conversion Unit machine crashing at Fiskerton during a three-engined landing on March 10, 1945. With the type already prone to 'swinging', the asymmetric forces acting on the aircraft, catching the 'rookie' pilot off guard, saw it swing off the runway, resulting in the undercarriage collapsing, and the aircraft to catch fire. Of the eight crew on board, two, the flight engineer and bombardier, were both badly hurt, and required hospital treatment. Humphrey Phillips was serving as the unit's Flight Engineer Leader at the time. KEY COLLECTION

"We did our external checks and clambered aboard, wondering what we might find. All seemed to be in order, and we began our start, run-up and cockpit drill, blissfully ignorant of the danger at hand."

Everything seemed normal as they taxied out and started the take-off run. The Lancaster steadily picked up speed along the runway until they had about 125mph indicated airspeed and the tail came up. "I could see Willie appeared to be lugging on the control column with unusual vigour as he wound back furiously on the elevator trim. He had a somewhat puzzled look on his face as he panted out: 'It doesn't want to come unstuck!'

"At last, long past the point of no return, the aircraft reluctantly left the runway, and we were finally airborne in a shallow climb. Quickly this changed to quite a steep climb with Willie now pushing hard on the control column to keep the nose down to build our airspeed and prevent us from stalling. He was furiously winding the trimmer forward again with his right hand to take off all the trim he had used to get us in the air!"

Although he had gained sufficient control to get a normal rate of climb out of the wayward bomber, Willie remained concerned. Humphrey recalled: "It was clearly taking it out of him physically as he instructed me to pull both the wheels and the flaps up to reduce drag and result in a nose-down change of trim. Having complied, he told me that the elevators felt locked and that he had only managed to gain control by an excessive use of the elevator trim control… which I had seen!"

Down to earth

"It was as we reached a thousand feet that the fun started!"

commented Humphrey, adding: "We had to make the first turn to port to stay in our left-hand circuit of the station… Willie was again having to use considerable physical force to get the aircraft to do anything. He managed to gasp out a somewhat cryptic message that he felt that the ailerons were now locking and began frantically winding the aileron trimmer to compensate. It was getting desperate now: He shouted: 'Think! What the hell can it be?'

"I tried to force my mind to work logically and systematically through the possibilities affecting both elevators and ailerons being overridden by the trim tabs. I could think of nothing… but my thoughts were interrupted by Willie's shout that we were not going to make it back to the runway. We needed to find a place to put down, and quickly!"

At this point the aircraft had achieved a semblance of stable flight maintaining altitude and speed on the downwind leg of the circuit – the airfield off to their left. And while good visibility is always a bonus (or is it a wanted?) when flying, it meant Humphrey couldn't see anything remotely like an adequate piece of flat land ahead or to the right to put the struggling bomber down on. "A minute or two passed," explained Humphrey. "We were nearing the next turn to port for the short crosswind leg. Somewhat more composed, Willie quickly briefed me

> **66** *Making my way aft, I was rather surprised to find one of our staff wireless 'ops' on the rest bed, making up his monthly hours!* **99**

on assisting him on the approach and landing. Between us we somehow managed to bring the mighty beast back down to earth… and even pulled off a creditable landing, all things considered! Willie was exhausted. We taxied the Lancaster back to dispersal without uttering a word."

The impossible

Briefly speaking about the symptoms and possible causes, both Humphrey and Willie agreed that the problem was a complete locking of the aileron controls, while the other flying controls, and especially the elevators, had also felt odd. Heading to the sergeants' mess, Humphrey joined the only table that was still occupied. He recalled: "A gaggle of my fellow engineers were chatting to a stranger. Although he was not, as it happens, just 'another engineer', but rather an operational 'type' from a neighbouring squadron.

"One of my friends commented on my somewhat harassed demeanour, and I was encouraged to give an account of what had happened. Naturally I expected some sympathy, but instead my story was greeted with looks and expressions of disbelief from all… except the stranger.

"With a cynical and rather patronising tone he said: 'It's obvious old chap. You two clots had 'George' in!' His statement was ▶

Having 'borrowed' parts from a crashed Lancaster, Humphrey Phillips devised this working, diagrammatical fuel system teaching aid while serving with No. 1656 CU.

followed by a moment or two of ominous silence, during which time my mind raced over the relevant facts, and I had a strange feeling in the pit of my stomach – George was the nickname given to the autopilot fitted to the likes of the Lancaster, Halifax, and Stirling.

"With something of a cold sweat, I spluttered: 'Impossible. Firstly, all of our George controls are wired 'out'; and secondly, it would have been impossible to fly the 'kite' manually with George engaged. We would not be here to tell the tale.'

"My statement provoked quite a heated discussion, lasting some minutes. I allowed the others to talk over themselves but made no further contribution to the debate.

"Instead, I proceeded to bolt my lunch and beat a hasty exit. Grabbing my bike from outside the mess, I pedalled furiously back to the dispersal. Climbing hurriedly into the aircraft and making my way forward, one glance in the cockpit revealed the awful truth: both of George's clutches were 'in'... the automatic pilot was fully engaged!"

Willie and Humphrey had just achieved what everyone had previously believed impossible. He later phoned Willie and thanked him for saving his life.

Too fussy

Given Humphrey's experience on both types, how did the Halifax and the Lancaster compare?

"The Halifax was a fairly crude aircraft, whereas the Lancaster was more refined – in every sense. The Halifax had comparatively poor aerodynamics and certainly didn't fly as well on three engines. The problems with its tail assembly were well documented at the time – and since – and they were constantly modifying the fins to find the answer.

"'She' could flip into a rudder stall far too easily and often, catching out all but the most experienced pilots – and even some of those lost their lives. There were more technical faults with a Halifax as well as specific 'quirks', such as the problems we had with the tailwheel. It was even possible for a Halifax to take off and leave its tail wheel on the runway.

"When we first started flying the Halifax, engineers were instructed to open the fuel cross-feed cock on take-off and close it immediately afterwards. The idea was that this would ensure that the flow of fuel was

constant to all engines during one of the most critical phases of flight.

"Unfortunately, the opposite was the case and leaving the cross-feed cock open actually starved two of the engines of fuel, causing the aircraft to crash. I remember clearly the urgent instruction we received to halt this practice with immediate effect.

"But that was part of the problem with the Halifax... it was too fussy, and too unnecessarily complicated. There were too many fuel tanks – the Halifaxes we flew had six fuel tanks in each wing. The hydraulics had too many remedies, and too many things that could go wrong. There were five ways of getting the undercarriage down – the hydraulic power was supplemented by cylinders that stored air under pressure to be used in an emergency, so in theory we should have been safer, but in practice it just over-complicated matters.

"Some Halifax flight engineers will no doubt argue that you were fine if you knew your stuff, but it was a great deal to take in. Choosing the right course of action in an emergency, when you are under real pressure, is the difference between life and death."

Less to go wrong

"Everything about the Lancaster was easier!" commented Humphrey. "The fuel system was simpler – there were only three self-sealing fuel tanks in each wing. The hydraulic system was easier, and the undercarriage less complicated. There was far less to go wrong and therefore it gave you greater confidence when you were in the air. You never heard of a Lancaster falling out of the sky for no known reason... the same could not always be said of the Halifax. That's not to say that the Lancaster was perfect. It was not!

"Ergonomics had not been uppermost in the designer's mind. The flight engineer's position in a Lancaster was as uncomfortable as it was in the Halifax. That said, the panel in a Halifax was actually rather well laid out, with the fuel tank gauges, oil temperature gauges, engine temperature gauges etc all logically displayed. The one in the Lancaster was rather more 'Heath Robinson'. Positioned behind and to the right of where you stood, or sat if you were lucky, it was less easily accessible."

Like the Halifax, the Lancaster suffered teething problems. "The bomb doors often failed to close properly – the front-end jack moving faster than the jack at the rear. This was a result of low oil temperature within the pipes that entered at the front and run the length of the bay.

"The Rolls-Royce Merlin XX engines, which powered both aircraft in the early days, also

LEFT: Pioneering flight engineer Humphrey Phillips built this fully working undercarriage mechanism rig to demonstrate its locking functions using parts and components he had 'scrounged'!

BELOW: The aircrew assigned to No. 626 Squadron pose at RAF Wickenby – Humphrey Phillips, can be seen on the very far left. Joining the squadron in November 1943, he flew 27 operations with '626' before returning to instructor duties.

suffered their fair share of problems – water tended to leak through the top cylinder joint, which could cause the engine to catch fire.

"The Merlin 22 had a modified joint and the problem was solved, but the Merlin 28 – built under licence in the US by Packard – also had a different diaphragm-operated carburettor, and the air intake was prone to icing up. This would cause them to 'surge' and, if not rectified quickly, the engines could be wrecked.

"Both aircraft suffered from 'swing' on take-off, and a severe crosswind could aggravate the situation and caused many accidents. It was also very difficult to train new pilots to land the Halifax well. 'She' was a

rather unforgiving aircraft... if you held off too high you didn't bounce, like you did in a Lancaster, you came down with a crunch, that could severely damage the aircraft. A good pilot, if he 'bounced' a Lancaster, could take off again, if full power was immediately applied. This was never the case with the Halifax..."

Of the Halifax, the late Jack Currie, the famed RAF instructor turned author said: "It always seemed reluctant to leave the ground and glad to be back down again. If left to fly itself, it would porpoise its way back to straight and level. It was, in fact, the ideal aeroplane to go to sleep in. But the instruments were arranged as if they had been flung in through the window and fitted where they landed. The Flight Engineer and I were in constant communication."

War winners

Humphrey eventually added to his two operational flights in 1942 with a full tour with the Lancaster-equipped No. 626 Squadron out of RAF Wickenby in Lincolnshire just as Bomber Command's main effort was being directed against the German capital in what was dubbed the Battle of Berlin.

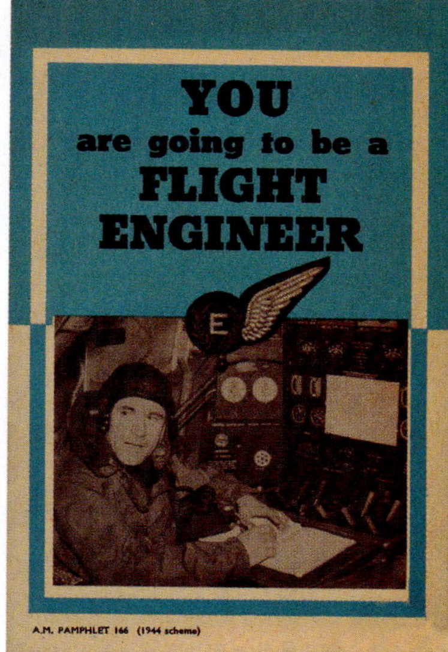

Joining the squadron in November 1943, he was hand-picked by Wg Cdr Philip Haynes to join his crew. It was flying with Haynes, that he was awarded the Distinguished Flying Cross for his actions that saved one of his fellow crew after their Lancaster was hit by a bomb dropped from another above them during a strike against an armaments factory in Essen on April 26, 1944.

Flying some 27 operations, he returned to instructor duties – seeing out the war as the Flight Engineer Leader of No. 1668 HCU at RAF Balderton in Nottinghamshire.

Despite his views, Humphrey was happy to recognise the achievements of both types – and their contribution to winning the war.

Although he conceded that not every flight engineer would share his opinions: "Ask the doyen of the flight engineer community, Flt Lt Ted Stocker DSO DFC, which aircraft he'd choose for a night 'op' to Cologne and he'd probably opt for the Halifax. Why? Because with your starboard wing ablaze, and the order given to bale out, you had a better chance of doing so safely from a Halifax!"

- In 2018, Humphrey Phillips became one of UK's oldest published authors when he released his memoirs *A Thousand and One - A Flight Engineer Leader's War from the Thousand Bomber Raids to the Battle of Berlin* with the author of this feature, Sean Feast – it is a fascinating insight into the heart and mind of a flight engineer and their often overlooked work. ■

A NOTE FROM THE EDITOR

While producing *Halifax*, I was made aware that a friend's grandfather, George Walker, had been a flight engineer on the Halifax while serving with No. 420 'City of London' Squadron, Royal Canadian Air Force, between August and October 1944. Seen here third from right, I'd like to dedicate this feature to George.

Jamie Ewan

MAKE DO AND MEND

Established in 1939 as Britain's new flag carrier, state owned British Overseas Airways Corporation was forced to improvise as it sought to gain a footing on the world's post-war air routes. David Ransted explores the fascinating, yet short-lived, career of BOAC's Handley Page HP.70 Haltons

During World War Two, in an agreement with the US, Britain concentrated its aircraft design and manufacturing efforts on bombers and fighters while transport aircraft were developed by America. This division of labour, driven by the urgency of the war effort and the different strengths of each nation's aircraft industries, allowed both countries to maximise their war production capabilities – the UK could concentrate on the aircraft needed for its immediate combat needs, while the US could focus on building the transport aircraft required to support the war effort and supply its allies. While not explicitly outlined in a single, formal document, this evolved through ongoing discussions and agreements related to the Lend-Lease Act established in 1941.

This arrangement worked well during the height of the conflict,

RIGHT: The Halton was based on the unarmed CVIII Halifax transport. Seen here at RAF Clifton near York, circa early 1946, PP236 joined BOAC as G-AHDO *Forfar* on August 13 the following year.
ALAMY-CHRONICLE

BELOW: The first HP.70 Halton conversion for BOAC – G-AHDU *Falkirk* – runs up at Handley Page's Radlett airfield, circa July 1946. Even for a stopgap, the Halton proved a disappointment in BOAC service.
KEY COLLECTION

however, it meant that as the end of the war approached, there were no new British transport designs in the pipeline.

The British Overseas Airways Corporation (BOAC) needed to re-establish itself on the world stage; British prestige was at stake. So was communication with the outposts across the Empire. Suitable, affordable aeroplanes were needed, and post haste.

BOAC agreed with a proposal from the Brabazon Committee – the influential group tasked to recommend the best way forward for the development of British commercial aircraft following World War Two. It suggested that use could be made of converted military types for civilian operations across the expected three-to-six-year interval period as an interim before new British airliners came online.

ABOVE: From London to the world… this was one of the many wonderful images captured by renowned photographer Charles A Sims of BOAC Halton G-AHDU *Falkirk* during its route proving flight to Cairo in August 1946.
KEY COLLECTION

> **It suggested that, as an interim before new British airliners came online, use could be made of converted military types for civilian operations across the expected three-to-six-year interval period**

Thus, in October 1945, BOAC leased three Handley Page Halifax CVIIIs from the Royal Air Force for route proving trials on its No.1 Line – then responsible for the long-range flag-carrier's African routes on airmail runs between Hurn Airport near Bournemouth to Accra on the Gold Coast (now Ghana) via Rabat in Morocco, and Bathurst (now Banjul) in Gambia. Powered by four 1,675hp 14-cylinder two-row Bristol Hercules 100 radial engines, the CVIII was a dedicated cargo-carrying version of the Halifax, that could be fitted with a deep detachable pannier, also known as the Universal Freight Container, in place of the bomb doors. Appearing very late in the war, this variant first flew in June 1945. Ultimately, just 98 were built.

Retaining their RAF markings, PP325, PP326, and PP327 were allocated to BOAC. With PP325

and PP326 typically kept 'online', PP327 was held in reserve as a source of spares. Despite the service operating from Hurn, this sub-fleet was based 'up the road' at Whitchurch, near Bristol, some 50 miles to the northwest.

The first flight operated by the type departed on October 13 that year with PP325 doing the honours. The frequency of this service was, at least initially, officially described as "on an ad-hoc basis with the aim of having a departure every other day".

Designated Flight 25W, the outbound aircraft would power out of Hurn at 2030hrs [all times local], arriving in Rabat at 0430hrs the following morning, Bathurst at 1500hrs, and finally Accra during the early hours of the third day – typically around 0030hrs. Return flights, prefixed 26W, left Accra at

0700hrs, reaching Hurn at 0930hrs the following day.

The Halifaxes covered this round trip of some 8,869 miles in an average time of 45 hours. It was found that while cruising at around 50% of take-off power, the aircraft had a true airspeed of 205mph. The experiment indicated that the converted Halifax could carry a load of ten passengers and around 3,500lb of cargo. Over the two-month trial period flying between Britain and Accra, the aircraft were flown at an operating intensity of 2,691 and 3,061 hours respectively, per aircraft, per year.

To the delight of all involved, the trial proved highly satisfactory, and, despite the intensity of operation, the humble Halifax ran free of the gauntlet of mechanical breakdowns, proving its reliability – something that did not go unnoticed by BOAC officials. The carrier soon confirmed its decision to employ a civilian version of the type while it awaited the arrival of Avro's 689 Tudor II, which was based on the firm's four-engine Lincoln. However, despite ordering 79 examples, BOAC never operated the type in the passenger role, the carrier ultimately cancelling its orders in 1947 amid performance issues and government pressures.

Consequently, BOAC ordered a dozen of Handley Page's proposed civilian derivative of its Halifax CVIII to be known as the HP.70 Halton, with deliveries scheduled for the late spring and early summer of 1946. In the meantime, PP325, PP326, and PP327 – by then registered with BOAC as G-AIAO, G-AIAR, and G-AIAS, respectively – were ▶

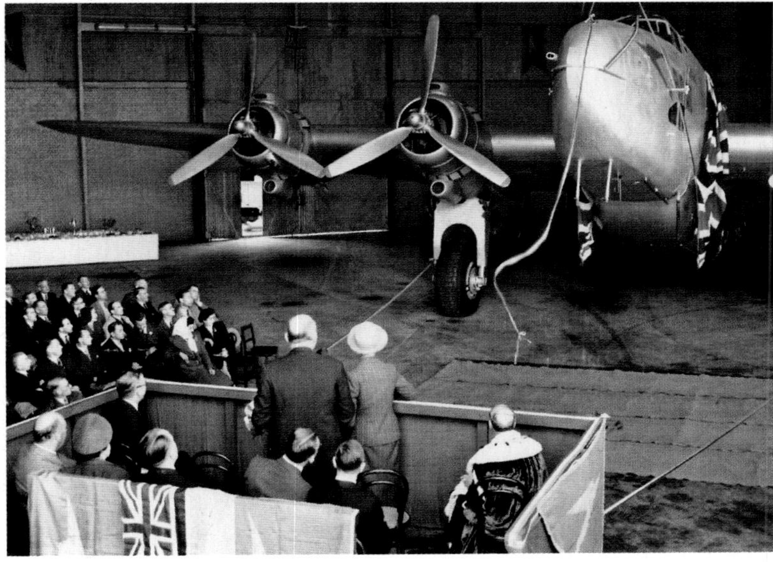

The first Halton delivered to BOAC, G-AHDU *Falkirk* – draped in the Union Flag – is christened by Lady Winster at Handley Page's Radlett airfield on July 18, 1946. ALL IMAGES BA HERITAGE CENTRE UNLESS STATED OTHERSWISE

retained and ferried to BOAC's Aldermaston base in Berkshire to train crew and engineers ahead of its first Halton delivery.

Design insight

The all-metal, four-engine, twin-tail Halifax was a mid-wing cantilever monoplane with a largely rectangular fuselage cross-section. Before the war had ended, Handley Page had gained experience in modifying the bomber variant for other uses. The first came in 1942, when it adapted Halifax IIIs and VIIs as jump ships for airborne forces and glider towing.

The second knowledge-building exercise came the following year when modifying bombers for RAF Transport Command for use as casualty, freight, and personnel transports. By removing turrets and guns, the aircraft could accommodate up to 24 troops, ten stretchers, or freight, while additional cargo could be carried in the detachable pannier that could be accessed via both fore and aft hatches.

The Haltons were built by Handley Page at their Radlett factory in Hertfordshire. However, since the firm's production lines were already at full capacity, including production of its elegant four-engined HP.81 Hermes airliner that could accommodate 40-82 passengers, they were flown to Short Brothers & Harland in Belfast to be kitted out to BOAC's requirements.

The carrier's Haltons were to be fitted with the panniers – pre-loaded, these would be winched into place. Boasting a generous 272cu ft of space, the panniers could carry 8,000lb of baggage, freight, and mail, and the likes, as well as cargo deemed too bulky to be loaded through the fuselage door. With the type's original glazed nose enclosed within a metal skin, this created additional space for storage. Of note, BOAC investigated converting the type's six underwing bomb cells – each capable of carrying 500lb of load – as additional cargo holds, although ultimately this was not pursued. Conversion further included provision of a large starboard-side entry door, a toilet, and square cabin windows – the latter differentiating the Halton from the military CVIIIs.

Delivery time

Although BOAC had initially placed its hopes in the Avro Tudor, as 1946 dawned it became clear that the type's service entry was still years away. In fact, it would be March 10 that same year before the prototype would get airborne for the first time.

With reluctance from the British Government to sanction the purchase of new American types, especially in scarce dollars, BOAC embraced the Halton – putting a brave face on its straightened resources. At a time when American carriers had the game changing Douglas DC-4 and

LEFT: This advert from the May 19, 1944 edition of *The Aeroplane* magazine subtly hints that Handley Page was looking at converting its Halifax for civilian use almost a year before hostilities ended. AVIATION ANCESTRY-WWW.AVIATIONANCESTRY.CO.UK

Lockheed Constellation, a converted former RAF bomber with a tailwheel hardly seemed to 'cut the mustard'. But BOAC had little option. The immediate post-war period found the carrier in limbo, unable to afford the latest equipment from overseas barring a handful of 'Connies' – and, in any case, it was expected to buy British – yet it was still awaiting the new home-grown types that were meant to 'define' its future.

The first example to be handed over to the carrier was G-AHDU – formerly PP310. Awarded its Certificate of Airworthiness (C of A) on July 10, 1946, just over a week later it was christened *Falkirk* by Lady Winster, wife of the then Minister of Civil Aviation, Reginald Thomas

LEFT: Officials and dignitaries pose with *Falkirk* – the flagship of the 12-strong BOAC Halton fleet and the first to be delivered – at Radlett on July 18, 1946. Sir Victor Tait, BOAC technical director, is far left, Capt W G Buchanan – one of the carrier's senior 'million-mile' pilots and the man responsible for training pilots on the type – seventh from left, and Handley Page founder, Sir Frederick Handley Page, fourth from right. GETTY IMAGES-TOPICAL PRESS AGENCY-FRANK HARRISON

Herbert Fletcher, 1st Baron Winster, before a crowd of onlookers at Handley Page's Radlett airfield – becoming the official flagship of the fleet.

At the ceremony, Lord Winster described the Halton as "the newest product of the oldest company in the aircraft industry" and recalled how Handley Page had produced some 6,000 Halifaxes for the war effort. With Sir Victor Tait, BOAC's then technical director, officially taking delivery of the aircraft on behalf of the carrier, it flew several passenger trips under the command of Capt W G Buchanan – one of BOAC's senior 'million-mile' pilots, and the man responsible for training its pilots on the type. As more of the carrier's Haltons were delivered, each was given a geographically or historically significant place name beginning with 'F'. Handed over on July 20, 1946, G-AHDM (ex-PP228) was dubbed *Falmouth*, G-AHDV (ex-PP314) which arrived on August 19, 1946, *Finisterre*, and G-AHDL (ex-PP224), accepted on September 18, 1946, became *Fitzroy*. Other names included *Fife* (G-AHDT, ex-PP308), *Folkestone* (G-AHDX, ex-PP316), *Flamborough* (G-AHDN, ex-PP234), and *Foreland* (G-AHDR, ex-PP269).

Post-war pragmatism

The cabin of the Halton was airconditioned and soundproofed to allow normal conversation. However, its narrow fuselage meant that only two semi-adjustable seats with fold-down tray tables (these, as across many British airliners of the post-war era, being manufactured by the Rumbold company) could

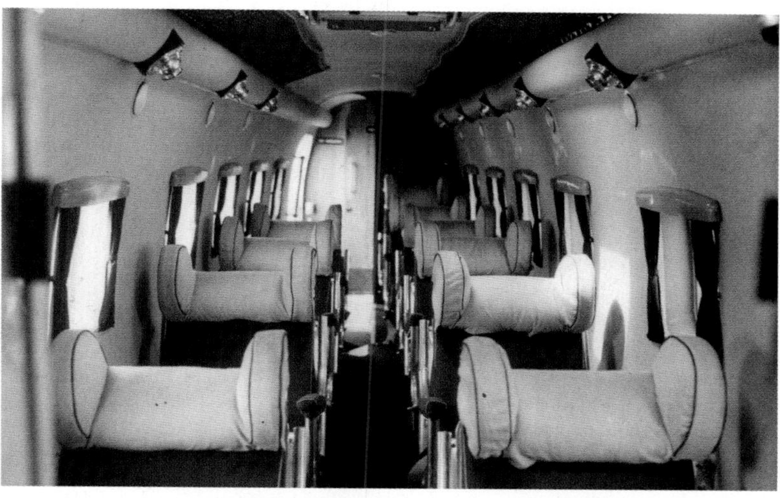

RIGHT: BOAC worked hard to disguise the wartime heritage of the Halton's interior – the aircraft being fitted out by Short Brothers & Harland in Belfast.

RIGHT: This view looking forward through the cabin of a Halton from abeam the starboard passenger entry door, reveals Handley Page's attempts to civilianise its bomber – including larger rectangular windows, soundproofing, fresh air vents, lighting, netting for storing luggage, carpets, and semi-adjustable seats with fold-down tray tables.

be fitted abreast – one either side of a central aisle. With four side-by-side rows installed, these, plus two additional seats on the port side, offered a total of ten.

Despite the cost constraints imposed by post-war austerity, a major effort was made to disguise the aircraft's utilitarian wartime heritage. Seat covers and armrests were finished in a dark blue fabric with white headrests – the latter accented with dark blue piping. The blue would become known as BOAC's trademark 'Corporation Blue'.

The cabin walls were finished in two shades of beige Vynide (a thin plastic alternative to the more expensive vinyl) with a lighter tone above the windowsill line, a darker shade below. The lower ▶

ABOVE: Ground personnel, with the aid of a Fordson tractor, tow G-AHDU at Radlett sometime during 1948. The prototype Halton conversion, this was the only example of the type to have its Certificate of Airworthiness (C of A) issued directly to BOAC. Going on to serve with the carrier until May 1, 1948, the aircraft was re-registered to Aviation Traders (AT) at Southend on September 24, that same year and quickly leased by Bond Air Services – then one of the major civil outfits carrying essential supplies into West Berlin from Wunstorf Aerodrome in West Germany during the Soviet blockade. Pressed into service, by the time 'Delta-Uniform' returned to AT in late June 1949, it had flown some 363 airlift sorties. With its C of A expiring on May 28, 1950, the aircraft was withdrawn from use for spares use and ultimately scrapped – it being officially cancelled from the register on March 25, 1954. KEY COLLECTION

eight inches of the sidewalls were protected by a material 'kicking skirt', while three independently operated lights were fitted along the cabin roof. In place of the Halifax's original round porthole windows, a large 12x15in rectangular window was installed beside each seat row – each of which was adorned with neatly tied back rust-coloured curtains. The tall, straight-sided cabin walls and high celling provided reasonable headroom, while netting above the seats allowed for storage space for hats, coats and small bags. Additionally, each seat row had an adjustable fresh air vent on either side of the cabin, a steward's call button, and individual lighting controls. Unusually for a civilian airliner, the main passenger entry door was on the starboard side of the rear fuselage, replacing the portside crew entry door of the military version. Inside the door, a small vestibule housing a wardrobe for coats and hats led to the main cabin. A cloakroom with toilet and washbasin, also decorated in beige and blue, was installed at the rear of the aircraft. A galley, equipped for serving hot meals, and which also served as the steward's accommodation, was installed forward of the passenger cabin, separated by swing doors. The

> **The experiment indicated that the converted Halifax could carry a load of ten passengers and around 3,500lb of cargo**

crew (which typically consisted of a captain, first officer, navigation officer, radio officer, flight engineer and steward) had a restroom that was located between the galley and the flight deck.

The Haltons were finished in a rather austere all-silver colour scheme with dark blue insignia. The BOAC name was painted in large letters on the forward fuselage underneath the flight deck windscreen, along with the Speedbird logo – the stylised emblem of a bird in flight designed in 1932 by Theyre Lee-Elliott – and the individual name

of the aircraft. The BOAC moniker featured again in much smaller form above the passenger entry door. With the aircraft's civilian registration added in large letters along the rear fuselage, the tailplane was emblazoned with a large Union Flag.

Route proving

On August 1, BOAC dispatched G-AHDU *Falkirk* from London Airport (today's Heathrow Airport) on a 7,000-mile route-proving round trip to the Sudanese capital Khartoum (via Algiers in Algeria, Tripoli's Castel Benito Airport in Libya, and Cairo in Egypt) commanded by Buchanan.

Lacking Gee or LOng RAnge Navigation (LORAN) equipment, the aircraft routed by QDM magnetic bearing fixes using the direction-finding loop or by the time-honoured means of a sextant

ABOVE: A magnificent image of BOAC Halton G-AHDU *Falkirk* over the bustling Egyptian capital Cairo during its route proving expedition of July 1946 – the aircraft under the command of Capt W G Buchanan.

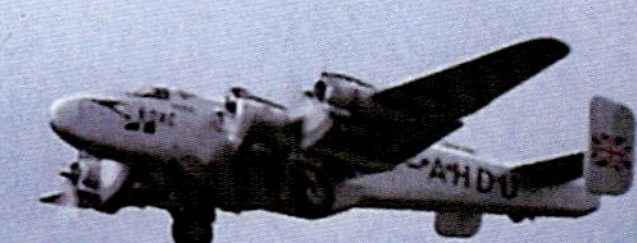

Halton G-AHDU *Falkirk* gets airborne out of Radlett during acceptance flights with BOAC in July 1946. Note the pair of Halifax A.IXs visible – RT900, left, and RT897, right. Two of the 40 examples of the paratroop transport/glider tug platform rolled out by Handley Page under Contract No. 3645 between June and September 1946, neither aircraft was taken up. Both were ultimately sold for scrap; RT900 on January 31, 1951, and RT897 a week later. KEY COLLECTION

BRITAIN — INDIA

YORK SPEEDBIRD — Four times weekly in each direction

SERVICE 9/10F

EASTBOUND

				L.S.T.	G.M.T.	Statute Miles	
LONDON	Airways Tml. Sun., Tue., Wed., Fri.		dep.	16.15	15.15	0	1st day
LONDON Airport			dep.	18.15	17.15		
BORDEAUX			arr.	20.45	19.45	459	
BORDEAUX			dep.	21.45	20.45		
TRIPOLI	Mon., Wed., Thu., Sat.		arr.	04.15	02.15	1584	
TRIPOLI			dep.	05.15	03.15		
CAIRO			arr.	10.35	08.35	2678	2nd day
CAIRO			dep.	13.30	11.30		
BASRA			arr.	19.15	16.15	3696	
BASRA			dep.	20.45	17.45		
KARACHI	Tue., Thu., Fri., Sun.		arr.	05.15	23.45	5006	
KARACHI			dep.	08.15	02.45		
DELHI			arr.	11.45	06.15	5674	3rd day
DELHI			dep.	12.45	07.15		
CALCUTTA			arr.	17.45	11.15	6494	

WESTBOUND

				L.S.T.	G.M.T.	Statute Miles	
CALCUTTA	Mon., Wed., Fri., Sat.		dep.	09.30	03.00	0	
DELHI			arr.	12.45	07.15	820	1st day
DELHI			dep.	13.45	08.15		
KARACHI			arr.	17.15	11.45	1488	
KARACHI	Tue., Thu., Sat., Sun.		dep.	03.15	21.45		
BASRA			arr.	07.15	04.15	2798	
BASRA			dep.	08.45	05.45		
CAIRO			arr.	12.45	10.45	3816	2nd day
CAIRO			dep.	18.00	16.00		
TRIPOLI			arr.	23.45	21.45	4910	
TRIPOLI	Wed., Fri., Sun., Mon.		dep.	00.45	22.45		
BORDEAUX			arr.	05.50	04.50	6035	
BORDEAUX			dep.	07.20	06.20		3rd day
LONDON Airport			arr.	10.05	09.05		
LONDON	Airways Terminal		arr.	11.05	10.05	6494	

HALTON SPEEDBIRD — Twice weekly in each direction

SERVICE 27/28F

EASTBOUND

				L.S.T.	G.M.T.	Statute Miles	
LONDON	Airways Tml. Tuesday, Friday		dep.	07.15	06.15	0	1st day
LONDON Airport			dep.	08.15	07.15		
TRIPOLI			arr.	16.40	14.40	1472	
TRIPOLI			dep.	18.10	16.10		
CAIRO			arr.	23.35	21.35	2573	
CAIRO	Wednesday, Saturday		dep.	22.30	21.30		2nd day
BASRA	Thursday, Sunday		arr.	05.50	02.50	3591	
BASRA			dep.	07.20	04.20		3rd day
KARACHI			arr.	16.30	11.00	4901	

WESTBOUND

				L.S.T.	G.M.T.	Statute Miles	
KARACHI	Monday, Friday		dep.	23.30	18.00	0	1st day
BASRA	Tuesday, Saturday		arr.	04.05	01.05	1310	
BASRA			dep.	05.35	02.35		
CAIRO			arr.	10.10	08.10	2328	2nd day
CAIRO			dep.	18.40	16.40		
TRIPOLI	Wednesday, Sunday		arr.	01.05	23.05	3429	
TRIPOLI			dep.	02.35	00.35		
LONDON Airport			arr.	09.35	08.35		3rd day
LONDON	Airways Terminal		arr.	10.35	09.35	4901	

The Local Standard Time for BRI...

for astronavigation. Unsurprisingly, this technique kept navigators busy over the desolate and featureless expanses of the Sahara Desert.

This first run was said to be intended purely as a routine affair to satisfy the Corporation, and particularly those most intimately concerned, the executives and staff of No. 1 Line, that everything down to the last detail was ready and in good order. The aircraft and its engines performed promisingly throughout its shakedown and returned safely to Britain on August 8.

Amongh those on board was Charles A Sims, reporter and principal photographer for *The Aeroplane*. He recalled: "Everyone on board had an important job to do, and in order to get the most out of the research work, conferences were frequent, mostly informal, and taking place during the flight as matters of moment arose. Conferences on this trip, both in the air and more formally on the ground decide the ultimate schedules, times of departures, loadings, and many other technical items. Nothing of major or minor importance is overlooked, from the details of a full-load take-off in the mid-day heat to the passage of the steward down the compartment with his plates of soup."

Sims described the Halton as being "comfortable and pleasant as any passenger aircraft on service anywhere. There is ample leg and elbow room, a very comfortable seat, and a window apiece for each passenger... One completely forgets that the Halton is a converted bomber."

It was his view, that "...if it can be taken as an augury, [this] means that the advent of the Haltons on service is going to bring a deal of credit to BOAC and considerable satisfaction to the fare-paying public."

Eager to strengthen its position on the world's expanding post-war airways, BOAC wasted no time in making its mark. In September 1946, with six of the type on strength, the corporation launched scheduled Halton services on its trans-Sahara and Cairo route – a daily link between BOAC's Bovingdon base in Hertfordshire and Cairo – replacing the carrier's Douglas DC-3 Dakotas then being used. The first flight was operated by G-AHDV *Falmouth* under the command of Capt R G Ballantyne who was another of the carrier's senior pilots with more than one million flown miles already under his belt.

Fleet list: BOAC's Handley Page H.P.70 Halton and H.P.70 Halifax CVIII – Registration/Model/Name/c/n/Formerly/Delivered/Fate

Halton:

G-AHDL Halton 1 *Fitzroy* 1308 PP224, RAF September 18, 1946. Sold to Aviation Traders, June 1948.
G-AHDM Halton 1 *Falmouth* 1312 PP228, RAF July 20, 1946. Sold to Aviation Traders, June 1948.
G-AHDN Halton 1 *Flamborough* 1318 PP234, RAF March 24, 1947. Sold to Aviation Traders, June 1948.
G-AHDO Halton 1 *Forfar* 1310 PP236, RAF August 13, 1947. Sold to Aviation Traders, May 1948.
G-AHDP Halton 1 *Fleetwood* 1341 PP268, RAF March 24, 1947. Sold to Aviation Traders, June 1948.
G-AHDR Halton 1 *Foreland* 1342 PP269, RAF July 7, 1947. Sold to Aviation Traders, May 1948.
G-AHDS Halton 1 *Freemantle* 1350 PP277, RAF August 24, 1946. Sold to Aviation Traders, June 1948.
G-AHDT Halton 1 *Fife* 1370 PP308, RAF June 4, 1947. Sold to Aviation Traders, June 1948.
G-AHDU Halton 1 *Falkirk* 1372 PP310, RAF July 10, 1946. Sold to Aviation Traders, September 1948.
G-AHDV Halton 1 *Finisterre* 1376 PP314, RAF August 19, 1946. Sold to Aviation Traders, June 1948.
G-AHDW Halton 1 *Falaise* 1377 PP315, RAF July 29, 1946. Sold to Aviation Traders, June 1948.
G-AHDX Halton 1 *Folkestone* 1378 PP316, RAF June 4, 1947. Sold to Aviation Traders, September 1948.

Halifax leased from RAF for route proving trials:

PP325/G-AIAO Halifax CVIII - PP325, RAF Leased, Oct to Dec 1945. Transferred to BOAC Training Unit at Aldermaston. Damaged beyond repair in crash landing, July 8, 1946. Spent two years being used as a ground instructional airframe.
PP326/G-AIAR Halifax CVIII - PP326, RAF Leased, Oct to Dec 1945.
PP327/G-AIAS Halifax CVIII - PP327, RAF Leased, Oct to Dec 1945. Used as spares source.

Leased from RAF to cover Halton grounding:

G-AHYH Halifax CVIII - 1334 PP261, RAF Leased Sept 24, 1946 to Oct 20, 1947. Returned to RAF.
G-AHYI Halifax CVIII - 1373 PP311, RAF Leased Sept 24, 1946 to July 10, 1947. Returned to RAF.
G-AIAN Halifax CVIII - 1344 PP271, RAF Leased Sept 2, 1946 to April 25, 1947. Returned to RAF.
G-AIAO Halifax CVIII - 1345 PP272, RAF Leased Sept 2, 1946 to April 25, 1947. Returned to RAF.
G-AIAP Halifax CVIII - 1354 PP281, RAF Leased Sept 2, 1946 to April 25, 1947. Returned to RAF.
G-AIAR Halifax CVIII - 1388 PP326, RAF Leased Sept 24, 1946 to July 10, 1947. Returned to RAF.
G-AIAS Halifax CVIII - 1389 PP327, RAF Leased Sept 2, 1946 to April 11, 1947. Written off, November 1946. Broken up at Aldermaston, April 1949.
G-AIID Halifax CVIII - 1379 PP317, RAF Leased Sept 24, 1946 to April 28, 1947. Returned to RAF.

Despite the promising start, once in service, the Haltons' lack of de-icing equipment meant the aircraft suffered from numerous hydraulic system maladies. Impacting BOAC's ability to deliver a reliable service, the type was withdrawn from service after just six weeks. The aircraft were returned to Handley Page for remedial work — notably including the installation of much needed de-icing capabilities. While this was being carried out, BOAC leased eight Halifax CVIIIs from the Air Ministry to cover the grounding: G-AHYH (ex-PP261) leased between September 24, 1946 and October 20, 1947; G-AHYI (ex-PP311) between September 24, 1946 and July 10, 1947; G-AIAN (ex-PP271) between September 2, 1946 and April 25, 1947; G-AIAO (ex-PP272) between September 2, 1946 and April 25, 1947; G-AIAP (ex-PP281) between September 2, 1946 and April 25, 1947; G-AIAR (ex-PP326) between September 24, 1946 and July 10, 1947; G-AIAS (ex-PP327) between September 2, 1946 and April 11, 1947; and G-AIID (ex-PP317) between September 24, 1946 and April 28, 1947. All but one of these were returned to the RAF, G-AIAS noted as being "written off" and

FAR LEFT: As *The Aeroplane*'s **Charles Sims put it:** "Conferences on this trip, both in the air and more formally on the ground, decide the ultimate schedules, times of departures, loadings, and many other technical items." Here, Mr E P Hessey (facing camera), Manager of BOAC's No.1 Line whose responsibility it would be to introduce the Halton smoothly into service, confers with Supplies Officer J Partridge and Aircraft Engineer N Jerram during the July 1946 route proving trip to Khartoum.

LEFT: BOAC's short-lived Halton service to Colombo took a gruelling four days to cover the 6,402-mile journey via Tripoli, Cairo, Basra, Karachi, and Bombay (now Mumbai)

BRITAIN – CEYLON

SERVICE 25/26F — *Once weekly in each direction*

HALTON SPEEDBIRD

EASTBOUND

			L.S.T.	G.M.T.	Statute Miles	
LONDON *Airways Terminal*	Monday	dep.	07.15	06.15	0	
LONDON *Airport*		dep.	08.15	07.15		
TRIPOLI		arr.	16.40	14.40	1472	} 1st day
TRIPOLI		dep.	18.10	16.10		
CAIRO		arr.	23.35	21.35	2573	
CAIRO	Tuesday	dep.	23.30	21.30		} 2nd day
BASRA	Wednesday	arr.	05.50	02.50	3591	
BASRA		dep.	07.20	04.20		} 3rd day
KARACHI		arr.	16.30	11.00	4901	
KARACHI	Thursday	dep.	07.00	01.30		
BOMBAY		arr.	10.10	04.40	5446	} 4th day
BOMBAY		dep.	11.40	06.10		
COLOMBO		arr.	16.45	11.15	6402	

WESTBOUND

			L.S.T.	G.M.T.	Statute Miles	
COLOMBO	Saturday	dep.	08.30	03.00	0	
BOMBAY		arr.	13.50	08.20	956	
BOMBAY		dep.	15.20	09.50		} 1st day
KARACHI		arr.	18.30	13.00	1501	
KARACHI	Sunday	dep.	23.30	18.00		
BASRA	Monday	arr.	04.05	01.05	2811	
BASRA		dep.	05.35	02.35		} 2nd day
CAIRO		arr.	10.10	08.10	3829	
CAIRO		dep.	18.40	16.40		} 3rd day
TRIPOLI	Tuesday	arr.	01.05	23.05	4930	
TRIPOLI		dep.	02.35	00.35		} 4th day
LONDON *Airport*		arr.	09.35	08.35		
LONDON *Airways Terminal*		arr.	10.35	09.35	6402	

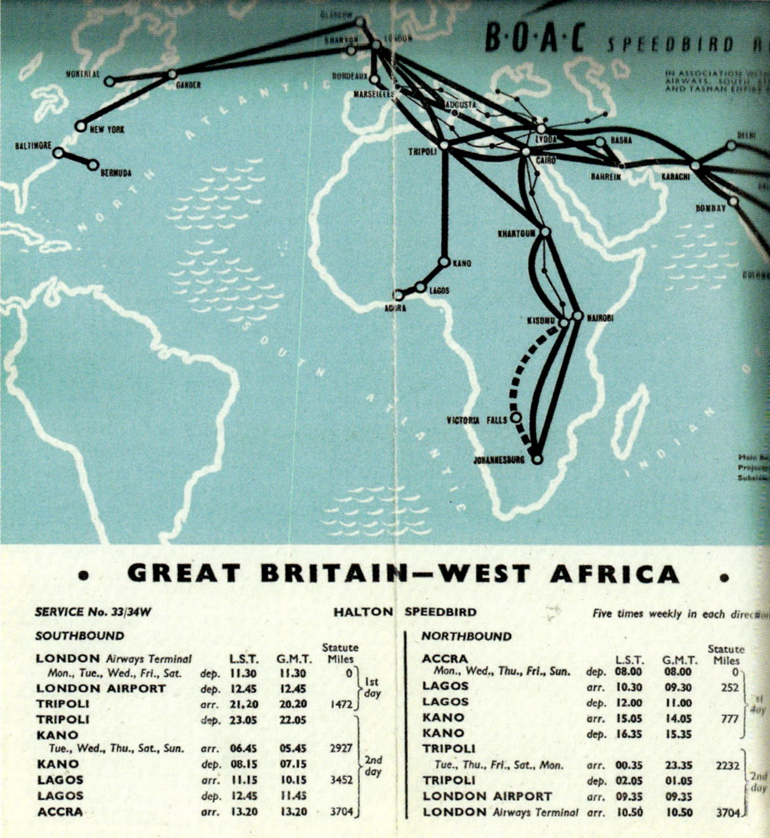

• GREAT BRITAIN—WEST AFRICA •

SERVICE No. 33/34W					HALTON SPEEDBIRD				Five times weekly in each direction

SOUTHBOUND

		L.S.T.	G.M.T.	Statute Miles	
LONDON *Airways Terminal*					
Mon., Tue., Wed., Fri., Sat.	dep.	11.30	11.30	0	1st day
LONDON AIRPORT	dep.	12.45	12.45		
TRIPOLI	arr.	21.20	20.20	1472	
TRIPOLI	dep.	23.05	22.05		
KANO					
Tue., Wed., Thu., Sat., Sun.	arr.	06.45	05.45	2927	2nd day
KANO	dep.	08.15	07.15		
LAGOS	arr.	11.15	10.15	3452	
LAGOS	dep.	12.45	11.45		
ACCRA	arr.	13.20	13.20	3704	

NORTHBOUND

		L.S.T.	G.M.T.	Statute Miles	
ACCRA					
Mon., Wed., Thu., Fri., Sun.	dep.	08.00	08.00	0	1st day
LAGOS	arr.	10.30	09.30	252	
LAGOS	dep.	12.00	11.00		
KANO	arr.	15.05	14.05	777	
KANO	dep.	16.35	15.35		
TRIPOLI					
Tue., Thu., Fri., Sat., Mon.	arr.	00.35	23.35	2232	2nd day
TRIPOLI	dep.	02.05	01.05		
LONDON AIRPORT	arr.	09.35	09.35		
LONDON *Airways Terminal*	arr.	10.50	10.50	3704	

"broken up at Aldermaston, April 1949". The improved Haltons returned to BOAC's Cairo route from June 2, 1947.

The British Overseas Airways Corporation opened its Bovingdon base during the summer of 1946 for its No.1 Line, which had decamped from its wartime base at Whitchurch. A former RAF and United States Army Air Forces (USAAF) base just to the northwest of London, not only did it become home to both the Halton fleet and its maintenance, but it was also designated an alternate to London Airport for BOAC in the event of weather diversions. Because of its elevation of about 160m, Bovingdon was often clear when London Airport, sat at 25m, was weathered in – especially during the winter months. Initially, BOAC with some 400 staff, shared the

> **" BOAC investigated converting the type's six underwing bomb cells – each capable of carrying 500lb of load – as additional cargo holds, although ultimately this was not pursued "**

airfield and its facilities with an RAF Fighter Command Communications Squadron, and a USAAF European Air Transport Service detachment, meaning both space and accommodation were at a premium. As a result, male staff moved into former USAAF quarters, while female employees were housed around the surrounding area.

Despite the type's grounding soon after entering service, Bovingdon had to be maintained and staffed and, by the following year, around 1,000 personnel were based there – at considerable cost to BOAC. As a result, as soon as hangarage became available at London Airport, the airline transferred its Halton fleet there, closing its Bovingdon base during early 1948. That said, it was still used for weather diversions.

Further afield

On July 1, 1947, Haltons replaced the Avro Yorks being used on BOAC's behalf by charter carrier Skyways' twice-weekly service between London and the Pakistani city of Karachi. Departing London at 0715hrs, it touched down in Tripoli around 1640hrs local time, and later Cairo at 2335hrs. After almost 24 hours in Cairo, the service continued, departing at 2230hrs and arriving in the Iraqi city of Basra at 0550hrs, and finally Karachi at 1630hrs – some 52 hours after leaving the British capital.

The following day, BOAC began thrice-weekly Halton services to the Nigerian city of Lagos via Casablanca in Morrocco, Dakar in Senegal and Accra, initially augmenting its DC-3s on that run, before ultimately replacing them later that same month as ▶

> **66** *However, the type was payload restricted on some of the longer sectors, further undermining its already poor economics* **99**

When BOAC was forced to ground its Halton fleet for needed modifications, it leased eight Halifax CVIIIs from the RAF – including PP281, which joined the carrier on September 2, 1946, as G-AIAP. Returned to the RAF on April 25 the following year, the aircraft was later acquired by Airtech at Haddenham Airfield in Buckinghamshire on October 24, 1948 (where it is thought to be seen in this image), and leased by Eagle Aviation and used, like many others, in the Berlin Airlift. Going on to fly the last civilian airlift into Berlin on August 15, 1949, it was destroyed in a fatal accident taking off from Calcutta's Dum Dum Airport in India on November 25, 1950, while operating a contracted BOAC service bound for Singapore. Two of the six crew on board were killed – the radio officer Dennis Carter, and flight engineer John Stoney. KEY COLLECTION

frequency grew. The first rotation was operated by G-AHDT *Fife*, with the routing taking a demanding 29 hours – of which 24 hours were spent in the air. On September 1, it was replaced by a more direct trans-Sahara routing as the corporation launched a five-weekly London-Tripoli-Kano (Nigeria)-Lagos-Accra service. The governor of Nigeria had reportedly complained about the journey time and pressed the corporation, via the Colonial Office, for a quicker trans-Sahara schedule. With this new routing providing a faster link to West Africa and the elapsed journey time dropping below 24 hours, the frequency was increased to six-weekly. However, the type was payload restricted on some of the longer sectors, further undermining its already poor economics. As a result, in May 1948 they were relieved by Avro Yorks, and the frequency reverted to its original five-weekly schedule.

On the trans-Sahara route, BOAC touted their four-engined all-British airliners. The flights departed London Airport at 1330hrs, arriving in Tripoli at 2055hrs. The following day they would arrive in Kano around 0550hrs, Lagos at 1015hrs and Accra at 1320hrs. The Haltons then rested overnight, departing for their return journey at 0800hrs the following morning. The northbound service arrived in Lagos at 1100hrs, Kano at 1535hrs, Tripoli at 0105hrs, and London Airport at 0905hrs. For this, BOAC charged a return fare of £67 to Tripoli, £153 to Kano, £158 to Lagos and £169 (the latter an eye-watering £7,850 in today's money!) to Accra.

The flights were scheduled to connect in Lagos with a local service to Dakar, in order to meet with the UK to South America services of sister corporation British South American Airways (BSAA). For context, BOAC's successor, British

NOTABLE INCIDENTS

The Halton had an excellent service record throughout its time with BOAC – but they did pick up a few 'scrapes' along the way. Somewhat inevitably during that early postwar period, instances of engine failure and shutdown, as well as relatively minor mechanical issues, were not uncommon. However, the individual aircraft's histories include some more unusual incidents.

May 15, 1947: G-AHDV *Finisterre* at Bovingdon. The port undercarriage collapsed while rolling out. The Captain, A R Onoszko, gave the order to "raise flaps". First Officer, Capt J G Naz responded by pulling the undercarriage lever instead of the flaps lever, resulting the aircraft coming to a stop with its port wing and engines resting on the ground, causing major damage to the aircraft. Owing to distortion to the undercarriage/flap lever quadrant – which caused the initial confusion – the undercarriage lever, when pushed to the 'down' position, was not locked by the safety lock. The quadrants were reinforced to prevent recurrence.

May 25, 1947: G-AHDL *Fitzroy* at Karachi. While on the ground, the Graviner fire extinguisher impact inertia switch, located close to the cockpit floor underneath the navigation officer's table, was inadvertently activated – most likely by a cleaner. While the aircraft was being towed, the duty electrician put the aircraft's master switch from 'ground' to 'flight' in preparation for his pre-flight checks, activating the system, which immediately discharged the fire extinguishers behind all four engines, to spectacular effect. No damage was caused.

July 16, 1947: G-AHDT *Fife* at London Airport. While parked, the aircraft was struck by the wingtip of an Air France Douglas DC-3 – the latter deemed to be taxiing too fast as it was being marshalled into position, damaging the Halton's pitot head.

October 18, 1947: G-AHDW *Falaise*, operating Flight 33W35, London to Castel Benito. Immediately after take-off on the outbound leg, the aircraft experienced severe aileron flutter – resulting in a subsequent loss of stability, which took the efforts of both pilots to maintain control. Reducing power, and using the outer engines (number 3 and 4) and rudder to fly the aircraft – the ailerons having almost no effect – the crew, led by Capt H Steen, carried out an overweight emergency landing after some 35 minutes in the air. It was discovered that the clevis pin securing the starboard aileron trim tab control arm to the trim tab was missing due to a maintenance error.

December 24, 1947: G-AHDR *Foreland*, operating Flight 33W86, Kano to London. Outbound from Kano, the pilot's escape hatch came adrift after take-off, having not been properly secured after it had been opened before departure to clean the windscreen. The aircraft returned to Kano for an emergency landing.

February 1, 1948: G-AHDW *Falaise*, operating Flight 33W119, Lagos and London. The aircraft overran the runway at Accra by some 30m after landing fast and long following a starboard undercarriage warning light –although it was in fact locked down. The aircraft, led by Capt A Gibson, passed over a ditch which crossed the run-off area. With no injuries or damage reported, no blame was attributed to the crew.

RIGHT: A line-up of freshly minted Haltons for BOAC awaiting delivery – headed up by G-AHDW *Falaise*. Registered to the carrier on June 27, 1946, the aircraft's Certificate of Airworthiness (C of A) was issued to the Ministry of Supply two days later. Flying its last BOAC service on April 8, 1948, it joined Bond Air Services on lease from Aviation Traders – the latter having acquired it on July 2, 1948. Going on to fly some 65 airlift sorties to Berlin, the aircraft was later scrapped at Southend after its C of A expired on December 24, that same year. It was officially cancelled from the register some two years later, on November 20.

ABOVE RIGHT: Seen here sometime between January and March 1949 looking somewhat worse for wear, with 'her' roundels painted out and civil registration seemingly spray painted on just forward of the tailplane, G-AHYI – formerly PP311 – was one of the eight Halifax CVIIIs BOAC leased from the RAF to cover its Halton services when the type was grounded, its leasing period lasting from September 24, 1946 through to July 10, 1947. KEY COLLECTION

RIGHT: The Halton service from London Airport (now Heathrow) to Cairo managed to complete the journey in a single day, leaving London at 0715hrs and arriving in Cairo at 2305hrs.

Airways, today operates a daily nonstop Heathrow to Accra service, with a scheduled flight time of 6hrs 35mins using a 331-seat Airbus A350-1000, an economy class ticket setting you back between £537 and £1,183 depending on the month of travel – summer months, obviously, being more expensive.

During the second week of June 1947, BOAC was forced to briefly suspend its Halton services to West Africa due to a lack of meteorological facilities. The Air Ministry had been compelled to close several of its 'met' stations across both West and Central Africa due to the high rate of demobilisation of RAF met officers – this not being helped by the lack of adequate, and immediate, replacements being available.

On July 14, 1947, BOAC launched the first ever commercial services from the West to Ceylon (today's Sri Lanka) using Haltons. The weekly service between London and Colombo, routed via Tripoli, Cairo (which included a 24-hour stop on the outbound leg, and a 12-hour lay-over inbound), Basra, and Karachi. Although the type successfully completed a route-proving flight three months earlier, in commercial operation the Haltons faltered. Despite the operational reliability of the type, it was unequal to the task over the long, gruelling flights, time after time. As a result, the Avro York took over the service on September 11.

The endgame

The Halton was never going to be a money-maker for BOAC. But its rugged dependability was appreciated, especially on the West Africa run, with its often-tumultuous weather conditions. Its robust airframe and undercarriage coped well with the extremes of weather and temperature, and the often less than pristine state of some of the runways down route. This was key in maintaining ▶

• GREAT BRITAIN — MIDDLE EAST •

SERVICE No. 39/40M HALTON SPEEDBIRD *Seven times weekly in each direction*

EASTBOUND			L.S.T.	G.M.T.	Statute Miles	
LONDON *Airways Terminal* Daily	dep.	07.15	07.15	0	
LONDON AIRPORT	dep.	08.30	08.30		Same day
TRIPOLI	arr.	17.05	16.05	158	
TRIPOLI	dep.	18.35	17.35		
CAIRO	arr.	01.05	23.05	2678	

WESTBOUND			L.S.T.	G.M.T.	Statute Miles	
CAIRO	Daily	dep.	21.00	19.00	0	
TRIPOLI	arr.	02.35	01.35	1094	
TRIPOLI	dep.	04.05	03.05		Same day
*BORDEAUX	arr.	10.50	09.50	2219	
*BORDEAUX	dep.	12.20	11.20		
LONDON AIRPORT	arr.	14.15	14.15		
LONDON *Airways Terminal*	arr.	15.30	15.30	2678	

*MARSEILLES will replace BORDEAUX while quarantine restrictions are in force and the arrival and departure times for MARSEILLES will be 1hr. 55 mins. earlier than those shown above.

SERVICE No. 29/30M DAKOTA SPEEDBIRD *Five times weekly in each direction*

EASTBOUND			L.S.T.	G.M.T.	Statute Miles	
LONDON *Airways Terminal* Tue., Wed., Fri., Sat., Sun.	dep.	08.45	08.45	0	
LONDON AIRPORT	dep.	10.00	10.00		1st day
MARSEILLES	arr.	14.50	13.50	615	
MARSEILLES	dep.	15.35	14.35		
MALTA	arr.	20.00	19.00	1335	
MALTA Wed., Thu., Sat., Sun., Mon.	dep.	08.45	07.45		
EL ADEM	arr.	13.40	11.40	1948	2nd day
EL ADEM	dep.	14.10	12.10		
CAIRO	arr.	17.05	15.05	2408	

WESTBOUND			L.S.T.	G.M.T.	Statute Miles	
CAIRO Thu., Fri., Sun., Mon., Tue.	dep.	09.00	07.00	0	
EL ADEM	arr.	12.15	10.15	460	1st day
EL ADEM	dep.	12.45	10.45		
MALTA	arr.	16.00	15.00	1073	
MALTA Fri., Sat., Mon., Tue., Wed.	dep.	05.15	04.15		
MARSEILLES	arr.	10.10	09.10	1793	
MARSEILLES	dep.	10.55	09.55		2nd day
LONDON AIRPORT	arr.	14.10	14.10		
LONDON *Airways Terminal*	arr.	15.25	15.25	2408	

SERVICE No. 31/32M DAKOTA SPEEDBIRD *Twice weekly in each direction*

EASTBOUND			L.S.T.	G.M.T.	Statute Miles	
LONDON *Airways Terminal* Tue., Thu.	dep.	06.55	06.55	0	
LONDON AIRPORT	dep.	08.10	08.10		1st day
MARSEILLES	arr.	13.00	12.00	615	
MARSEILLES	dep.	14.00	13.00		
MALTA	arr.	18.25	17.25	1335	
MALTA Wed., Fri.	dep.	07.00	06.00		
EL ADEM	arr.	11.55	09.55	1984	2nd day
EL ADEM	dep.	12.25	10.25		
LYDDA	arr.	16.25	14.25	2593	

WESTBOUND			L.S.T.	G.M.T.	Statute Miles	
LYDDA Thu., Sat.	dep.	08.30	06.30	0	
EL ADEM	arr.	13.00	11.00	645	1st day
EL ADEM	dep.	13.30	11.30		
MALTA	arr.	16.45	15.45	1258	
MALTA Fri., Sun.	dep.	04.30	03.30		
MARSEILLES	arr.	09.25	08.25	1978	
MARSEILLES	dep.	10.25	09.25		2nd day
LONDON AIRPORT	arr.	13.40	13.40		
LONDON *Airways Terminal*	arr.	14.55	14.55	2593	

BOAC's presence among the world's airways, and Britain's Empire and Commonwealth links while it both gradually recovered from wartime conditions, and awaited more modern, comfortable, and efficient types.

Despite BOAC's best efforts, the Halton was far from ideal on the long, arduous routes assigned to it, and on December 31, 1947, it was withdrawn from the London-Cairo link.

And so it was, less than two years after the type had entered service with the corporation and less than a year after returning to service following their grounding, BOAC's final Halton service was flown between May 3-4, 1948 – G-AHDX *Folkestone* closing the type's chapter on the London-Accra route. Across the routes once served by the Halton, Avro Yorks quietly took the mantle.

Unlike other types, such as the Hermes and Canadair Argonaut, which were drafted back into employment after their retirement from the BOAC fleet, there would be no reprieve for the Haltons. Within a month of the final passenger flight, two of the aircraft (and available spares) had been sold to Freddie Laker's Aviation Traders based out of the airfield at Rochford (today's London Southend Airport) in Essex. With it acquiring another eight in June, it bought the remaining pair in September.

BOAC's faithful Haltons went on to fly with some of Britain's independent airlines, including charter carriers Lancashire Aircraft Corporation and Westminster Airways. Along with other civilianised Halifaxes which became the workhorse of many small cargo carriers, several added a noteworthy spell to their histories as freighters during the Western Allies' frantic efforts to resupply West Berlin by air between April 1948 and May 1949 after the Soviet Union blocked road and water transport routes. The type's "tough as old boots" original design proved particularly adept in handling conversions to haul diesel oil (for which regular lorry tanks could replace the panniers), as well as staples like flour and coal. In all, Halifaxes and Haltons flew more than 8,000 sorties in aid of the beleaguered city.

Given BOAC's loss of significant money during its early years, the Halton, with its ratio of six crew to ten passengers, did little to shore up the carrier's already weakened finances. Although the type helped re-establish Britain's commercial aviation links to important markets, it contributed to BOAC's wider losses with every round trip it operated – a fact that was even cited in parliament when the state-owned carrier's financial plight was discussed.

> **66** *Given BOAC's loss of significant money during its early years, the Halton, with its ratio of six crew to ten passengers, did little to shore up the carrier's already weakened finances* **99**

That said, the conversions of the Halifax and Lancaster (into the Halton and Lancastrian, respectively) represented a makeshift expediency, while BOAC eagerly awaited the new wave of British airliners, the Tudor, Hermes and, ultimately, the de Havilland Comet. As it was, BOAC would not register a profit until the early 1950s, despite the best efforts of its widely dispersed staff.

While the unglamorous Halton may never have been loved, its contribution was acknowledged. The 12-strong fleet had been a worthy stopgap – safe and reliable – that had helped keep Britain connected to the wider world at a time when the resources and finances of both BOAC and the nation were spread extremely thinly.

● Acknowledgements. The author would like to express his thanks to Jim Davies and Adrian Constable of the British Airways Heritage Centre for their assistance in sourcing material for this article. ■

LEFT: An atmospheric, if poor quality, shot of BOAC Halton G-AHDL *Fitzroy* running up. Later acquired by Westminster Airways, this aircraft was "damaged beyond economical repair" in a non-fatal landing accident at RAF Schleswigland in Germany following an airlift sortie to Berlin during the night of March 31-April 1, 1949 – the three crew were unhurt.

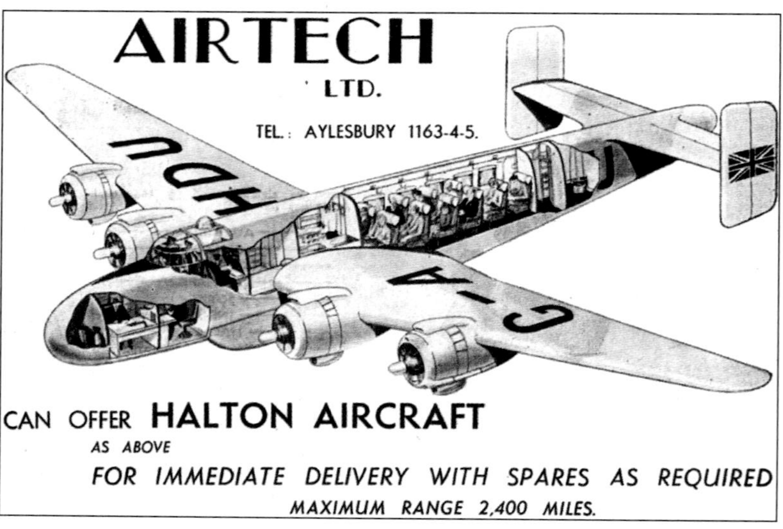

LEFT: Following their retirement from BOAC, Haltons gained a second lease of life across the independent/spares sectors thanks to firms such as Airtech at Haddenham Airfield in Buckinghamshire, which specialised in servicing and conversion/modification work on the type – as this advertisement from the September 16, 1948, issue of *Flight* shows. AVIATIONANCESTRY.CO.UK

Published in *Aeroplane*, **November 19, 1943.** AVIATION ANCESTRY/WWW.AVIATIONANCESTRY.CO.UK

SUBSCRIBE TODAY
TO YOUR FAVOURITE MAGAZINE!

965/25

THE DESTINATION FOR
HISTORIC & MILITARY ENTHUSIASTS

Visit us today and discover all our publications

SCAN ME

SCAN ME

Aeroplane is still providing the best aviation coverage around, with focus on iconic military aircraft from the 1930s to the 1960s.

Britain at War - dedicated to exploring every aspect of the involvement of Britain and her Commonwealth in conflicts from the turn of the 20th century through to the present day.

and subscribe to your favourite magazine...
/collections/subscriptions

**Free 2nd class P&P on BFPO orders. Overseas charges apply.*

HALIFAX III

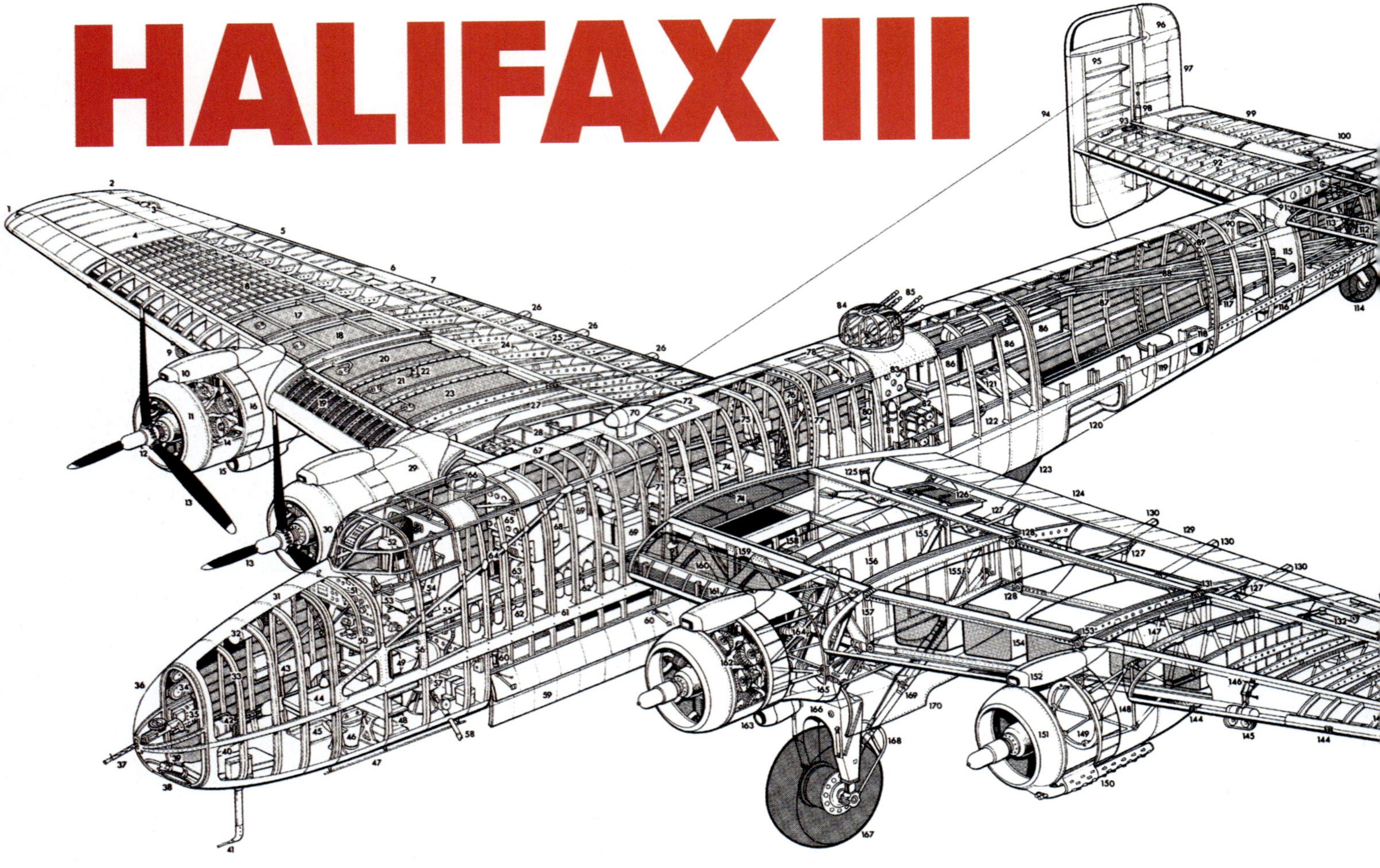

1	Starboard navigation light (Green)	32	De-icing fluid tank	63	Parachute stowage
2	Formation light	33	Nose section frames	64	Front fuselage diagonal bracing strut
3	Aileron balance weight	34	Spare ammunition drums	65	Flight engineer's control panel
4	Wing skinning	35	Bomb aimer's control panel	66	Astral dome
5	Starboard aileron	36	Nose glazing	67	Fuselage skin plating
6	Aileron servo tab	37	0.303in Vickers 'K' GO gun	68	Hydraulic accumulator
7	Trim tab	38	Bomb aiming panels, optically flat	69	Batteries
8	Wing stringer construction	39	Bomb sight	70	D/F loop aerial fairing
9	Landing/taxiing lamp	40	Bomb aimer's prone position couch	71	Nose/centre section joint frame
10	Carburettor air intake duct	41	Pitot tube	72	Cabin roof escape hatch
11	Exhaust collector ring	42	Parachute stowage	73	Heater duct
12	Propeller hub pitch change mechanism	43	Navigator's folding seat	74	Rest bunks, port and starboard
13	De Havilland three-bladed propellers	44	Chart table	75	Hydraulic accumulators
14	Bristol Hercules XVI radial engine	45	Ventral escape hatch	76	Escape ladder
15	Oil cooler intake	46	Camera	77	Fuselage/rear spar joint frame
16	Cowling air outlet flaps	47	Aerial rail	78	Rear escape hatch
17	No.6 fuel tank, capacity 123 imp gal	48	Radio transmitters and receivers	79	Fuselage upper longeron
18	No.5 fuel tank, capacity 122 imp gal	49	Radio operator's control panel	80	Upper turret ladder
19	Leading edge oil tank	50	Rudder pedals	81	Flare stowage
20	No.4 fuel tank, capacity 161 imp gal	51	Instrument panel	82	Sea marker stowage
21	No.3 fuel tank, capacity 188 imp gal	52	Co-pilot's and flight engineer's folding seats	83	Turret mounting ring
22	Fuel tank breather	53	Control column	84	Boulton Paul A III mid-upper gun turret
23	No.1 fuel tank, capacity 247 imp gal	54	Pilot's seat	85	Four 0.303in Browning machine guns
24	Trailing edge ribs	55	Cockpit floor level	86	Tail gun turret ammunition boxes
25	Starboard flap construction	56	Cabin side windows	87	Rear fuselage frame construction
26	Starboard fuel jettison pipes	57	Radio operator's seat	88	Ammunition feed tracks
27	Starboard main undercarriage wheel bay	58	Trailing aerial winch	89	Tail fuselage joint frame
28	Inboard wing section bomb cells	59	Bomb-bay doors (open)	90	Tail gunner's access door
29	Starboard inner engine cowlings	60	Bomb door operating Jacks	91	Tailplane mounting
30	Asymmetric windscreen	61	Main floor/bomb-bay support longeron	92	Starboard tailplane construction
31	Nose skinning	62	Oxygen bottles	93	Rudder hinge control
				94	Aerial cable

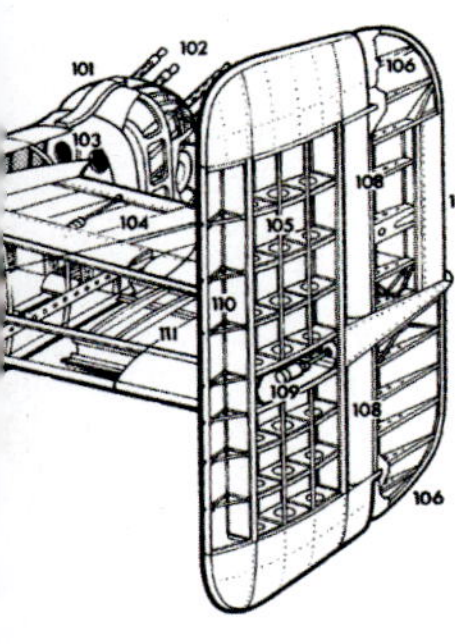

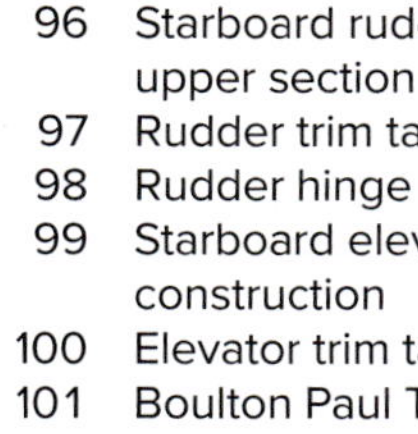

95	Starboard tail fin
96	Starboard rudder upper section
97	Rudder trim tab
98	Rudder hinge post
99	Starboard elevator construction
100	Elevator trim tab
101	Boulton Paul Type E tail gun turret
102	Four 0.303in Browning machine guns
103	Turret sliding doors
104	Port elevator
105	Port tail fin construction
106	Rudder upper and lower sections
107	Rudder trim tab
108	Rudder aerodynamic balances
109	Trim tab control jack
110	Leading edge bracing struts
111	Port tailplane
112	Rudder and elevator control hinges
113	Tailwheel strut
114	Semi-retractable tailwheel
115	Rear fuselage bulkhead
116	ARI 5122 radar bombing control units
117	Tailplane control rods
118	Master compass
119	Elsan toilet
120	Crew entry door, opens in and upward
121	Flare launch tubes
122	Main fuselage floor level
123	H2S radar bombing antenna fairing
124	Port inner flap
125	Flapjack
126	Dinghy stowage
127	Flap control rods
128	Rear spar inboard section attachment joint
129	Port outer flap
130	Port fuel jettison pipes
131	Rear spar outer panel attachment joint
132	Trim tab controls
133	Aileron hinge control
134	Trim tab
135	Aileron servo tab
136	Port aileron
137	Aileron balance weight
138	Formation light
139	Port navigation light (Red)
140	Wing rib construction
141	Front spar
142	Leading edge nose ribs
143	Armoured leading edge
144	Cable cutters
145	Retractable landing/ taxiing lamps
146	Lamp operating jack
147	Outer engine mounting ribs
148	Engine bearer struts
149	Engine mounting ring
150	Flame suppressor exhaust pipe
151	Exhaust collector ring
152	Carburettor intake duct
153	Outer wing panel joint
154	Port wing fuel tanks
155	Main undercarriage jacks
156	Port mainwheel bay
157	Inner wing panel front spar joint
158	Wing bomb cell long-range fuel tank, capacity 96 imp gal
159	Front spar girder construction
160	Leading edge No.2 fuel tank, capacity 62 imp gal
161	Engine control runs
162	Port inner Bristol Hercules XVI engine
163	Oil cooler air intake
164	Inboard engine bearers
165	Main undercarriage hinge mounting
166	Messier main undercarriage leg
167	Port mainwheel
168	Tyre guard
169	Folding retraction strut
170	Mainwheel door

SPECIFICATIONS – HALIFAX III

General characteristics

Crew	Seven (typical)
Length	71ft 7in (21.82m)
Wingspan	Early production aircraft: 98ft 10in (30.12m); Late production aircraft: 104ft 2in (31.75m)
Wing area	98ft wingspan, 1,250ft² (116.12m²); 104 ft wingspan 1,280ft² (118.91m²)
Height	20ft 9in (6.32m)
Aerofoil	Root: NACA 23021; Tip: NACA 23007
Undercarriage track	24ft 8in (7.5m)
Empty weight	37,870lb (17,178kg)
Max take-off weight	65,000lb (29,484kg)
Fuel capacity	1,986 Imp gal (9,028lit)
Powerplants	Four Bristol Hercules VI or XVI air-cooled 14-cylinder radial piston engines with power output of between 1,615hp (1,204kW) and 1,675hp (1,235kW) each
Propellers	3-metal bladed de Havilland Hydromatic constant-speed fully feathering, 13ft (3.96m) diameter

Performance

Maximum speed	277mph (445 km/h)
Cruising speed	225mph (362 km/h)
Range	1,700 miles (2,735 km)
Service ceiling	20,000ft (6,096m)
Take-off distance	1,150yds (1,051.5m)
Landing distance	1,100yds (1,005m)

Armament

Primary	Four 0.303in (7.7mm) Browning II machine guns in Boulton Paul Type A mid-upper turret, and four 0.303in (7.7mm) Browning II machine guns in Boulton Paul Type E rear turret
Alternative/additional	One 0.5in (12.7mm) Browning AN/M2 machine gun in a ventral Preston Green mount; one 0.303in (7.7mm) Browning II machine gun in nose
Bomb load	Varying between 7,500 and 13,000lb (3,401 and 5,903kg) and consisting of combinations of 4,000lb High Capacity (HC), 2,000lb Armor-Piercing (AP), 2,000lb HC, 1,000lb Medium Capacity (MC), 500lb MC or 250lb MC bombs, or various quantities of 4lb incendiaries installed in Small Bomb Containers or Cluster Projectiles, three 1,500lb (839kg) Parachute Anti-Shipping Mines

WHAT THEY FACED: Located on the Ruhr's northern edge, on the line of advance for the Allied armies, the western German town of Gladbeck was heavily bombed by No. 6 and 8 Groups on March 24, 1945. Of the 175 aircraft dispatched, 153 were Halifaxes – including MZ759/NP-Q *Wizard of Aus* of No. 158 Squadron out of RAF Lissett in North Yorkshire. Hit by anti-aircraft fire over the target area, the aircraft – then a 72-mission veteran, seen here falling to earth ablaze – was the sole casualty of the raid.

On board MZ759 that fateful day was pilot WO Ernst Yule Yeoman, flight engineer Sgt John Rodd Williams, navigator Flt Sgt John Edward Dennis Taylor, bomb aimer Flt Sgt James Brown, wireless operator/air gunner WO William Henry Hulme (Royal Australian Air Force), air gunner Flt Sgt Gordon Davis Lunn, and air gunner FO Walter Harold White. While it is thought all seven manged to escape the stricken bomber, only Taylor, Lunn, and White survived.

While in service with Bomber Command, the Handley Page type flew 82,773 operations and dropped 227,805 tons of bombs, while 1,833 aircraft were lost, with many thousands more of their aircrew killed – their average age being just 23. KEY COLLECTION